BRITAIN and IRELAND

Country Inns and Back Roads

The Swan Hotel, Bibury, Gloucestershire

BRITAIN and IRELAND

Country Inns and Back Roads

**Sixth Edition
1990–91**

Country house hotels,
bed and breakfast, traditional inns,
farmhouses, guest houses,
and castles

**Norman T. Simpson
The Berkshire Traveller
with Jerry Levitin**

Harper & Row, Publishers, New York
Grand Rapids, Philadelphia, St. Louis, San Francisco
London, Singapore, Sydney, Tokyo, Toronto

TRAVEL BOOKS BY NORMAN T. SIMPSON

Country Inns and Back Roads, North America
Country Inns and Back Roads, Britain and Ireland
Country Inns and Back Roads, Continental Europe
Bed and Breakfast, American Style

COVER PAINTING: A view of Gold Hill in Shaftesbury, Dorset, England. This artist's rendering represents the scene behind St. Peter's Church overlooking the countryside of southwestern England.

DRAWINGS: Janice Lindstrom

ISSN 0893-1186
ISBN 0-06-096494-4
90 91 92 93 94 FG 10 9 8 7 6 5 4 3 2 1

Contents

BRITAIN and IRELAND

Country Inns and Back Roads

Preface

In the last two years, since the fifth edition, a number of developments have taken place regarding country house hotels in Britain, most notably in the Cotswolds and adjacent areas of the West Country. Quite a few of the stately manor houses that have been run for years as successful country house hotels by their owners have been sold to corporations. Usually, the reasons are economic ones. Rising costs and higher taxes make it difficult for a private person to hold on to a valuable piece of property. Corporations appear to be the only ones around with enough money to buy these places. When they take over, invariably, the manor house is enlarged, many new guest rooms are added, everything is remodelled and redecorated, and the rooms are flooded with amenities. Conference rooms are created. Tour groups are encouraged. What was once a relaxed country house hotel of twenty rooms or fewer where the owner took personal charge and the atmosphere was warm and friendly tends to become a big business, by its nature cold and impersonal. Everything looks good, often more beautiful than before, decorated by designers in country style, yet it is no longer the sort of country hotel I have always advocated—the hospitable place that welcomes you as a person.

This new type of country house hotel fills a certain niche, and is fine for that, but it is not suitable for the American traveler who wants an adventure in England, who wishes to have a true flavor of the English people and their country. Therefore, many of the hotels that have appeared in past editions have been replaced in this sixth edition with smaller, privately-owned establishments.

Another development, this time in central London, has been the creation of small country-style hotels in residential areas. Often a company is formed to purchase several strategically located townhouses of interesting architecture and develop them into small hotels of about 25 rooms. Then, a manager is hired to choose his staff and transmit his character to the establishment. I have no objection to this arrangement if the service is

The Rising Sun Hotel, Lynmouth, North Devon

personal and the place well-managed. It offers a good alternative to the traveler who wishes to stay in London, but not in one of the large hotels.

Let me hasten to say that there are still many, many privately-owned country inns and hotels up and down and all around the back roads of England, and even in London. I had to search for them, but I found them. They are there for you to enjoy.

Many country house hotels and inns are now offering what they call "leisure breaks" if you book for more than one night at any time of the year or "winter breaks" during the off season. Often, there is quite a savings. I suggest you inquire if this option is available whenever you book.

One final note. A number of hotel managers have asked that I emphasize to American guests that in Great Britain's hotels there is a "ground floor"—the "first floor" being one story up. Apparently, there have been some unhappy Americans who have asked for the first floor rooms, not realizing they would have to walk up a flight a stairs to get there. Of course, if there is a "lift" (elevator), it isn't a problem, but most country inns provide only the stairs.

In Britain and Ireland I set out to find the same qualities that I look for among inns in North America: warm, friendly, personal lodgings that are the expression of the owner and his or her family. For the most part, these are proprietor-managed places and provide the opportunity for the traveler to get "the feel of the country."

As in North America, I looked for inns and country house hotels that I felt would continue to operate for many years to come. I searched for a feeling of stability.

If the reader finds as much about *people* as he does about half-timbered houses, hearty roast beef, Irish sunsets, Scottish castles, and English antiques, it is because I believe the heart and soul of these accommodations are the proprietor, his family, staff, and the guests themselves. The setting, food, lodgings, service, furnishings, diversions, and surroundings, of course, are of prime importance, but the main factor that makes this journey unique and enjoyable is personal involvement.

HOW THE BOOK IS PLANNED

I've divided this book into the principal touristic sections of Britain, plus London and Ireland. A large map of England shows these sections, and there are separate maps for Scotland and Ireland.

Each of these sections has its own keyed map showing the approximate location of every accommodation. Of further assistance is the Index, which lists the hotels alphabetically as well as showing rates and last times for dinner orders. There's also a map in this section showing the location of every county.

The italicized paragraphs following each narrative account of my visits contain essential information about the amenities offered and nearby recreational and cultural attractions. Reasonably explicit driving directions are also included.

To understand the italicized factual information, the following explanation may prove helpful:

NAME OF HOTEL, Village, (nearby larger town), County, Postal code.

TELEPHONE NUMBER: This is in two parts: The first number in parenthesis is the STD code. When outside of the immediate area of any of the accommodations, step into the nearest friendly red phone booth and dial all of the STD number plus all of the numbers that follow. In some cases, where an operator may be necessary, I have included the name of the individual exchange.

Many U.K. points can be dialed direct from overseas. The country code for England, Scotland, Wales, and Ireland is 011-44 plus the STD code and the individual number.

CREDIT CARDS: Except as noted, all places accept some major credit cards such as American Express, Barclaycard, MasterCard, or Visa. British traveler's checks are excellent.

RATES

Rates for a room for two people for one night with breakfast, except where noted, are included in the Index of this book. They are not to be considered firm quotations, but should be used as guidelines only. The traveler who is willing to travel British-style (booking a room with a shared bath) will appreciate the lower rates.

MAKING RESERVATIONS

A travel agent can frequently be the traveler's best friend. These people are professionals and know how to make the necessary contacts for reservations. Since a very high percentage of the hotels and inns pay travel agents' commissions, this should not be an additional expense for the traveler. However, in some cases, the smaller accommodations do not pay commissions, and the travel agent is entitled to charge the client a fee equal to the usual commission. It's also reasonable for the travel agent to charge the client for the cost of telephone calls or telex messages.

The best way to assure a firm reservation is to contact the inn or hotel by telephone and then send a deposit, which is held against the first night's stay.

HOW TO TELEPHONE GREAT BRITAIN
TO MAKE A RESERVATION

If you are calling from North America, you may directly dial the numbers that are in this book. The first thing to do is to dial 011 if you want a station-to-station call, or 01 for calls requiring operator assistance (collect, person, etc.). Next, dial 44, the country code. Now refer to the telephone number given for each accommodation. One very important point: if calling from North America, omit the first zero; otherwise, dial the number as given. If direct international dialing is not available in your area, you will still get the dial rate on a simple station call; just dial 0 and give the details of your call.

If telephoning from point-to-point *within* Great Britain, read the instructions carefully that are posted in each telephone booth and be sure to dial the 0, which is omitted when dialing from North America to Great Britain.

The most economical way to telephone Great Britain is to call between 6:00 p.m. and 7:00 a.m., local North American time (British time is 5 hours later than Eastern Standard Time). This is for a call that does not require operator assistance. It costs about 25% more to dial direct between 1:00 p.m. and 6:00 a.m., and about 50% more to dial between 7:00 a.m. and 1:00 p.m. Operator-assisted calls are considerably more expensive. AT&T Information Service can fill you in on further details; dial toll-free 800-874-4000.

TELEPHONING THE UNITED STATES FROM BRITAIN

Before picking up a telephone to make an international call in a hotel or inn, it is wise to inquire as to the house policy on surcharges. International calls placed in a hotel or inn may be subject to stiff surcharges, unless the establishment is a participant in AT&T's TELEPLAN, which sets a uniform limit on such surcharges.

There are various ways to cut these extra telephone expenses if it is necessary to make out-of-country calls. Collect calls might have a small surcharge, as would be the case with credit card calls, if they are allowed. The person-to-person charge on a credit card call probably still would be less than the surcharge. Another method would be to place your call and ask your U.S. party to call you right back. To save time, you would want all the necessary numbers handy—access numbers, country and city codes, hotel and room numbers. Or, if possible, you could simply set up a schedule of places and times when you could be reached from the U.S.

The least expensive method, with no surcharge, is to call from main post offices, international airports, railway stations, or telephone buildings. Some public pay phones can handle international calls. Be sure to have a pocketful of change at the ready. (Be aware that, unlike American public telephone systems, British pay-telephones are on computers. When making any calls, you must keep an eagle eye on the display screen or listen for a warning signal so that you can quickly insert more change, otherwise you are in danger of being cut off in midsentence.)

AT&T has an International Information Service, from which all sorts of advice on international telephoning may be obtained. They publish two informative booklets and maintain a toll-free service at 800-874-4000.

LUGGAGE

For years I've been making two- or three-week extended trips to the U.K. and the Continent, using only carry-on luggage consisting of a garment bag and a soft travel bag. This eliminates any waiting for luggage or any other type of delay. The garment bag holds one jacket, which is necessary for the evening meal, and one pair of suitable dress trousers. I also include at least one sweater, an additional pair of trousers, and a raincoat, which serves many purposes. I usually carry three drip-dry shirts and three drip-dry shorts, and four pairs of wool socks. Of course, this means that I am doing a hand laundry every night, which, under the circumstances, will dry in just a few hours. The ladies will have a different list, but keeping your luggage to a minimum will simplify your travels all the way around.

CANCELLATIONS

In Britain, acceptance of a hotel booking by telephone or in writing is generally regarded as a legally binding contract. If it's necessary to cancel, advise the hotel immediately. If they are unable to re-let the room, the hotel may be entitled to claim compensation—usually two thirds of the agreed price—and any deposit would be included as part of this payment. Ask your travel agent about travel cancellation insurance.

AIR FARES TO BRITAIN AND IRELAND

I have been very satisfied with British Airways. They have the most flights from the United States, at the most convenient times. In addition, they fly continuously to other major cities throughout Europe.

Even in these days when escalating air fares keep pace with the rising cost of jet fuel, I find that it's possible to shop around and get bargains. All airlines have standby tickets that require an obvious flexibility of schedule. When this doesn't suit my convenience, I order my ticket in advance under one of several plans that effect a savings.

Although other airlines fly directly to Ireland, I've always found Aer Lingus extremely satisfactory.

ARRIVING IN BRITAIN

Visitors to England will, for the most part, arrive in London at one of two airports, although another gateway to the British Isles that is growing in popularity is Prestwick Airport, Glasgow, Scotland.

Heathrow

The large and somewhat complicated Heathrow Airport, just outside London, is most efficiently designed. Part of the hassle is reduced by luggage trolleys and moving walkways. Immigration and Customs are easily negotiated, and the traveler emerges into the International Arrivals Section, where currency can be exchanged and information about lodgings can be obtained if you haven't already done so. This is also where there are literally hundreds of people waiting for arriving friends and guests. Many of them have small signs with the name of the arriving person printed on them—that's how chauffeurs and other people meeting strangers get together.

Luggage is now handled very swiftly at Heathrow, and a tip of twenty pence per bag is usual, although the services are supposed to be free of charge.

It is possible to take a bus from Heathrow to Gatwick.

The most convenient way to the center of the city is the Airbus. Airbus 1 (A1) proceeds to Victoria Railway Station with stops along the way. The A2 goes to Paddington Station and the A3 to Euston Station. It takes about an hour and costs about five dollars.

A taxi will take a shorter time, but it is still at least an hour and fifteen minutes during the rush hour. The fare will be about forty dollars plus tip.

One of the best ways to get into London is to use the Underground, which runs from Heathrow right to the center of the city. Follow the signs in the airport and use the moving walkways. This is another good argument for keeping the baggage to a carry-on weight.

If you have an overnight wait, I understand that the Sheraton-Heathrow provides very convenient accommodations, with free bus service to and from London and a coffee shop and pub that serve good, inexpensive food.

Gatwick

Charter flights deplane at Gatwick, but it now has many scheduled flights from North American cities.

Gatwick maintains that it has very fast baggage service, and there are little lounges with television sets that announce the arrival of the baggage for each flight.

Flightline 777 is a nonstop bus service between Victoria Coach Station at 164 Buckingham Palace Road in London and Gatwick. It stops just outside the terminal on the upper level. Victoria Coach Station, not to be confused with Victoria Bus Station, is about a half a mile from Victoria Railway and Underground Station. Coaches leave Gatwick every half hour all day long and then hourly in the evening. It takes about an hour and ten minutes and, of course, longer at the rush hour. The price is four dollars one way. A taxi costs forty dollars.

Often regarded as the most practical way to get to and from Gatwick is the train from Victoria Station. At Gatwick, the train stops inside the terminal on a lower floor. At Victoria, take the entrance next to the National Tourist Information Office to Platform 15. Trains leave every fifteen minutes all day long and every hour through the night. It is about a fifty-minute journey, although I understand that the express cuts it down to thirty minutes. The fare is six dollars.

There is an airport hotel at Gatwick in case you cannot get out or cannot get to town. The new ring road, M25, that encircles London eliminates the necessity of driving through the city to go north or northeast.

DEPARTING LONDON

As noted earlier, the Underground is a quick, reliable, direct method of getting to and from Heathrow Airport, and the train is the best way to and from Gatwick. For overseas flights, I find it's best to arrive at least ninety minutes ahead of time. You can always enjoy yourself watching the fascinating crowds after being ticketed or going through Passport Control. Major overseas airlines all have special reservation numbers for checking vital departure information.

RENTAL CARS

After much trial and error I found the most satisfactory car rental arrangements in both Britain and Europe, from the standpoints of convenience and cost, could be made through AutoEurope-Maine, whose offices in North America are at P.O. Box 1097, Camden, Maine 04843. The toll-free number for the U.S. is 800-223-5555 (Maine: 800-342-5202). For Canada it is 800-458-9503. Arrangements can also be made to pick up cars in principal cities and airports in Britain and drop them off in other countries.

I always advise travelers not to plan on driving their rented cars in the city of London. Take the Underground or the airport coach to center London and then a cab to your hotel. Pick up a rental car when leaving the city. The AutoEurope-Maine cars can be picked up and/or dropped off in London or at Heathrow, Gatwick, or Prestwick airports, or many other points.

Many experienced travelers visit London at the conclusion of their trip, engaging a rental car on arrival at the airport and spending the first night at one of several countryside accommodations listed in this book. At the end of their travels, the car can be dropped off at one of various locations, including Edinburgh, Glasgow, York, Oxford, Cambridge, Exeter, or even Heathrow or Gatwick. At some locations there is no charge for drop-off. The trick is to take the train back to London and avoid the traffic.

DRIVING TIPS

In Britain, automobiles are driven on the left-hand side of the road. This should not alarm anyone, since it's very easy to make the adjustment. I'd suggest an automatic rather than a stick shift automobile. A U.K. operator's license is not necessary.

Enter the roundabouts (traffic circles) on the left and circle clockwise. The traffic already in the circle has the right of way.

The *A–Z Great Britain Road Atlas,* published by Geographers' A–Z
Map Company Ltd. in Kent, is available in many American bookstores,
especially stores that specialize in travel books. If you can't locate a copy,
ask your bookstore dealer to order it for you. The cost, about $11.00, is
well worth the price, for all of the little country roads are included. It kept
me from getting lost and helped me find a number of inns on the back
roads.

MAPS

The *A-Z Great Britain Road Atlas,* published by Geographers' A–Z
Map Company Ltd. in Kent, is available in many American bookstores,
especially stores that specialize in travel books. If you can't locate a copy,
ask your bookstore dealer to order it for you. The cost, about $11.00, is
well worth the price, for all of the little country roads are included. It kept
me from getting lost and helped me find a number of inns on the back
roads.

USING BRITRAIL IN BRITAIN

Experiencing the English countryside by train can be a comparatively
inexpensive and pleasant way to travel throughout Britain. In addition to
its usual schedule, which covers a passenger network of 12,000 miles,
Britrail has a number of special offers, among which is a plan for travel on
the red buses and Underground in London.

A Britrail pass cannot be purchased in Britain, and must be obtained
before you leave the United States. Britrail vouchers must be exchanged
for tickets at Victoria Station in London. For complete information, write
or call:

Britrail Travel International
630 Third Ave.
New York, NY 10017

Telephone: 212-599-5400

COUNTRY INNS IN BRITAIN AND IRELAND

For the past twenty-three years I have defined the word "inn" in North America as a certain type of lodging that conveys something of the innkeeper's personality, along with friendly hospitality and service in unique surroundings.

However, I've discovered that in Britain the term "inn" has a more specific meaning. It's a type of pub (public house) that has a license clearly defining the hours when it must be open or closed. When overnight accommodations are available in a pub, they are frequently called inns. These are sometimes the old traditional inns, with colorful and imaginative names. The food and accommodations range from simple to sophisticated.

The popularity of traveling in Britain in recent years has seen the emergence of the "country house hotel." For the most part, these are sizable houses built a hundred or more years ago by affluent Britons for pleasure and residence away from the city. Today, they have been converted into very good, smallish hotels, usually set in several acres of grounds and woodlands, and located away from the towns and villages. They are not, by strict interpretation, inns. Proprietorship usually runs the gamut from retired naval and military types to younger couples who, like some North American innkeepers, are establishing new careers. If a British country house hotel were located in North America, it would be known as a country inn. If North American country inns were to be transferred to Britain, they would be called country house hotels.

The third category is the guest house. These are frequently in farms and private homes. Breakfast and dinner are usually served in the family dining room, and besides sharing the living room, there is usually that wonderful institution, only to be found in Britain, the residents' lounge, where there's usually a small "telly," a fireplace (or an electric fire), and many books and magazines.

The final type of establishment is the B&B, which is short for "bed and breakfast." Some B&Bs are splendid, others leave something to be desired. I have included as many of the former as possible.

I wish to thank Barbara and Grant Winther for their input and research into Great Britain.

DINING IN THE BRITISH ISLES

Basically, menus in Britain and Ireland fall into three categories. First, there's pub food, which is usually salads, sausages, cold cuts, meat pies, and pâtés. Pub food is most generally served at midday.

Some lunch and nearly all dinner menus include hearty British food such as roast beef and Yorkshire pudding; various cuts of lamb, veal, ham, and poultry, which might include pheasant, partridge, and other game birds.

At dinner, British dishes frequently share the spotlight with French cuisine, both traditional and *nouvelle*. I found a great many French chefs working in British kitchens.

There are local food specialties in various parts of Britain. Most of the time they are easily recognizable on the menu.

The latest times dinner may be ordered vary greatly from one place to another, and these times are listed in the Index in the back of the book.

England

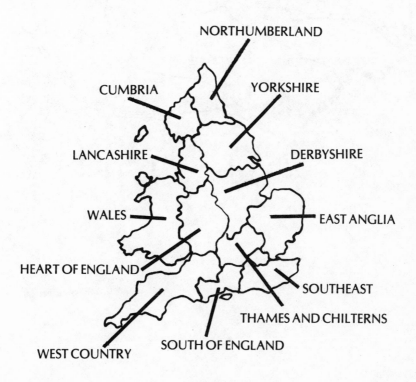

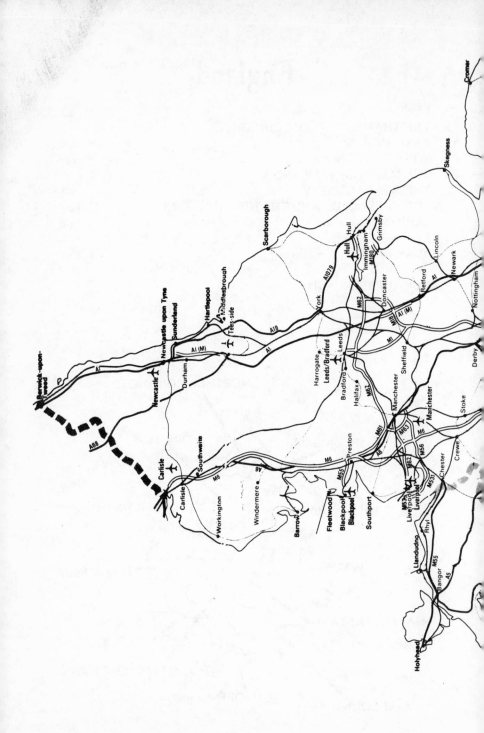

LONDON

Sooner or later, almost everyone visiting Britain goes to London, and well-a-day that they do because London is alive with interest, fun, and excitement. In this book I will not attempt an overview of this great city, but hope that the reader will be encouraged to visit London, walk as much as possible, and feel free to mingle, not only with the Londoners, but also the thousands of other visitors. I have walked the London streets very late at night in complete safety.

Now a word of caution and some advice for the first-time visitor to London. Do not attempt to drive an automobile within Greater London! The ground transportation from Heathrow or Gatwick is speedy and frequent. You will not need a car in the city of London. If you land at Heathrow, and your baggage can be handled conveniently, it is possible to take the Underground to center London, where a cab can then be taken directly to your hotel. (Please see "Arriving in Britain" in my introductory notes.)

Getting around London is easy. The London Underground is fast and efficient, goes everywhere, and is good for excursions that are some distance away. The double-decker buses, as well as the green buses, provide an opportunity to see London aboveground. The hotel concierge can supply a very essential map that gives all of the bus lines by number, and it's quite common to see tourists standing in front of a chart on a post, reading the numbers of the buses that are going to stop there. (See "Using Britrail in Britain" in my introductory notes.)

There are dozens of books about sightseeing in London; one of the best is London, Your Sightseeing Guide, *published by the British Travel Authority.*

London Hotels

Because almost everybody traveling to Britain will be planning to stop in London for a few days, I have included a group of moderate-sized London hotels in various price categories. (See rates in Index.)

Many of these hotels have representatives in the United States, but they can also be contacted directly for reservations. A telephone call at the low-rate time is well worth the effort. Once a reservation is made it should be followed up as soon as possible by an air-mail letter with a deposit.

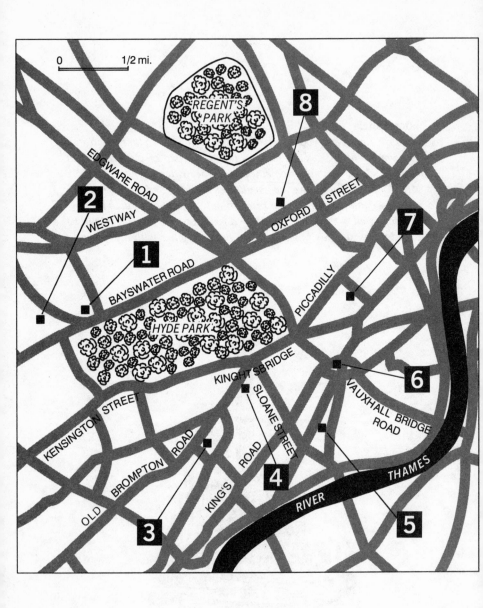

0   1/2 mi.

REGENT'S PARK

8

EDGWARE ROAD

2

WESTWAY

1

BAYSWATER ROAD

OXFORD   STREET

7

PICCADILLY

HYDE PARK

KINGHT SBRIDGE

6

SLOANE STREET

VAUXHALL BRIDGE ROAD

KENSINGTON STREET

OLD BROMPTON ROAD

KING'S ROAD

4

3

RIVER   THAMES

5

THE ABBEY COURT
20 Pembridge Gardens, London

On a quiet street in Kensington, just off Bayswater, with bus service and an underground station half a block away, is a small luxury hotel called The Abbey Court. Masterminded by Nicholas Crawley, the former entrepreneur who was behind the creation of several successful country house hotels, this handsome establishment is a townhouse built around 1830. Two years ago it was carefully restored and renovated; each of its twenty-two rooms was uniquely designed and decorated with interesting prints and paintings, unusual fabrics, and numerous antiques. There are fresh flowers and potted plants around the halls and parlor, and personal touches in the rooms, such as a tin caddy of cookies, bottles of mineral water, a selection of novels, and terrycloth bathrobes. All bathrooms are ensuite, tiled in Italian marble, and contain whirlpool baths as well as showers. A large and delicious continental breakfast is brought to the room if desired, and light meals and drinks can be provided at any time. Service is excellent.

"We pay attention to detail," said manager Graham Chapman. "Our bed sheets are made of Egyptian cotton, and they are lightly starched. After a tiring day, they are nice to slide between."

They were, believe me.

THE ABBEY COURT, 20 Pembridge Gardens, London W2 4DU. Tel.: (01)221-7518. Telex: 262167 ABBYCT. Fax: (01)792-0858. A 22-guestroom (private baths), 5-story Victorian without elevator, in Kensington near the Gardens, one half block from Nottinghill Gate Underground Station and bus services to Heathrow and all areas of London. Open year around. No pipes or cigars in bedrooms. No pets. Breakfast extra. Light meals available. Graham Chapman, Manager. (See Index for rates.)

THE HOLLAND PARK HOTEL
6 Ladbroke Terrace, London

The green front door on the Victorian townhouse opened as I came up the walk, and a tall gentleman introduced himself as the Manager, Richard Taylor.

"I saw you coming from the window," he said with a smile. "Do you have a reservation?"

"No, I'm just here to look around. I understand the same people who own The Abbey Court own this hotel."

"That's correct."

"I was curious to see if the two places were alike."

"Oh, no." His smile grew even wider. "I believe you'll see we are very different." He led me into the attractive sitting room with a large window that overlooked a back garden. A young lady, no doubt a guest, sat at a corner desk writing postcards.

"In cold weather," Richard said, lowering his voice, "we light the gas fireplace. It gives an even more comfortable look to the room." He returned to the front hall, and I followed him up the staircase.

There are twenty-three individually decorated bedrooms, ranging from a cozy single to a spacious family room. The only similarity between this hotel and The Abbey Court is that both are renovated Victorian townhouses on quiet streets in Kensington. The Holland Park does not claim to be a luxury hotel. A few rooms share bathrooms. There are not as many upscale amenities. But it is a very attractive place with a relaxed atmosphere, and the price, which includes continental breakfast served in the room, is certainly reasonable for London.

There is a secluded, informal garden for guests and their visitors' use. According to Richard, during the summer months, the residents like to sit outside and drink coffee or tea (facilities for making both are in the rooms) or simply read books.

"We aim to be a small, friendly hotel that feels like home," he said as he opened the green front door for me.

It's a good aim, and they hit the mark.

THE HOLLAND PARK HOTEL, 6 Ladbroke Terrace, London W11 3PG. Tel.: (01)727-5815. A 23-guestroom (75 percent private baths) Victorian townhouse hotel (essentially a bed and breakfast) in Kensington, close to shops and restaurants, West End stores, theatres, Earls Court, and Olympia exhibition halls. Near #12 and #88 buses, Holland Park and Nottinghill Gate Underground Stations and A2 bus from Heathrow. Breakfast included. Light meals obtainable. No pets. Richard Taylor, Manager. (See Index for rates.)

In Britain, acceptance of a hotel booking by telephone or in writing is generally regarded as a legally binding contract. If it's necessary to cancel, advise the hotel immediately. If they are unable to re-let the room, the hotel may be entitled to claim compensation—usually two thirds of the agreed price—and any deposit would be included as part of this payment.

Rates for a room for two people for one night with breakfast, except where noted, are included in the Index of this book. They are not to be considered firm quotations, but should be used as guidelines only.

NUMBER SIXTEEN
16 Sumner Place, London

Since the number of the address is also the name of this small hotel on a lovely residential street in the South Kensington area, a person could easily pass by and not know what has been created out of four townhouses built in 1848 and preserved for their fine architectural design.

A recent refurbishment program has done much to bring a fresh, light atmosphere to the interior of the hotel. English designer fabrics were used to complement a variety of stylish wallpapers. A mix of antiques and comfortable furniture sets a tone of quality. Although General Manager Timothy McDonald has had assistance from design consultants, he has the flair for knowing just what should go where and how to choose a piece of art—he loves art—and build the decor around it.

I was fascinated with a large painting in the reception room. "Who did this?" I asked Timothy.

"It was painted by Cyril Fradon, a South African, in 1967. Actually, it is his version of a painting by Velasquez, *Las Meninas,* which is in the Prado in Spain. This represents the Court of King Charles I."

"The figure down here looks like a dwarf," I said, inspecting the painting closer.

"Yes, it is a dwarf. That is Sir Jeffery Hudson, an honored member of the courts of both Charles I and Charles II. One of the reasons we have this painting is because we also have a lifesized stone statue of Sir Jeffrey in the garden."

Well, of course, I had to hurry out into the beautiful garden, which stretches across the back of the hotel (winner of the "London in Bloom" competition), to pay my respects to Sir Jeffrey.

One of the few hotels in the British Isles to have received the Cesar award for excellence from the Good Hotel Guide, Number Sixteen, with its two pleasant sitting rooms, private bar, large garden, conservatory, and thirty-three elegant bedrooms—each with a special name—is a little hotel whose individuality is a joy to behold and its comfort, a blessed haven.

NUMBER SIXTEEN, 16 Sumner Place, London SW7 3EG. Tel.: (01)589-5232. Telex: 26638. Fax: (01)584-8615. A 33-guestroom (31 private baths) bed and breakfast hotel in 4 Edwardian townhouses. Close to Harrods, museums, Hyde Park, Kensington Gardens. South Kensington Underground Station nearby with direct transportation to Heathrow. Continental breakfast included. Complimentary soft drinks. Open all year. No pets. Timothy McDonald, Manager. (See Index for rates.)

Directions: After arriving at Heathrow Airport, take the underground to South Kensington Station and ask directions to 16 Sumner Place; it is just around the corner. Otherwise, take the regular airport bus to central London and then take the short cab ride to the hotel.

THE BEAUFORT
33 Beaufort Gardens, London

The only indication that this Victorian brick building, neatly trimmed in white woodwork and accented with wrought iron railings and plants, might be a hotel is a discreet sign near the front door: *The Beaufort.* A young woman welcomed me in the hallway as if I were a member of her family, asked me to sign the guest book on a nearby table, and gave me not only a key to my room but one to the front door as well. She then indicated a well-stocked bar to one side of the sitting room. "All drinks are complimentary here. Pour your own whenever you like."

The emphasis on personal consideration for guests is one of the reasons this small, stylish hotel, five-storied with an elevator, is so successful. Its location, perfectly situated on a quiet cul-de-sac, lined with London plane trees, in the middle of bustling Knightsbridge, is another reason. The famed department store Harrods is just around the corner, and within a short walk are the National Museum of Science, the Victoria and Albert Museum, Hyde Park, and Kensington Gardens. In the guest rooms, every amenity possible is found, including a decanter of brandy, a nest of tiny chocolate eggs, videos, fresh flowers, and a bowl of fruit. A light supper menu is available if desired.

The Beaufort is the brainchild of Diana Wallis, a former "television presenter" (once producer for David Frost) and television news reporter. One of her programs was a thirteen-week series on interior design, a harbinger of things to come. In 1985, she decided to leave television and, combining her organizational ability with her flair for decoration, plunged into the creation of a London hotel with a "country-house atmosphere." It took her two years to turn the run-down hotel into the elegant building it is today, with light and airy rooms of marbled wallpapers, bleached furniture, and printed fabrics reminiscent of English gardens. Her husband, Michael, chose over 300 watercolor paintings, mostly florals, to hang on the walls. An artist was hired to paint a series of delicate *trompe l'oeil* arch designs on the parlor walls. Everything is done to create a peaceful environment.

The following morning, a sumptuous continental breakfast was served in my room. As I sat at the circular, glass-topped table, drinking freshly-squeezed orange juice, I gazed out at the trees and had a hard time believing I wasn't in the countryside.

THE BEAUFORT (Pride of Britain), 33 Beaufort Gardens, London SW3 1PP. Tel.: (01)584-5252. Telex: 929200. Fax: (01)589-2834. A 28-guestroom (private baths) primarily bed and breakfast Victorian townhouse on a quiet street, centrally located, near Knightsbridge Underground Station. Closed Christmas week. No pets. Breakfast included. Light meals available. Diana Wallis, Owner. Jane McKevitt, Director. (See Index for rates.)

EBURY COURT HOTEL
26 Ebury Street, London

Fifty years ago Diana Topping bought two houses on Ebury Street in the Belgravia district of London and started a small hotel. Later, she added three more buildings, bringing the total number of guest rooms to thirty-nine. Although not all have private baths, "there is a move toward fully equipping them," said Diana's daughter, Marianne Kingsford, who, along with her husband, Nicholas, is now taking over the hotel's management. "Mother is slowing down a bit," she went on, "but still takes part in what goes on around here."

The Ebury Court is not an elegant hotel. It doesn't try to be. The only bar is a "Members Club," although hotel residents may be served from it everywhere but on the club premises or in the front hallway. Guest rooms do not contain all the amenities found in luxury hotels, and the upstairs halls tend to be narrow and winding. However, rooms are bright, often with color-washed walls, and they are comfortable and clean, a number containing fine pieces of antique furniture. For example, one room has a four-poster bed, another a half-tester. Furthermore, the price of your stay, modest for London, includes a full English breakfast.

A number of staff members have been employed at the hotel for many years. In the cozy green and white restaurant, located in the basement where private nooks and crannies abound, I discovered that the chef had worked at the restaurant for twenty-nine years. Then I learned that the assistant chef had been there for thirty years. "Recently, she retired," said Marianne. "At the age of eighty-six, she didn't feel quite up to helping out with the lunches anymore."

One afternoon, as I sat in the lounge pondering the newspaper's theater section, Nicholas Kingsford's cheerful face appeared in the doorway. "If you need any help there, our head porter is good at arranging theater tickets." He laughed at my look of surprise. "Everyone who works here," he said, "likes to pitch in to help if they think a guest has a problem."

It is this kind of friendliness that keeps guests returning to Ebury Court time and time again, whenever they come to London.

EBURY COURT, 26 Ebury Street, London SW1W OLU. Tel.: (01)730-8147. Fax: (01)823-5966. A 38-guestroom Victorian hotel (private baths for 11 rooms). Close to Buckingham Palace, Westminister Abbey and the West End theatre district. Three minutes' walk from Victoria Station and 2 minutes' walk from the Heathrow Airbus (A1) at Grosvenor Gardens. Open all year. No pets. No pipes in restaurant. Breakfast, lunch, and dinner served to nonresidents. Diana Topping and Nicholas and Marianne Kingsford, Proprietors. (See Index for rates.)

Rates for a room for two people for one night with breakfast, except where noted, are included in the Index of this book. They are not to be considered firm quotations, but should be used as guidelines only.

For room rates and last time for dinner orders, see Index.

THE GORING HOTEL
Beeston Place, Grosvenor Gardens, London

Long considered one of the innovators in the London hotel business, The Goring Hotel has managed to retain its quality and style, in part because Mr. Goring, he himself a revered institution, is still in charge. It is said he sleeps in various bedrooms in his hotel to make certain they are kept up to a high standard.

The Goring is located within walking distance of the Thames Embankment, as well as the Royal Parks, Westminster Abbey, and the Houses of Parliament.

Departures and arrivals from Gatwick Airport are transported directly to or from nearby Victoria Station by train.

The Goring manages to be sedate and informal at the same time. One of its virtues is the fact that there is a beautiful lawn and garden in the rear, providing views of the posteriors of a group of small London townhouses.

THE GORING HOTEL, Beeston Place, Grosvenor Gardens, London SW1W OJW. Tel.: (01) 834-8211. Telex: 919166. An 87-guestroom family-owned hotel near Victoria Station and Pan Am Air Terminals. Breakfast, lunch, tea, dinner served daily to non-residents. William Cowpe, Manager. (See Index for rates.)

DUKES HOTEL
35 St. James's Place, London

Dukes, like the Stafford, is located close to Piccadilly and the London theater district, although both of them are very quiet. Dukes was originally composed of "chambers" for the younger sons of the nobility; it has been a hotel since 1908. I've included it in *CIBR, Britain* since the first edition.

Dukes is probably the closest thing to a private London club—the essence of restrained elegance with a friendly and accommodating atmosphere. It's located on one of the few remaining streets in London enjoying romantic gas lighting.

The *London Times* is left at each door every morning. Although the dining room, which has been considerably enlarged, is open for breakfast, most of the guests prefer to enjoy breakfast in their rooms.

All of the rooms are furnished in a classic style with all the modern conveniences. They are on the medium-to-small size.

To find Dukes one has to have a sharp eye. You turn off St. James's Street, and about 200 yards on the left there is an entrance to Dukes between two buildings. There is a very small car park, used only for leaving your car while you check in. A valet parking service is provided.

I have a feeling that Beau Brummel, the arbiter of London fashion, who lived at 39 St. James's Place, would thoroughly approve of Dukes today.

DUKES HOTEL (Prestige Hotels), 35 St. James's Place, London SW1A 1NY. Tel.: (01)491-4840. Telex: 28283. Fax: (01)493-1264. A 36-guestroom and 26-suite luxury Edwardian hotel in the heart of London's West End. Open every day. Breakfast, lunch, tea, and dinner served to nonresidents. Adjacent to Green Park and Buckingham Palace. Richard Davis, Managing Director. David Dowden, House Manager. (See Index for rates.)

DURRANTS HOTEL
George Street, London

When I walked through the carved double doors into the small lobby where brass lamps glowed softly on wood paneling, I felt transported back to Georgian England. Indeed, the Durrants Hotel really was a coaching inn back in the 1790s. Two centuries later, the atmosphere is still there.

Since 1922, ownership of the hotel has remained with one family. "We feel here," said manager James Speed, "that it is important to preserve the traditions of the past." When the hotel was recently renovated, strict attention was paid to keeping part of old England while giving guests all the modern conveniences for comfort in the well-appointed bedrooms.

On the ground floor are four intimate lounges with unique fireplaces, intricate ceiling moldings, and antique furniture. The George Bar and Pump Room give the feeling of a 19th-century London Club, and the dining room could be a scene from Dickens's *Pickwick Papers*. It was worth taking time to walk through the public rooms and curved halls to peruse the collection of prints and paintings, many showing scenes of early London. Especially interesting, in the breakfast room, are the rare prints of English male characters by Spy, and, just off the lobby, a painting done in 1792 of W.H. Durrant, a family member of the original owner. Also, the Victorian clock that chimes from the stairway deserves special attention.

Located in the heart of the West End, the Durrants is close to the fashionable shopping streets of the Marylebone, an area considered a village by locals. Within walking distance are Marble Arch, Hyde Park, Piccadilly, and the theatres.

DURRANTS HOTEL. George Street, London WIH 6BJ. Tel.: (01)935-8131. Telex: 894919 Durhot. Fax: (01)487-3510. A 94-guestroom (85 private baths) pleasant Georgian hotel off Manchester Square, opposite the Wallace Collection, a few blocks from Oxford Street and Marble Arch. Near Bond Street Underground Station. Open every day of the year. Breakfast, lunch, tea, and dinner served to nonresidents. James Speed, Manager. P.J.W. Humphreys, Director. (See Index for rates.)

HARRODS

I was browsing in the meat shop at Harrods, one of London's great department stores.

What a glorious fantasia of sights and enticing aromas greeted me! It was Elysian at the very least.

The first things I saw hanging from the domed ceiling, mind you, were hundreds of hams, sausages, pumpernickels, salamis, and dozens of their relatives in the "wurst" family. A great many of them were imported from different countries in Europe, and there were numerous items that were totally new to me.

Below them was a large center section of cases with such delights as pork pies, steak-and-kidney pies, ham pies, and chicken pies. There were twenty-seven varieties of salads, including oriental, Spanish, Russian. The displays themselves were beautiful. There were tins of caviar and small fish, and dozens of varieties of pâté. There were jellied eels, absolutely sumptuous-looking bacon, and beautiful quiches. I walked around the center at least three times planning picnics and cold buffets.

To further add to my delight, all around the outside of this square were counters with gorgeous displays of fowl, including turkey and pheasant. There were cuts of pork, lamb, veal, beef—just about everything. Particularly intriguing was the display of fish, including kippers, shellfish, halibut, sole, Scottish salmon, and many others. There was also a large fish sculpture in ice.

All of these great treats were beautifully displayed in a setting of intricately tiled pillars and ceiling. There were many colors of tiles forming a fascinating succession of patterns.

The next stop was the cheese department, equally exciting. There were all kinds of cheeses done in all forms—in crocks, jars, cans, sliced, in cases for slicing, and hanging from the ceilings. There were cheeses from all over the world—Beaumont, Brie, Port Salut, Jarlsburg, provolone, to name a few. There were cases of cheese of all colors—yellow, green, white, and speckled cheeses. I saw wheels of cheeses and cheese pâtés.

The aroma and sights are still in my mind.

In Britain, acceptance of a hotel booking by telephone or in writing is generally regarded as a legally binding contract. If it's necessary to cancel, advise the hotel immediately. If they are unable to re-let the room, the hotel may be entitled to claim compensation—usually two thirds of the agreed price—and any deposit would be included as part of this payment.

It's not that the distances are very long in the British Isles, it's the many diversions along the way that sometimes make it impossible to estimate traveling and arrival times. Last order times for dinner are included in the Index so that you can see what time you must arrive in order not to find the kitchen door locked. If you are going to arrive later, call ahead—there isn't a hotel/inn listed here that will not make some provision to feed you if they know you can't make it before the kitchen closes.

THE THAMES AND THE CHILTERNS
Counties of Oxfordshire,
Buckinghamshire, Bedfordshire
and Berkshire

The Thames Valley and the Chilterns extend from the London city limits to the western borders of Berkshire and include Oxford, the edge of the Cotswolds, and Bedford to the north.

The Thames meanders through towns and villages and eventually through London. It ripples down from its source in the Cotswold Hills, gathering momentum and becoming a full-fledged, navigable river. It passes through the peaceful countryside, historic towns, and lush meadows and by lovely old inns and waterside gardens; negotiates locks, rushing weirs, and leafy backwaters; slices between the wooded hills of Goring Gap; and slides lazily by Windsor, taking in memorable views of the town and castle.

The Chiltern Hills, many of which are crowned with ancient beech groves, are located roughly to the northwest of London, and the narrow country roads leading out of High Wycombe, Chalfont, and Wendover provide a very pleasant alternative route to Oxford.

The Thames and Chilterns are rich in history, architecture, and tradition. There are hundreds of years of family history to explore, and every one of its many great houses has its own unique story—of great men and wicked men, men who won battles, built empires, and gambled away fortunes.

THE THAMES AND THE CHILTERNS

THE FEATHERS HOTEL
Market Street, Woodstock, Oxfordshire

It was 3:30 in the afternoon when I drove into Woodstock, a historic town within walking distance of Blenheim Palace. I found a parking space next to the brick archway which leads to the back of The Feathers Hotel, where the public entrance to the bar is located. For a moment I imagined what it might have been like in the 17th century when horse-drawn carriages clattered through the gateway to let passengers out in the courtyard where now stood groups of chairs around umbrella-topped tables.

Later in history, part of this coaching inn was a butcher shop then a ladies' sanitarium. Today, the handsome brick building, its white woodwork decorated with window boxes and hanging baskets full of bright flowers, has returned to its original intention—an inn to serve tired travelers. I was one.

Wearily, I followed the porter past an exceptionally beautiful flower arrangement and a glass case containing a stuffed owl, then up a little staircase to my room.

Later, Manager Tom Lewis joined me downstairs in the paneled lounge where a fire was lit and I sipped refreshing tea, feeling better by the minute. I asked him about the birds I had seen in numerous cases about the hotel.

"It's Mr. Gray's personal antique collection," he replied, "and the reason why he named his hotel The Feathers. Sorry he isn't here right now. He enjoys talking about the pieces."

In the evening, I pursued the bird theme further by eating breast of guinea fowl filled with spinach, hazelnut, and savoury crumbs, as a main course served with basil and tomato strips. Unbelievably good.

When I commented to Tom how impressed I was with the warm, good old-fashioned service, he told me the owner recruits his personnel based on personality. Then he sets about training them. "You see, Mr. Gray wants his hotel to be more like a home, where everything looks worn in but not worn out."

It's one of many reasons why people keep returning to dine and stay at The Feathers Hotel.

THE FEATHERS HOTEL, Market Street, Woodstock, Oxfordshire. Tel.: Woodstock (0993)812-291. Telex: 83147 VIA OR G. Fax: Woodstock (0993)813-158. A 15-guestroom (private baths) hotel in a 17th-century coaching inn within walking distance of Blenheim Palace. Close to Oxford and the Cotswolds. Open all year. Full English breakfast included. Breakfast, lunch, tea, dinner, bar snacks served to nonresidents. Gordon Campbell Gray, Owner. Tom Lewis, Manager. (See Index for rates.)

Directions: From London, follow M40 which goes onto A40 to Oxford. Follow signs to Stratford/Woodstock on A34. On reaching Woodstock, turn 2nd left after Blenheim Palace gates.

THE MANOR CHADLINGTON
Chadlington, Oxfordshire

"Why did you do it?" I asked my host, David Grant, as we sat in front of the fireplace in the drawing room of his newly opened country house hotel. I was referring to the fact that he and his wife, Chris, had sold their much larger, successful hotel in Yorkshire, to purchase a run-down manor house of historical significance in the stone village of Chadlington in Oxfordshire and thrown heart and soul into turning it into the elegant country house hotel it is today.

"I suppose we were quite mad, really," he replied, "to start all over again from scratch, but we realized we couldn't run a large hotel in a personal way. The smaller you are, the easier it is to single-mindedly offer what we really like when we go ourselves."

Set in eighteen acres of grounds, including a vegetable garden, with peaceful countryside stretching in all directions, Manor Chadlington is a listed building from the 16th century, with fine interior architectural details. While David runs the hotel and restaurant, besides overseeing a quality wine cellar, Chris is the head chef. She insists on creating an imaginative variety of meals to complement their home. Her motto: "Present the freshest food with the finest flavor."

Much is offered here at Manor Chadlington. Each of the seven spacious rooms (eventually there will be twelve) is decorated quite differently, in high style, not just the usual floral chintz but bolder patterns, more interesting color combinations, and special hand-painted touches such as designs on mirror frames, a mural on the wall behind one of the bathtubs, and butterflies on the partially domed ceiling in one of the most luxurious bedrooms.

Here is a retreat from the fast-paced world, yet only an hour by train from London.

THE MANOR CHADLINGTON, Chadlington, Oxfordshire OX7 3LX. Tel.: (0608)76711. A 7-guestroom (private baths) country house hotel of 16th-century origin. Open all year. Equidistant between Cheltingham and Stratford, 17 mi. from Oxford and close to the Cotswold villages. Breakfast included. Dinner for nonresidents restricted to several tables by appointment. No pets. Chris and David Grant, Proprietors. (See Index for rates.)

Directions: From Oxford, take A34 north. Exit at Chipping Norton and take the Burford Rd., A361, south for about 3 mi. Chadlington is marked to the left. The Manor is beside the church in the village. Charlbury, 3 mi. away, is a mainline train station connecting to Paddington Station in London.

THE GOLDEN PHEASANT
The High Street, Burford, Oxfordshire

I was first attracted to The Golden Pheasant when I saw its logo on a brochure—a striking rendition of a pheasant perched on the limb of a tree, a country scene beneath. The inn was located in Burford, and I remembered once visiting the town, full of charming old stone houses and antiques shops.

Ben Sands, son-in-law to the owners, met me in the lobby and showed me around. The hotel proved to be a great find. From the residents' lounge through the dining room and up into the guest rooms, I could see that great care had been taken to meet the needs of travelers and give them beauty and atmosphere besides. In many areas old timbers and interior stone walls had been exposed. Halls, so often drab in hotels, had been freshly papered. I was even more impressed with two exceptionally fine bedrooms on the top floor where high, sloped ceilings and beams invoked medieval times. Each of the two rooms had four-poster beds, one dating back to the 17th century.

"I liked this building right away," Ben declared. "It has the oldest set of property deeds in Burford. Parts of the building date back to the 14th century. In the 15th century, a woolen merchant lived here. In 1737, it became a pub."

Ben, who has always lived in the Cotswolds and previously managed a hotel in Stow, came here four years ago to oversee the inn's restoration for his wife's parents. He stayed and is now the manager.

Besides being a quality hotel, The Golden Pheasant is also a fine restaurant. French and English dishes are served at tables covered with linens; candles are lit at night, and a fire is set on the raised hearth when evenings are cold. Both dinner menus and à la carte meals are available. In the summer, people enjoy eating outdoors on a back courtyard near the large car park.

THE GOLDEN PHEASANT HOTEL, The High Street, Burford, Oxfordshire. Tel.: Burford (099382)3223. A 12-guestroom (private baths) inn in a 15th-century stone building, strategically located for visits to the Cotswolds. Close by are the Wildlife Park and the Country Farm. Breakfast included. Breakfast, lunch, tea, and dinner served to nonresidents.

William and Anne Barrett, Owners. Ben Sands, Manager. (See Index for rates.)

Directions: Turn off right at Burford roundabout from A40 Oxford to Cheltenham.

LE MANOIR AUX QUAT'SAISONS
(The Manor of Four Seasons
Great Milton, Oxfordshire

It was 7:30 on a Monday evening. Already nine people had gathered in the yellow salon, some perusing the menu and wine list, others enjoying a cocktail, and others sampling from a plate of tiny appetizers set before them. I had just finished mine, enjoying each tantalizing taste, when the waiter informed me my table was ready.

Thus began a memorable experience, a nine-course dinner that included button mushrooms filled with a snail mousse, served with a Hermitage wine sauce; roasted monkfish, masked with savory breadcrumbs and served with a saffron-scented cream; and roasted teal, served with fresh diced quinces. At the conclusion, three little desserts were presented separately: a tulip of red fruits with a raspberry sorbet, followed by a delicate Malibu soufflé with banana sorbet, then a crème caramel with sliced pears. No, wait, that was not all. I retired to the salon for coffee and a small tiered tray of petite fours.

On Monday nights the restaurant at Le Manoir is closed to the public. Only residents of its ten guest rooms enjoy the superb cuisine of Raymond Blanc, head chef and owner of Le Manoir aux Quat'Saisons, a manor house that dates from the 15th century. On other nights there is a wide menu choice, although the restaurant itself remains small and intimate. This one night a week the gourmet menu is set, and I ate every morsel of every course. Yet so balanced was the meal, with just the right amount presented, and so smooth the service that at the end of the two-hour feast I felt pleasantly full and decidedly relaxed.

What is amazing about Raymond Blanc is that he is completely self-taught. "I fell into cooking by accident," the slender dark-haired Frenchman said. "I was a waiter in a pub, and one day the chef did not arrive. I found myself with a cookbook in one hand, a spoon in the other, a kettle before me, and only my imagination and taste to give me courage." Not only did he become the chef of the pub, but two years later received a Michelin star for his achievement. At Le Manoir he has *two* Michelin stars and awards from just about every gastronomical society in the world.

Lest you think it is only the food that makes this country house hotel famous, let me hasten to say there is much more. The decor is elegant, yet retains a country feeling. There are multitudes of exquisite flower arrangements (Raymond's mother-in-law does them.) Each guest room has a silver-leafed decenter of Madeira and a bowl of fruit that looks like a Renoir painting. The twenty-seven-acre grounds are spectacular. Everything is the finest, including the service. From the moment I stepped into the front hall and received a gracious welcome to the time I climbed back into my car, I felt royally treated in this country palace. True, it is expensive here. However, with a staff of 75 and so many amenities, it could hardly be otherwise.

LE MANOIR AUX QUAT'SAISONS, Great Milton, Oxford, Oxfordshire OX97PD. Tel: (0844) 278-881. Telex: 837552. Fax: (0844) 278-847. A 10-guestroom (private baths) 15th-century manor house with swimming pool and extensive landscaped grounds (11 more guestrooms to be completed by late spring 1990). Closed Dec. 21 thru Jan. 19. Two nights minimum on weekends. Kennels on grounds for pets. Only 12 mi. from Oxford; 45 mi. from London. Breakfast included, served in room. Dinner available to nonresidents every day except Mon. Luncheon available on special arrangement. Raymond Blanc, Owner. Nicholas Dickinson, Manager. (See Index for rates.)

Directions: From London take the M40. Exit at junction 7. Turn left onto A329, going south, then right at Great Milton's 2nd turning. Hotel is 200 yards on the right.

THE RED LION HOTEL
Henley-on-Thames, Oxfordshire

I debated about including The Red Lion Hotel, since it hasn't yet completed its remodelling and isn't yet exactly what I consider a country inn, but because of its fascinating history, its location close to Heathrow Airport, and the careful process of restoration that promises to bring back its old character, I decided it should be brought to the traveler's attention. Furthermore, the town itself is interesting, and the hotel has wonderful views of the Thames and the stone Henley Bridge built in 1786.

Long before the Norman Conquest in 1066, Henley stood by the River Thames. Sometime in the 16th century, The Red Lion came into existence. Strategically located on the old coaching road between London and Oxford, at one time at least seventeen coaches stopped here daily. In 1632 Charles I stayed at the inn. His coat of arms, painted above the fireplace in his room, has been preserved. Other royalty and important personages have visited. In commemoration, the rooms in which they stayed bear their names today.

A year ago, the owners of Durrants Hotel (see the London section) bought The Red Lion and embarked on the gigantic task of reconstruction and refurbishment. The ground floor and half of the rooms, all individually designed, are finished and tastefully appointed in a manner that complements the age of the inn. Completion of the rest is to be done unobtrusively, one room at a time, and is scheduled to be finished by the end of 1990.

THE RED LION HOTEL, Henley-on-Thames, Oxfordshire RG9 2AR. Tel.: (0491)572-161. Fax: (0491)410-039. A 26-guestroom (21 private baths) 16th-century coaching inn across the street from the River Thames. Open all year. Breakfast not included. Breakfast, lunch, and dinner available for nonresidents. Has an à la carte menu and bar snacks. Henley Royal Regatta, end of June. Short drive from Heathrow Airport. Durrants Hotel, Ltd., Proprietors. Jean-Paul Leveque, Resident Director. (See Index for rates.)

Directions: Take A4 from Heathrow Airport to Maidenhead, then A423 to Henley-on-Thames.

THE GREY SPIRES OF OXFORD

Long before I had walked along the High or stood at the Carfax, the main crossroad of Oxford, or had seen for myself the Magdalen College deer park, or admired Wren's Sheldonian Theatre, or browsed in Blackwell's Bookstore, I had dreamed of being in Oxford.

I expected to find a quiet town basking in the afternoon sun with groups of undergraduates casually strolling to appointments with their tutors, or trotting toward the cricket field, or dreaming on the river bank.

Instead, I found a vibrant, active city where town and gown alike enjoy the fruits of learning and pleasure. The quadrangles of the thirty-four colleges, each providing a superb example of almost every architectural period, are woven into the fabric of the commercial and residential life of the town.

Oxford has left its mark on some of the world's intellectual and literary giants. A list of scholars and graduates is a veritable "Who's Who" of English letters. Balliol College claims John Wycliffe, Adam Smith, Robert Southey, Matthew Arnold, and Algernon Swinburne. Thomas Moore, Robert Burton, John Ruskin, and W. H. Auden were members of Christchurch.

Magdalen Hall looked down upon a youthful John Keats.

Perhaps of more contemporary interest is the fact that J.R.R. Tolkien was a Fellow and a Professor of English Language and Literature at Merton from 1945 to 1959.

Cardinal Wolsey, Roger Bacon, Geoffrey Chaucer, Shakespeare, Alexander Pope, Jane Austen, Wordsworth (a Cambridge man who wrote two sonnets about Oxford), Thomas Hardy, Henry James, and Dylan Thomas visited Oxford and came under its sway.

For an interesting satirical contrast between Oxford and Cambridge, first read Sir Max Beerbohm's novel, Zuleika Dobson, *and then read* Zuleika Goes to Cambridge. *The latter is attributed to "S. Roberts," which may be a Beerbohm pseudonym.*

WOODLANDS MANOR
Clapham, Bedfordshire

This is a place where you are likely to meet American businessmen. Owner Richard Lee tells me that there are a number of American companies based in Bedford, including Texas Instruments, Prime Computers, and National Semiconductors.

I could see why they would like to stay in this gracious Victorian manor house. There is a pleasant and comfortable drawing room with many groupings of sofas and chairs, the dining room is inviting with its white linen and rose-and-white Limoges china and silver settings, and I understand the food is excellent.

The guest rooms that Mr. Lee showed me were quite attractively decorated. Some of the bathrooms boast rather unusual tortoise shell, marbleized walls, and fixtures in harmonizing colors.

All of the guest rooms have televisions, radios, and telephones, and such other amenities as hair dryers and trouser presses.

The dinner menu offers ten possible starters, including a fan of baked avocado, pear, and Stilton cheese with a spicy tomato sauce, curried mushrooms and pistachio nuts in a puff pastry, and a smoked mackerel mousse with a horseradish sauce. Among eight choices for the meat course were Dorset veal, pan fried with white wine and cream and Stilton cheese, roast breast of duckling with plum and port wine sauce, and calf's liver pan fried with sage, sliced onion, and bacon. A special menu is available for vegetarians.

The manor house is surrounded by a pleasant lawn with trees and gardens, and there are chairs and tables with umbrellas, where drinks are served when the weather permits.

WOODLANDS MANOR, Green Lane, Clapham, Bedfordshire MK41 6EP. Tel.: (0234) 63281; Telex: 825007. A 21-guestroom (private baths) Victorian manor house on the outskirts of the busy and historic town of Bedford, a few miles from Cambridge. Continental breakfast included in tariff. Restaurant serves breakfast, lunch, and dinner. Reservations neces-

sary. Open year-round except Christmas week. Convenient to Woburn Abbey and the John Bunyan Museum in Bedford and the many cultural and historic attractions in Cambridge and Oxford. Trout fishing on the River Ouse and other recreational activities also available nearby. Two dogs in residence. Richard Lee, Proprietor. (See Index for rates.)

Directions: From London, take the M1 to the A1. Turn off on the A603 to Bedford. In Bedford take the A6 toward Clapham. Continue 2 mi. to Green Lane on the right.

FLITWICK MANOR
Flitwick, Bedfordshire

I think of Santa Claus when I think of Somerset Moore—he has that jovial, jolly quality that makes you feel happy to talk to him. I was trying not to eat *all* the delectable cookies on the tea tray Debbie, his manager, had placed before me, while he was telling me the story behind his remarkable collection of beautiful antique porcelain covered sardine dishes. You might want to ask him about them.

With his reputation as a fine chef, Somerset and his wife, Hélène, opened Flitwick Manor as a restaurant, and with its success they were soon able to move forward with their dream of creating a country house hotel.

They had chosen an impressive property for their endeavor. Standing on high ground above the town, this estate has a recorded history dating back to the 11th century, and the present manor house is of 17th- and 18th-century origins. The drive up to the house is lined with lime, or linden, trees, most of which are 250 years old. Somerset is justly proud of

all the magnificent trees on the grounds, many of which have been listed by the Forest Commission. You should ask him about them—especially the juniper *recurva,* which I couldn't get over.

There are fifty acres of grounds, including woodland, a three-acre lake, an 18th-century grotto (called a "folly") with an ornamental pond, and gardens, both cultivated and wild. Somerset makes sure there are some wild areas for his bees. You'll want to ask him about those, too.

The reception area has an interesting, somewhat primitive feeling, with its simple brick fireplace, rather rough parquet floor, and medieval chairs. However, the sitting room is quite different. Paneled in lovely honey-colored pine, with a marble-faced fireplace and elegant furniture and fittings, it provides quite a luxurious feeling.

In fact, the entire house is most luxurious. I saw nearly every guest room, and was really impressed with the decoration—the furnishings, the choice of colors and fabrics—and, in short, the total aspect of every room. Even the bathrooms are outstanding. I don't think I've ever seen such an array of amenities, from every sort of toiletry, including razors, combs, and cosmetics, to baskets of fruit and an incredible assortment of both alcoholic and nonalcoholic drinks on the "honesty" drink tray. Every room also has a Scrabble game and a pack of cards in addition to television, a radio, and a telephone.

There isn't a view from a window that isn't enchanting, whether it's lawn, trees, and gardens, the cedar of Lebanon tree, a meadow, the pond, the lake, a village on a hill far away, or the kitchen garden with fruit trees, beehives, chickens, and a brick wall covered with wisteria.

Even the halls and landings display beautiful and unusual antique pieces and paintings. You should ask Hélène about those.

It goes without saying that the lounge and dining rooms are lovely. I was extremely disappointed that I couldn't stay for dinner. The cuisine is basically English with some French influence, and the menu lists a really mind-boggling selection of dishes for every course, with an emphasis on fish and other seafood. There are various mouth-watering treatments of lobster, crab, salmon, oysters, trout, eel, clams, shrimps, and sea bass. For instance, there is lobster cooked with brandy, cream, and truffles or a fillet of Scotch salmon in a puff pastry with asparagus tips and a sauce Maltaise. I noticed several starred items, which presented "a new concept in low-calorie eating." It's impossible for me to convey the full scope of the menu. You'll have to see it. Their brochure describes their sources for provisions, and I'm sure if you asked Somerset, he'd show you the kitchen.

Flitwick is in an excellent spot for seeing some of the interesting sights in Bedfordshire, particularly the Woburn Estate, with a stately house, a fabulous art collection, and a 2,000-acre park with rare deer. There is also the Fabergé collection at Luton Hoo, a house of descendants of Russian czars, and many other places of interest. You should definitely ask Somerset about them—I think you'll agree he's a lot of fun to talk to.

FLITWICK MANOR, Flitwick, Bedfordshire MK45 1AE. Tel.: Flitwick (0525) 712242. Telex: 825562. A 16-guestroom (private baths) luxurious country house hotel in the rolling countryside of Bedfordshire, halfway between Oxford and Cambridge. All bed sizes. Breakfast included in the tariff. Lunch and dinner served to the public; reservations imperative on weekends. Open year-round. Croquet lawns, hard-surface tennis court, putting green, snooker, walks, Wellies, and bicycles on grounds. Woburn Estate, Luton Hoo, and other stately homes, golf, Silverstone motor racing, squash, swimming, horseback riding, surfing, and windsailing nearby. One cat and one dog in residence. Mr. and Mrs. Somerset Moore, Proprietors; Janet Abbot and Debbie Bullock, Managers. (See Index for rates.)

Directions: From London, take the M1 north to the A5120 or 512. About 3 mi. from turnoff watch for entrance on the left.

It's not that the distances are very long in the British Isles, it's the many diversions along the way that sometimes make it impossible to estimate traveling and arrival times. Last order times for dinner are included in the Index so that you can see what time you must arrive in order not to find the kitchen door locked. If you are going to arrive later, call ahead—there isn't a hotel/inn listed here that will not make some provision to feed you if they know you can't make it before the kitchen closes.

EAST ANGLIA
Counties of Sussex,
Essex, Suffolk, Norfolk,
and Cambridgeshire

East Anglia starts at the Thames estuary and runs north to King's Lynn and the Wash. It bulges into the North Sea to the east, and its coastline is opposite Europe. To the west it borders the Thames, the Chilterns, and the Heart of England.

Essex is the county closest to London. Its great attractions are the seaside towns and villages and the historic town of Colchester.

In the 13th century, Flemish weavers settled in Suffolk and established a cloth trade that was to make the county one of the great centers of medieval England. Some of the towns in midcounty like Long Melford and Lavenham still have great churches, houses, and colorful cottages. Suffolk is Constable country and the great English painter saw great beauty in the quiet pastoral scenes near Dedham. Newmarket is a famous racing center.

Norfolk has the famous inland waterways known as the Norfolk Broads. These reed-fringed lagoons are thought to be the remains of Saxon peat diggings that are now flooded and connected by a complex network of six rivers. Norwich is its ancient capital, and there are castles and many great houses in this section. Norfolk is also well known for its seaside resorts.

Cambridgeshire, besides being the site of the famous university, also has the cathedral town of Ely, where the King's School was founded by Alfred the Great. Other towns include Kimbolton, where Mary, Queen of Scots, was imprisoned for a time; Soham, one of the last areas of natural habitat for fenland wildlife; and St. Ives.

Many individuals from East Anglia have left their mark on England, if not the entire world. The great landscape painter John Constable was inspired by the tranquil countryside. Sir Isaac Newton was seated in the garden of this manor in nearby Lincolnshire when he formulated the law of gravity as he watched an apple fall from a tree. Oliver Cromwell, the Protector of England, attended the grammar school which is now the Cromwell Museum in Huntingdon.

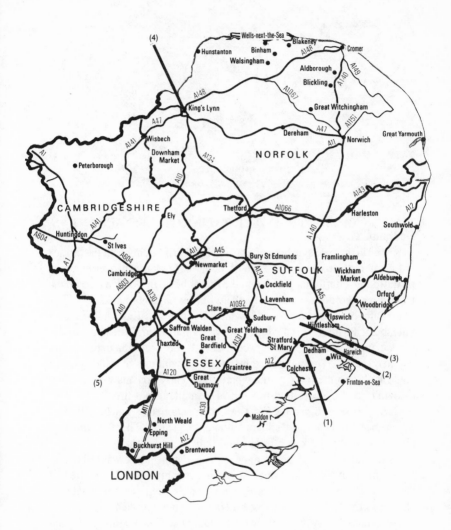

EAST ANGLIA

MAISON TALBOOTH AND LE TALBOOTH RESTAURANT
Dedham, Essex

Seated in the pale sunshine of a promising April forenoon on the terrace of Le Talbooth on the banks of the River Stour, I was nearly overwhelmed by daffodils—daffodils growing in the flower beds, in wooden tubs on the terrace, on the dock—masses of them on the opposite banks.

Le Talbooth is a beautiful, old, white building with Tudor half-timbers interspersed with red brickwork. The wrought iron furniture and marble-topped tables on the terrace would shortly be accommodating other luncheon guests. Through the stone mullioned windows of leaded glass, I could look into the lounge area where some early arrivals were already enjoying good conversation in front of a small, bright fire.

Gerry Milsom joined me for a few moments before lunch. "We still have time to run over to Dedham Village," he said. "There's something over there that I think you might find rather extraordinary."

As we walked across the lawn, he told me that the house was built early in the 16th century. "The name 'Talbooth' probably derives from the fact that tolls were collected at the bridge. It may have been used to collect tolls also from the barges that worked their way from Harwich."

I remarked on how beautifully the building had been restored. "By the 1930s," he said, "the house was in a sad state of disrepair. Abandoned lime kilns occupied the site of the River Room, and the oak timber frame of the house, so characteristic of East Anglian domestic architecture, was concealed by the original lime plaster, crumbling and long past making good.

"We arrived on the scene in 1952 with everything in a near-shambles. It took a lot of time and a lot of work, but we finally opened. During the first week, the takings were 27½ pence!"

I might add, parenthetically, that now Le Talbooth is a rousing success and a founding member of the prestigious Pride of Britain Partnership.

As we sped over the country road towards the village of Dedham, Gerry explained that there are two establishments; one is the restaurant Le Talbooth, and the other is a country house hotel with the appropriate name of Maison Talbooth.

In the village I saw the old grammar school attended by the painter John Constable. Gerry pointed out a brick building with a sun dial on the front. "This building, Sherman Hall," he said, "has direct connections with the General Sherman who gained some notoriety during the American War Between the States."

Maison Talbooth is an elegant country house hotel with fine views of the Constable countryside. As Gerry says, "We work on the assumption that everybody who comes here really has a first-class home, and they don't want to experience anything less than they are accustomed to."

There was no reception desk; instead, we were met in the reception hall by a very attractive hostess who obligingly showed me through the individual rooms and suites, all with sumptuous furnishings. The bedrooms were beautiful, but words fail me on the subject of the bathrooms. Each of the ten was entirely different, and two of them had round sunken bathtubs large enough for two people. Very contemporary.

During the half-mile return trip to the restaurant, Gerry commented that the Vale of Dedham is known throughout the world because of the many Constable paintings. "There is a painting, hanging in the National Gallery of Scotland, of Le Talbooth itself in a view across the vale. We're fortunate enough to have a copy."

I still have fond memories of lunch, which included a delicious slice of pork brought to the table on a silver carving tray. The kitchen is staffed with enthusiastic men and women well versed in the art of French cuisine, who also turn out such regional specialties as Yarmouth herring with cream cheese, Colchester oysters, and Suffolk stew.

Gerry proved to be a walking fount of information about the virtues and attractions of East Anglia, and his last word before my departure was, "I hope all of your readers will visit East Anglia. It's the uncrowded, natural England for which so many people are searching."

MAISON TALBOOTH AND LE TALBOOTH RESTAURANT (Pride of Britain), Stratford Rd., Dedham, Colchester, Essex CO7 6HN. Tel.: (0206) Colchester 322-367. U.S. reservations: 800-323-7308. A 10-guestroom (private baths) luxury hotel and restaurant located about 8 mi. from the ancient city of Colchester. Lunch and dinner served every day. In the heart of Constable country, it is very convenient to many of the Essex and Suffolk cultural, scenic, and recreational attractions. Tennis, swim-

ming, riding, golf, fishing, available nearby. Gerald Milsom, Proprietor. (See Index for rates.)

Directions: Follow A12 from London. Above Colchester, watch for exit at Stratford St. Mary and Dedham. Follow road down hill. Take right turn toward Dedham. Maison Talbooth is ½ mi. on right.

DEDHAM HALL
Dedham, Essex

"This entire area—the Vale of Dedham—is a walker's and painter's paradise." Bill Slingo and I were taking a stroll about the grounds at Dedham Hall as he explained some of the many interesting aspects of this splendid guest house.

"Actually," he continued, "the Vale of Dedham is a wide valley through which flows the River Stour, the boundary between the counties of Essex and Suffolk. John Constable discovered its wonderful, paintable qualities and it was made famous by his landscapes. Fortunately, the Ministry of the Environment has declared it an area of outstanding beauty and national importance, so it's changed very little since he painted it."

As we made the turn around Dedham Hall, he indicated a timber-framed, white plastered house with one side almost completely of glass. "Because so many of our guests are interested in painting, we made this old 14th-century building available for painting courses that are held throughout most of the year. Visiting tutors are experienced in oils, water colors, and pastels. I do a bit of picture framing here if it's desired."

There are ten very comfortable guest rooms at Dedham Hall, and besides the full English breakfast, which includes homemade bread or

croissants, Elizabeth Slingo provides a hearty dinner. Most of the eggs and meat come from the Hall grounds, and she's very proud of the home-grown vegetables. Dinner is served at 7:30 p.m., but reservations are necessary no later than 9:30 a.m., because everything is cooked to order.

"There are two sitting rooms and a small bar in the oldest part of the house, which dates back to 1380," Bill commented. "Relaxing there in the evening is sometimes one of the best times of the day."

Our turn around the grounds brought us back to the front entrance, and I could see the often-painted tower of Dedham Church rising above the trees. The village of Dedham and the surrounding countryside remain one of the most beautiful and unspoiled areas in England. Small wonder that John Constable was so inspired.

DEDHAM HALL, Dedham, Colchester, Essex CO7 6AD. Tel.: (0206) Colchester 323027. A 12-guestroom (8 rooms with private baths) guest house in the heart of Constable country. Rates include breakfast. Dinner served to houseguests and friends with 12-hr. advance notice. Closed Jan. and Feb. Inquire about painting courses held frequently with visiting tutors. Most conveniently located to enjoy Dedham Vale and wonderful walks in the country. Mr. and Mrs. William Slingo, Proprietors. (See Index for rates.)

Directions: Take Dedham exit from A12; follow through village and look for guest house sign on the left.

THE OLD VICARAGE
Higham (near Colchester), Suffolk

We American Anglophiles who watch "Masterpiece Theatre" regularly are certainly familiar with English countryside and with English country houses. That's why, when I stopped off at the Old Vicarage, I felt as if I had been there before. It's really a private house, because there is no sign indicating that there are accommodations available. The Parkers are country people who have "a few guests now and again." I think the great appeal is that it is indeed a private family; however, Meg Parker has a way of taking people up and making them feel as if they are very much part of everything that is going on.

I phoned from about a mile away in the center of the village and had no difficulty following her directions to reach the pink house. There were other personal guests visiting at the time, and for a few minutes we all gathered in the comfortable drawing room and talked travel, discovering that we had all visited several of the same places.

The guests went off to play tennis on the courts just outside the door, and Meg and I stayed long enough to have a late-morning cup of coffee and to get acquainted.

"That's the River Brett just behind us," she pointed out. "It joins Constable's favorite river, the Stour, just a little bit farther on. You know we are right on the Essex and Suffolk borders."

While we were talking we were joined briefly by a couple of friendly dogs, who rendered their approval of me and then went outside to enjoy the June sunshine. Meanwhile, we could hear the sounds of the tennis game going on, and another guest came through to take a plunge in the swimming pool.

The house itself, like other East Anglian structures, is Elizabethan in design. There are six guest rooms, three of them with private baths and the other three share two bathrooms. A full breakfast is included and Meg mentioned that there are times when she invites her guests to use the kitchen to prepare a light evening meal for themselves.

We continued our chat, strolling around the grounds and the most impressive garden. She pointed out that the sweet little church that adjoins the Vicarage dates back to the 14th century. "It is a typical small wool church," she explained, "so-called because the people who lived up here were all in the wool business. The church is still in use today, and on Sunday the church bells are rung by the village carpenter."

I think you'll have a lot of fun finding the Old Vicarage, but you'll have even more fun as a guest.

THE OLD VICARAGE (Wolsey Lodges), Higham (near Colchester), Suffolk. Tel.: (0206-37-248) Higham 248. A 5-guestroom (4 pty baths) private home in the Constable country of Suffolk. Double and twin beds available. Full breakfast is included in the room rate. Open all year. Tennis court and swimming pool on grounds. Boats and fishing on river. Conveniently located for excursions to the Suffolk coasts, as well as e.joying the footpaths and back roads. Meg Parker, Proprietress. (See Index for rates.)

Directions: Take the Stratford St. Mary exit from the A12 (halfway between Ipswich and Colchester), and follow the road toward Dedham and Langham to Stratford St. Mary. In Stratford St. Mary, there is a turning marked Higham; follow this 1 mi. and look on the right for a pinkish house with a black barn and 3 pink deer beside a sign marked "Church."

THE NORFOLK BROADS

It's hard for anyone to suppress a smile when the term "Norfolk Broads" is introduced into the conversation. Double entendre aside, the Norfolk Broads are among the greatest attractions of this section of East Anglia. These reed-fringed lagoons are thought to be the remains of Saxon peat diggings now flooded and connected by a complex network of rivers.

*Hidden canals link vast acreages of water drained from the local coun-
tryside, offering ideal waterways by which to explore the broadlands.
There are more than thirty large water areas contained in the triangular
area between Norwich, Lowestoft, and Sea Palling. Along with the canals,
lakes, and rivers, they provide some two hundred miles of water for
cruising and sailing.*

*The essential character of the Broads can only be properly appreciated
from a boat and there are boat liveries and tour operators in such centers
as Roxham, Horning, and Potter Heigham.*

*One of the best ways to view the Broads by car is to take the main road
between Ormesbey St. Margaret and Rollesby.*

*From Norwich to Great Yarmouth, the country is as flat as Holland, and
like Holland, boasts windmills—five, if not more, can be seen along this
stretch. In this part of the world, flat means beautiful.*

CONGHAM HALL
King's Lynn, Norfolk

I had no trouble knowing which direction was west. From the great
window in my bedroom overlooking the rear lawns of Congham Hall I
could see the wonderful, lowering Norfolk sky moving in, leaving an ever-
diminishing streak of red across the horizon. In some places this might
bode a fair day on the morrow; however, in England the weather can be
capricious, and the television in my room had informed me only a few
minutes before that a string of showers from the southwest would soon be
coming across the heart of England and into East Anglia.

However, in the spring one travels in England on a day-to-day basis, and
this had been a beautiful day, starting with cheery good-byes to Gerald
Milsom at Maison Talbooth in Dedham, and continuing on up to Bury St.
Edmunds for a visit at the Angel, and then north through the wonderful
Thetford Forest, past the gates of Sandringham, the Queen of England's
estate.

Now I was at Congham Hall, a Georgian manor house built in the
mid-18th century and set in forty-four acres of beautiful parkland. Strolling its paddocks, orchards, and country gardens, travelers can unwind and
enjoy their holiday.

The conversion from a country house into a luxury hotel in 1982 has
been accomplished by Mr. and Mrs. Trevor Forecast, with careful regard
to its original classic interior. They brought with them considerable
experience as hoteliers in other parts of Britain.

The entrance hall spans the depth of the house, with a view of the park
at the far end. All of the guest rooms have a view of the surrounding
parkland or the adjacent fields. There is a pleasant mix of conventional
rooms and suites. The furnishings are both modern and traditional.

Dinnertime beckoned me below and I could hear the sound of merry tunes being played on a piano in the drawing room. I took one of the comfortable chairs, and the headwaiter immediately presented me with the evening menu. He explained that everything is cooked to order and so guests are able to make their choices in comfort in the drawing room. When their dinner has been prepared, they are then seated in the dining room.

The starters presented problems right away, they were so enticing. The first course was poached salmon, and the main courses included lightly grilled lamb livers, fillet of sole, roast fillet of pork, roast breast of duck for two, and roast saddle of venison. An eight-course meal is served here, including coffee and petit fours.

As the pianist drifted from Victor Herbert to Noel Coward, I was called in to dinner, and I found an attractively decorated dining room in rose-pink and lily. Dinner was most rewarding, and the sweets menu was quite in character with everything else. I chose hot spiced pears served in red wine and fresh homemade vanilla ice cream. I took coffee in the drawing room, lost in a reverie enhanced by the gentle sounds of the piano.

Congham Hall is a wonderful example of what is fortunately happening in many former country houses as they are being converted into excellent small hotels.

CONGHAM HALL (Pride of Britain), King's Lynn, Norfolk PE32 1AH. Tel.: Hillington (0485) 600250. U.S. reservations: 800-323-7308. An 11-guestroom (private baths) country house hotel at Grimston, just 6 mi. from King's Lynn. Twin and double beds available. Breakfast, lunch, and dinner served. Open year-round. Centrally located to enjoy a visit to Sandringham, uncrowded beaches, tiny fishing villages, horseback riding, golf, bird sanctuaries, and the Norfolk Broads. Swimming pool, tennis court, and cricket on the grounds. Not suitable for children under 12. Pet kennels and stabling available. Mr. and Mrs. Trevor Forecast, Hoteliers. (See Index for rates.)

Directions: From King's Lynn follow A149 to the roundabout and pick up A148. Grimston is the nearest local village for Congham Hall—not Congham Village.

BURY ST. EDMUNDS

Shall I risk saying it at least once more? The traveler to Britain who goes from London to Stratford-on-Avon and on to the Lake Country and then to Edinburgh has really experienced about five percent of this enchanted isle. Witness East Anglia in general and Bury St. Edmunds in particular.

Bury St. Edmunds is the crown of East Anglia. Here in the vast Norman Abbey were buried the remains of King Edmund, martyred in A.D. 869 by heathen Danish invaders.

For centuries the town was a premiere center for pilgrimages, and it may come as a surprise to learn that at the Abbey high altar, twenty-five barons of England swore on the 20th of November, 1214, that they would enforce the observance by King John of the Magna Carta.

The main attraction of the town is the Abbey of St. Edmund, whose history is much too complicated for me to even attempt here. Suffice it to say that it is one of the great ancient monuments of England, and even though its architecture, reflecting over a thousand years of renovations and changes, is confusing, nonetheless it continues to attract travelers from all parts of the world.

THE ANGEL HOTEL
Bury St. Edmunds, Suffolk

"The Angel at Bury." The place to stay in Bury St. Edmunds is the Angel Hotel. It is on the old market square directly across from the Great Abbey gatehouse. It so delighted Charles Dickens that he resided there twice when giving readings of *David Copperfield*. His room, Number 15, is preserved today exactly as if he had just left it.

If first impressions are the most memorable, then the lasting impression of the Angel would be its Georgian facade, covered from top to bottom with vines that turn deliciously crimson in the autumn. This is but the first of many lasting impressions, not the least of which is a dining room, in the basement of the Angel, that has vaulted ceilings dating from the 11th century. There has been an inn or some kind of accommodation on this site almost from the time that the original abbey became an object for pilgrimages.

Since my first visit some years ago, I have been an enthusiastic supporter of travel in East Anglia, but I must confess that innkeeper Mary

Gough really added considerably to my knowledge and appreciation of the area. Mary pointed out to me that East Anglia has strong links with the early settlers in America. "Two-thirds of the Mayflower Pilgrims came from Suffolk and Norfolk, and Thomas Paine was born in nearby Thetford."

She also told me that the Angel has been at the center of Bury's life for over seven hundred years. It's been used as a polling place and also as the Council House.

"We think we have a lot to offer the American visitor who has most probably visited Britain before. This is the real historic and living England, and we do not promise to make an American feel at home. At Bury, he will find none of the popular American hamburger stands or fast food restaurants. What he will find is a beautiful town, one of the undiscovered gems of this sceptered isle, amongst some of the loveliest, most gentle, quiet countryside and villages Britain has to offer. One might say that Bury is the hub of East Anglia and we're within a convenient drive of the racing at Newmarket, the great houses of Blickling, Sandringham, and Ickworth, and of course Cambridge is just a short distance away. It's not just the past, but the present and the future that makes the area so fascinating."

The Angel Hotel is very comfortable, and all of the guest rooms have private bathrooms and are all individually decorated. There are quite a few four-poster beds and private suites. Many of the guest rooms and the dining room look out across the square to the Abbey gatehouse.

THE ANGEL HOTEL, Bury St. Edmunds, Suffolk IP33 1LT. Tel.: (0284) 3926. Telex: 81630 Angel G. U.S. reservations: 800-323-5463. Telex:

286778 Barr Ur. A 42-guestroom (private baths) in-town hotel in East Anglia, just a few paces from the site of the famous Norman abbey. Twin and double beds available. Breakfast, lunch, and dinner served daily. Open year-round. Conveniently located for access to East Coast ports and ferries in less than two hours. Almost all of the recreational, cultural, and historic attractions of East Anglia within easy driving distance. Andrew Donovan, Manager. (See Index for rates.)

Directions: Once in Bury St. Edmunds, make inquiries for the Angel Hotel. It is on Angel Hill.

CAMBRIDGE AND THE FENS

Cambridge is a city of colleges and bridges. Clare Bridge, Trinity College Bridge, and the Bridge of Sighs span the river on the Backs, those picturesque banks of the Cam, with their peaceful green lawns running down to the river, shaded by willows, and carpeted with daffodils in the spring.

Cambridge University was founded in the 13th century and now consists of several different colleges, some of which are well known, including Emmanuel, Jesus College, Magdalene College, and Trinity College. Much to my surprise, I discovered that I was not the first writer to visit Cambridge, and that several of my predecessors, including Michael Drayton, wrote about it in 1622; Daniel Defoe had some comment about scandalous assemblies at unseasonable hours; Charles and Mary Lamb visited the town and the university, and Mary wrote about the excessive amount of walking that was necessary. Henry James spoke of the "loveliest confusion of Gothic windows and ancient trees, grassy banks, and mossy balustrades, of sun-chequered avenues and groves, of lawns and gardens and terraces, of single-arched bridges spanning the little stream."

North of the elegant landscaping of Cambridge's gardens and parks lie the Fens, an expanse of flatland now farmed and yielding cabbages, potatoes, carrots, sugar beets, and every other green and root crop. They proliferate in the rich black peat soil. There have been attempts to drain this land as far back as the Roman occupation, but it remained for a rather improbable figure in history, Charles II, to institute a scheme to drain large areas with the aid of Dutch experts. Now the water is confined to innumerable drains and rivers, many of which are higher than the shrunken peat land around them.

Cambridge and the Fens have many historic buildings, museums, Cromwell memorabilia, cathedrals, archeological sites, wildlife, nature trails, windmills, and sports. As far as I know, it is also possible to hire a punt, a romantic way to see Cambridge from the river.

SOUTHEAST ENGLAND
Counties of Sussex, Kent, and Surrey

All roads in Southeast England originate from (or lead to) London, consequently, almost every weekend, the motorways and main roads from London's Marble Arch are abuzz with small English cars being driven on the left-hand side of the road, at slightly-less-than-breakneck speed, through the pleasant countryside to the three southeast counties and the towns and villages of Chichester, Brighton, Eastbourne, Hastings, Rye, Folkstone, Dover, and Canterbury.

Surrey, the county closest to London, has beautiful hills, woods, and heathland, including Lythe Hill, the highest point in the south of England. There are many "great houses" in Surrey, and it has been the scene of some of the stirring events of England's past, including Runnymede where King John signed the Magna Carta in 1215 on the bank of the River Thames.

The county of Sussex, divided into East and West Sussex, extends from the southern borders of Surrey south to the coast, and eastward to Kent. Sussex has delightful combinations of peaceful forest, undulating downland, and attractive seaside towns and villages.

The South Downs (high rolling hills) sweep across Sussex from the border of Hampshire to Eastbourne, and there are several of the famous hill figures carved on the sides of the hills. Some of these are rather ancient, but a surprising number have been created since 1900. The Glyndebourne Opera is also in Sussex, as is the city of Chichester and its harbor.

The Kentish coast bends around Southeast England for 126 miles and is replete with many resort towns. This is the land of Anne Boleyn, Henry VIII's second wife, who was beheaded (and whose ghost still walks); Winston Churchill, whose home, Chartwell, is now maintained by the National Trust; Charles Darwin; and General Wolfe, who figured prominently in the history of the New World. It is a place of many cathedrals, abbeys, churches, castles, and ruins. One of the principal attractions is the old city of Canterbury with its famous cathedral.

Oddly enough, this section of England is not the prime objective for North American visitors who are far more apt to go from London north to Stratford-on-Avon, the Lake Country, and on to Edinburgh.

SOUTHEAST ENGLAND

MERMAID INN
Rye, Sussex

"Good night, Norman, I will see you at breakfast. Will 8:30 be suitable?" That was Michael Gregory speaking, owner and innkeeper of the Mermaid Inn in Rye. We had spent a most congenial evening in the dining room with a dinner of good England roast beef and Yorkshire pudding, and then in the lounge over second cups of coffee.

Naturally, most of the talk centered around the Mermaid. "How old is it, Michael?" I asked. "Do you really know?"

"Well, we think it was rebuilt in 1420 after the French had burned the town in 1377 on one of their frequent raids. Local legend says that the inn was visited by Queen Elizabeth I when she came to Rye in 1573.

"The inn has seen and made its own episodes in history," he commented. "During the Reformation many priests were sheltered here during their flight to France."

He took me upstairs to point out the initials "JHS" in one of their bedrooms. "This was the symbol of the escaping clerics," he said. Then he showed me the secret staircase, which was probably used many times as members of the clergy slipped away from their oppressors. In the huge

Back Lounge of the inn I saw the "Priest's Hole." "Just take a look up the chimney," he said. "That's another hiding place. A bit warmish, but quite safe.

"The history of the inn has always reflected the history of the town. Perhaps the most exciting period was during the times when smugglers' gangs were the bully boys of Rye. One group called the Hawkhurst Gang didn't do our reputation any good at all. They sat about in the windows of the inn cursing and carousing with their loaded pistols on the tables, and no magistrate would interfere with them.

"In February, 1735, a smuggler named Thomas More, who was out on bail, went to the Mermaid and dragged the bailiff by his heels from his room and into the street, taking the bail bondsman's warrants with him. The bailiff was taken to a ship in the harbor but was eventually rescued by the captain of another ship. I could go on at great length about famous people who visited here," Michael said, "and, of course, the ghosts."

Jan Lindstrom's drawing of the inn shows the Elizabethan half-timbers and entrance arch. The entrance hall reflects the motif of the entire building. The walls are faced with oak paneling and the timbered ceiling is supported by a kingpost. In a way, four centuries just fall away.

Michael and I said good night and I walked up the staircase past "Dr. Syn's Lounge," which is another whole piece of Mermaid tradition.

I fell asleep quickly, but in the middle of the night I awakened, hearing whispers in the hall and a clicking sound like the cocking of an ancient pistol. Footsteps went down the passageway and stairs and then it was quiet. When I asked Michael about it the next morning, he just smiled.

MERMAID INN, Rye, Sussex. Tel.: (0797) 22-3065. Telex: 957141. A 27-guestroom (private baths) traditional inn located in one of England's most historic ports, 65 mi. from London. Open all year. Breakfast, lunch, dinner served to non-residents. Reservations may also be made for the Royal Hotel in Deal. M. Gregory, Resident Owner. (See Index for rates.)

Directions: From London, take A21 through Tunbridge Wells, and then A268 from Flinwell directly to Rye. There are dozens of alternate routes.

For room rates and last time for dinner orders, see Index.

In Britain, acceptance of a hotel booking by telephone or in writing is generally regarded as a legally binding contract. If it's necessary to cancel, advise the hotel immediately. If they are unable to re-let the room, the hotel may be entitled to claim compensation—usually two thirds of the agreed price—and any deposit would be included as part of this payment.

RYE AT DAWN

Michael Gregory told me that Rye was fascinating at sunrise, and an early morning walk over hill and dale and into the town, with all its fascinating little shops, proved him to be altogether correct. The old houses and the flowers lining the cobbled streets; the church at the top of the hill with its ancient churchyard graves; Battings Tower, built in 1250, and redolent of English history; and that place on the hill where stood (until a bombing in 1940) the garden house of Henry James, who had lived there from 1898 to 1916, were all part of a magical sunrise walk through Rye.

POWDERMILL HOUSE
Battle, East Sussex

Douglas Cowpland was straightening me out about the Battle of Hastings. "First of all, it really is not the Battle of Hastings," he said, as we walked out toward the small pond in the front of this spacious Georgian country house. "The fact is that it should simply be called 'The Battle.' We are in a part of Battle Abbey Estate, originally six thousand acres; we have about fifty acres here. The Abbey itself was built in honor of the dead, and the original ruin is still there. You can walk from our grounds to the battlegrounds, and if you look to your left over the hedge, you'll see what is actually *the* 'Battleground.' We're in sort of a valley here, and for many years there were stories that the whole area flowed with blood. Of course, it really was the water washing through the ironstone in the area, creating a reddish tinge."

I could have listened to Douglas for hours, because I've always been intrigued by the events of 1066. In fact, this entire area is now called "1066 Country," and there's much to see and do relative to those portentous days, which certainly changed the life of all of us on both sides of the Atlantic.

However, Powdermill House occupied my immediate interest, particularly for the fact that it is a pure Georgian house and is filled, as far as my relatively unpracticed eye could see, with authentic Georgian antiques. This is because Douglas and his wife, Julie, are also well-known antique dealers with a shop in the village of Little Common, a few miles from Battle.

There are six guest rooms in the main house and others are in some buildings that are being reconstructed. To add to the fun of the stay, there are tennis courts and a lake with many Canada geese, resident Muscovy ducks, swans, white geese, and other birds and wildlife. There is also a small herd of rare Hebridean sheep.

"We're trying to encourage a wildlife park in that area over there beyond the lake," he said. "There are times when the visiting and resident wildlife are quite numerous."

At the time of my visit, Powdermill House was in the process of complete rehabilitation. However, I saw all of the guest rooms in the main house and also the drawing room, the dining room, and a room set aside as a new dining room that would be in use when this book goes to press. All will have Georgian furniture.

Julie Cowpland explained to me that dinner consists of a choice of starters and one main course, which, of course, is different every night, plus desserts and coffee.

Back to our little stroll at the pond. Douglas reached inside a bag and threw something that looked like food pellets on the surface of the water. Immediately, at least a dozen trout leaped out of the water, and the placid surface churned with activity for about thirty seconds before our finny friends disappeared into the deep.

POWDERMILL HOUSE (Wolsey Lodges), Powdermill Lane, Battle, East Sussex. Tel.: Battle (04246) 2035 or Cooden (04243) 5214. A 14-guestroom Georgian house converted into a picturesque guest house. Dinner served by appointment. Open all year. Located near Rye and Hastings. Adjacent to the grounds of Battle Abbey and the scene of the famous Battle of 1066. Swimming pool and lakes located on the grounds.

Three dogs and one cat in residence. Douglas and Julie Cowpland, Proprietors. (See Index for rates.)

Directions: From London take A21 toward Hastings. At Battle turn right on Powdermill Lane. From Brighton take A259. Turn off at Little Common and follow the road signs to Battle.

CANTERBURY

Canterbury dates back to Roman times and was used by the Romans as the seat of government for the tribes of Kent. In A.D. 597 St. Augustine traveled from Rome and converted the King of Kent and restored some of the town's earlier Christianity. The present cathedral dates from 1070 and was the scene of the brutal murder of Archbishop Thomas à Becket for his denial of the king's authority over the Church. It remains to this day one of the great and inspiring attractions in the United Kingdom.

In addition to the abbey and cathedral, it is possible to view the city wall bastions: the West Gate; Grey Friars, the first Franciscan settlement in England; the Weavers, a house for Flemish weavers in use in the 16th century; and the Poor Priests' Hospital, now used as the regimental museum.

Canterbury is a compact, inspiring city. Perhaps nowhere else is it possible to see so much history within a few hundred yards. It is a real center of English religion and learning.

Although not a native of Kent, Geoffrey Chaucer (1340?–1400) has proved to be the best press agent for Canterbury. The celebrated Canterbury Tales *is made up of the stories of a group of pilgrims, representing all types of English life, as they journeyed through the April sunshine and showers from the Tabard Inn in Southwark (near London) to Canterbury and back. Chaucer apparently finished twenty-one of these humorous, earthy tales that reveal his love of nature and his fellow man.*

It is said of Chaucer that he found English a dialect and left it a language.

HOWFIELD MANOR
Chartham Hatch, Canterbury, Kent

I was enjoying a second cup of coffee with Clark and Janet Lawrence in the wonderful, spacious kitchen of Howfield Manor, in the heart of the countryside and only ten minutes away from the cathedral city of Canterbury.

Breakfast had been outstanding—the orange juice freshly squeezed, the eggs from a local farm, and all the jams and marmalades made by Janet.

Clark is an American and Janet is English. They were explaining how this charming country manor had recently added a new wing blending in with parts of the building that date back to the 11th century. Each room has its own bath and other amenities such as trouser press, hair dryer, and alarm clock.

We were now talking about the fun they have as hosts. "We would like to have a place for people to stay that is as nice as their own homes. People traveling today expect much more than just the bare essentials of the room. They want comfort, service, good bathrooms and towels, decent food, and most of all, the opportunity to talk to somebody knowledgeable about all of the things to do in the area."

As far as the latter is concerned, Clark pointed out to me that it is well to keep in mind that you can't do Kent in a day or even two, and it is preferable to find a central point from which to enjoy all of the many beauties and attractions of the area, including visits to Dover, Folkestone, and Deal.

Dinner at Howfield Manor is a set menu and by reservation only. Guests are seated family-style in the beamed dining room. Janet explained that she does a number of things, including salmon that comes from Scotland and cheese soufflés.

"I use lots of cream because the cream is so fantastic down here. What we aim for is good home cooking."

"Janet also does braised lamb with an egg-and-lemon sauce that's marvelous," said Clark.

The oldest part of the house, which is now the kitchen, dates back to 1181, when it was a chapel. The well used by the monks is in the dairy, which is now the Lawrences' private sitting room.

HOWFIELD MANOR, Chartham Hatch, Canterbury, Kent CT4 7HQ. Tel.: Canterbury (0227) 738294 or 738495. A 5-guestroom restored country house, just a few moments from Canterbury Cathedral. Dinner, bed, and breakfast. Open year-round. Conveniently located to enjoy all of the cultural and recreational attractions in the area, including a great many castles; Chartwell, once the home of Winston Churchill; Great Dixter, Mount Ephraim, and other famous gardens. An ideal stop-off point going to and from the Continent. Not well-suited for children under 14. Clark and Janet Lawrence, Proprietors. (See Index for rates.)

Directions: Take the M2/A2 from London to a point just outside of Canterbury. Look for a Little Chef/Esso service station and watch for Chartham Hatch U-turn. Do not take U-turn, simply take the side road that goes off to the right. Howfield Manor is just a few minutes away.

KENNEL HOLT HOTEL
Cranbrook, Kent

Kennel Holt was one of the first places I visited in England. It was an Elizabethan, beamed, manor house, and today it is a country house hotel set in five acres of landscaped grounds with a natural pond, rosebeds, croquet lawn, and cobnut walks. It still sits at the end of a secluded lane, 300 yards from the main road, overlooking a wooded valley in the heart of the rolling orchard country of Kent.

There are eight guest rooms, all with color TV and private bathrooms.

There are over fifty historic houses, gardens, and castles within easy driving distance of Kennel Holt. I'm afraid I can't list them all, but I will mention Chartwell, Sir Winston Churchill's family home.

Kennel Holt would make an excellent first and last stop for guests using Gatwick and Heathrow airports. I should imagine that the peace and quiet, and the comfort of the log fires in the residents' sitting rooms would be most reassuring to all guests.

Kennel Holt is also just an hour away from London by train (Charing Cross Station).

If you'd like to have the pleasure of staying at a country house hotel and don't want to drive down into the country, you can be collected at Staplehurst Station and enjoy a few days in the Kent countryside.

KENNEL HOLT HOTEL, Cranbrook, Kent TN17 2PT. Tel.: (0580) Cranbrook 712032. A 10-guestroom country house hotel (all private baths) 50 mi. from London. Rates include dinner, bed and breakfast, and early morning tea. Minimum 2-night stay required with advance reservation. Color TV, video, radio and phone in rooms. Open Apr. to Nov. Central location for touring Kent. No credit cards. Two dogs, three cats, four rabbits, and six ducks in residence. David and Jana Misseldine, Resident Owners. (See Index for rates.)

Directions: Cranbrook is 1 mi. southeast at the A262-A229 crossroads, which is 10 mi. south of Maidstone. The hotel is on the A262 between Cranbrook and Goudhurst.

LITTLE THAKEHAM (COUNTRY HOUSE HOTEL)
Storrington, West Sussex

I was walking through the pergola with the warm April sun on my back. The pergola, as hotelier Tim Ractliff explained, was the name given to the rose arbor, which leads through the orchard and provides a view into the woods in the south. "It sort of links up the house with the surrounding lawns and gardens," he said.

Speaking of gardens, this might well be called the Little Thakeham Country House Hotel and Gardens, because the gardens are indeed a most important part of the entire experience. They include paved walks, numerous varieties of flowering shrubs, and specimen trees. The long approach to the house is lined with walnut trees. Gertrude Jekyll, a leading landscape designer of the last century, created the Little Thakeham gardens.

I walked up toward the house, which appears ageless but was actually built around 1902. Tim remarked that the South Downs, visible in the distance, actually protect this section of Sussex from the rigors of the coast. The climate here is really quite mild.

Dominating the first floor of the house is a great hall with a marvelous fireplace and a minstrel gallery. Everything is done in beautiful beige stonework. There's another huge fireplace in the dining room. The an-

tiques are most impressive, and mullioned windows create a wonderful manor-house feeling.

I've visited many British country house hotels and each of them has a unique identity and personality of its own. Although there are some similarities, it is impossible to become confused, and one never loses the sense of the particular place of each and its most favorable and special conditions.

The situation at Little Thakeham is exceptional because if the guests want to do nothing there is ample opportunity to enjoy reading, walking, motoring, a dip in the swimming pool, and the peace and quiet that the British look for continually. On the other hand, the Americans literally may want to do something, and there are visits to the nearby Glyndebourne Music Festival and the seacoast town of Brighton, as well as a game of tennis or croquet on the grounds. At the end of the day, it is wonderful to come back and sit in the lounge, meet and talk with other people, and feel completely as if for a moment you are home.

Dinner is a four-course set meal with a starter, a fish dish, and one main course that changes every evening. There are frequent evening concerts of chamber music, with wonderful sounds reverberating in the great hall.

Little Thakeham is less than an hour from Gatwick and probably a little bit farther from Heathrow Airport.

LITTLE THAKEHAM (COUNTRY HOUSE HOTEL) (Pride of Britain), Merrywood Lane, Storrington, West Sussex. Tel.: Storrington (09066) 4416. U.S. reservations: 800-323-7308. A 9-guestroom country house hotel located south of London on the edge of the South Downs and not far from Brighton. Breakfast to houseguests, luncheon by appt., dinner served to the public. Open year-round. Minimum stay of 2 nights required. Conveniently located to visit Goodwood, Petworth, Parham Park, and Arundel Castle. The nearby Chichester Theatre is open during the summer, as well as Glyndebourne. Swimming pool, grass tennis court, and croquet lawns on grounds. Other outdoor recreation nearby. Two dogs in residence. Timothy and Pauline Ractliff, Proprietors. (See Rates for index.)

Directions: From London take the A24 Worthing Rd., and about 1½ mi. after the village of Ashington bear right, off the dual carriageway. Follow the lane for 1 mi., and then turn right to Merrywood Lane. Little Thakeham is 300 yds. on the right. It's easy to get lost in this section of Sussex, so be prepared to make inquiries.

For room rates and last time for dinner orders, see Index.

THE WOODED LANES OF SUSSEX

Surrey and West Sussex have some extremely attractive back roads that wander through forests, border meadows, and follow the course of the many brooks and rivers. It is easy to get lost on them, but not "perilously" so.

It is beautiful in springtime, especially during the daffodil season, and I found myself stopping to look at gnarled old trees with ivy growing up the trunks, and lingering by the meadows with centuries-old stone and thicket walls. In the spring the rock gardens appear with all the lovely spring colors.

In this part of England what are called speed bumps in North America are known as "sleeping Bobbies."

GRAVETYE MANOR
(Near East Grinstead) West Sussex

The memories of my first visit to Gravetye (as it is known) were immediately revived as I followed the winding drive through the parklike grounds and saw the weathered stone and oaken door of the front entrance. The Sussex countryside was bathed in the light of an autumn sun, heightening the muted tints of beige, brown, and russet. The flowers of autumn in the famed Gravetye gardens, encouraged by the warmth, turned their faces toward the sun.

Gravetye is an Elizabethan manor house, built about ten years after the defeat of the Spanish Armada. According to the records, Roger Infield built it for his bride, Katherine Compton. Their initials, "R" and "K," are carved over the entrance to the formal gardens. To add to the romantic note, the likenesses of Roger and Katherine are carved in oak over the fireplace in the master bedroom.

The manor's most notable owner, William Robinson, had a worldwide reputation as one of the greatest gardeners of all time. He bought Gravetye and the one thousand acres on which it stands in 1884, and lived there until he died, well into his nineties, in 1935. It was here that he realized many of his ideas for the creation of the English natural "garden style," now admired and copied all over the world. His book, *The English Flower Garden,* is still in demand. His simple good taste is much in evidence both inside and outside of the manor house. He paneled the interior with wood from the estate and enriched the rooms with chimney pieces and fireplace furnishings kept entirely in the Elizabethan mode.

Today, the proprietors are Susan and Peter Herbert, who have devoted time, effort, and considerable investment in carrying on Mr. Robinson's ideals, while at the same time preserving much of the tradition and antiquity. The Herberts' five children range in age from 4½ to 33 years old, so a future line of assistant innkeepers seems assured. In fact, the eldest has already begun his career at Gravetye.

The menu for lunch and dinner is basically French, but a note points out that if the guest's preference is for *simply* cooked food, this can be accommodated. Even now while writing this paragraph, my mouth begins to water at the thought of their parfait of chicken livers, with a delicate hint of port and the contrasting sharpness of green peppercorns. The "sweet" menu is a Mozart sonata.

There are basically two types of guest rooms. One group is done in the grand manner with canopied beds and walls that are intricately paneled. The master bedroom is a classic—the furniture is "manorial" to say the least.

The other type of room is a bit smaller and has a more modest demeanor. However, all of Gravetye's rooms enjoy the most fabulous views over the gardens and surrounding forest.

"Garden" is a key word at Gravetye. In a country where gardening is a national sport, the gardens here, covering many acres, are some of the most impressive I've ever seen. For example, the kitchen garden has over a full acre of leeks, parsley, endive, chicory, spinach, dill, thyme, mint, hyssop, broccoli, french beans, radishes, lettuce, and several different types of berries and fruits. Naturally, these all appear on the table. The Herberts have also developed their own smokehouse, producing smoked salmon, duck's breast, and venison. Fresh herbs are grown all year round under artificial climate conditions in the spacious glasshouses.

Thanks to Roger Infield, William Robinson, and Susan and Peter

Herbert, Gravetye Manor has been preserved and is entering into its most useful and exciting period, because it is available for all of us to enjoy.

GRAVETYE MANOR (near East Grinstead), West Sussex RH19 4LJ. Tel.: (0342) Sharpthorne 810567. Telex: 957239. A luxuriously appointed 14-guestroom country manor hotel, 30 mi. from London. King, queen, and twin size beds available. Open all year. Lunch, dinner served to non-residents. Beautiful gardens on grounds as well as trout fishing, croquet, and clock golf. Golf and horseback riding nearby. This area has many famous houses and gardens for touring. Suitable for children over 7 years old. No credit cards. Peter Herbert, Managing Director. (See Index for rates.)

Directions: From London, leave M23 at Exit 10, taking the A264 towards East Grinstead. At roundabout take 3rd exit marked Haywards Heath and Brighton (B2028). Continue through Turner's Hill, and 1 mi. south of village, take left fork towards West Hoathly. Proceed for about 150 yds and turn left up Vowels Lane. Hotel on right after 1 mi. (Hotel drive 1 mi. long.)

Rates for a room for two people for one night with breakfast, except where noted, are included in the Index of this book. They are not to be considered firm quotations, but should be used as guidelines only.

It's not that the distances are very long in the British Isles, it's the many diversions along the way that sometimes make it impossible to estimate traveling and arrival times. Last order times for dinner are included in the Index so that you can see what time you must arrive in order not to find the kitchen door locked. If you are going to arrive later, call ahead—there isn't a hotel/inn listed here that will not make some provision to feed you if they know you can't make it before the kitchen closes.

THE SOUTH OF ENGLAND
Counties of Hampshire and Dorset

These counties, about two-and-a-half-hours' drive southwest of London, include the woods and heaths of the New Forest, the megaliths of Stonehenge, the great cathedrals of Winchester and Salisbury, Thomas Hardy and Jane Austen country, and among other great houses, Broadlands, the treasure-filled residence of the late Lord Louis Mountbatten.

Broadlands is located in Hampshire and contains an impressive collection of art, as well as numerous mementos of Mountbatten's naval and Asian campaigns. The River Test, one of Britain's trout streams, runs through the grounds of Broadlands, south of the town of Romsey and near Southampton.

Dorset has uplands rising to 900 feet and a splendid coastline. This is the country embodied in many of Thomas Hardy's novels, and where examples of the thatcher's art can be seen in countless villages.

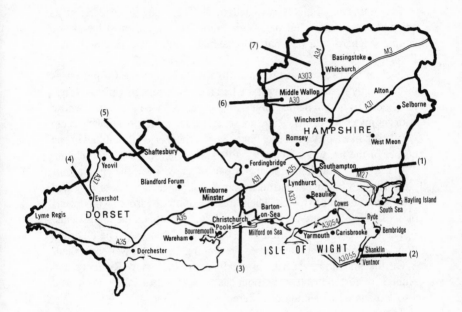

THE SOUTH OF ENGLAND

THE OLD HOUSE HOTEL
Wickham, Hampshire

"This is a duck's nest coal-burning hearth." Annie Skipwith was showing me the guest rooms at the Old House in Wickham. We were in a most attractive second-floor guest room, where the stately windows overlook the other Georgian town houses on the hollow square in the center of town.

Everything about this inn was delightful. The young innkeepers, Richard and Annie, were full of *joie de vivre*. They are a most handsome couple. Richard is a debonair Englishman, and Annie is a delightful French girl.

Each of the twelve guest rooms is totally different. The furniture was refinished by Richard. The upstairs hall has some engaging prints, originally done by a man named Gould, and curtains have been found whose patterns match the prints. There are several small things that make it seem very much like a private house. For example, there is a little cabinet in one corner of the hallway downstairs, filled with carved pieces and china.

In the back of the house, formerly part of an old barn, the guest rooms have exposed beams, beautiful flowered wallpaper in tones of blue and green, and curtains to match. There was one double bedroom with dozens of books. In fact, there are books in every guest room on the nightstands.

There are porcelain doorknobs on the paneled doorways and all of the floors in this house of many levels are shining clean and well varnished.

On the first floor, a series of small lounges all show Richard's and Annie's interest in prints. One room has some excellent sailing prints and also a mounted collection of different-sized keg taps.

The restaurant is part of the old converted barn and has exposed beams with a big window that overlooks the garden in the rear. This is an excellent breakfast room.

The menu is made up of French provincial dishes. For lunch that day I had a dish with green peppers, tomatoes, onions, and garlic cooked in spices and herbs and then topped with a whisked egg white that, when put in the oven, turns into a four-inch meringue. It was just right. Other main courses were pot-roasted chicken and escalloped veal and sirloin served with tomatoes and garlic sauce and topped with olives.

In discussing the inn clientele, Richard said that for the most part people stayed for one night, although many businessmen stay here while traveling during the week. "They like our little garden in the rear and our countryside is appealing." Please note that the hotel guest rooms are not available on Saturdays and Sundays.

THE OLD HOUSE HOTEL, The Square, Wickham, Hampshire PO17 5JG. Tel.: (0329) 833049. A 12-guestroom (private baths) in-town hotel, 9 mi. west of Portsmouth. Closed Sat. and Sun., 2 wks. in July and Aug., 2 wks at Christmas, and 1 wk. at Easter. Lunch and dinner served to non-residents. Restaurant closed all day Sun. and also for lunch on Mon. and Sat. Pleasant rose garden on grounds. Sailing and golf nearby. Mr. and Mrs. Richard Skipwith, Proprietors. (See Index for rates.)

Directions: From London take M3 southwest to Exit 5 and follow A32 to Wickham, 45 min. from Motorway exit.

LUCCOMBE CHINE HOUSE
Shanklin, Isle of Wight

Ah, the Isle of Wight! I have always heard much about it—the connection with Queen Victoria, its strategic position as an offshore naval base, and its present popularity for holiday excursions.

The day was marvelous; I had driven across Sussex and Hampshire, and at Portsmouth I found the foot ferry to Ryde. I left my luggage at the ferry entrance and drove about two blocks away to the multistoried car park.

I had decided to try the ferry that did not take autos (there are others that do). After a very pleasant voyage, along with many dozens of other holiday-seekers, I arrived at Ryde, where a train was waiting on the pier. My journey continued along the famous Sunshine Coast through several little towns, finally ending at Shanklin, where my hostess, Stella Silver, awaited my arrival with a car.

Stella proved to be as enthusiastic as she was informative and I got a running history of the island, as well as interesting information about the flora and fauna as we drove through the village of Shanklin. The road went out into the country with occasional glimpses of the sea.

She turned down into a sheltered and secluded valley (chine) and entered a long private drive with lovely ferns, trees, lawns, and a profusion of hydrangeas. I had arrived.

The house itself has an interesting history and is definitely Victorian in feeling, although there are Tudor half-timbers and casements on the upper stories. The Silvers have made it very attractive and homelike rather than grand. It looks like what it is—a comfortable, upper-middle-class home. The bedrooms are sensibly decorated with period pieces, but there is an emphasis on comfort, with wool blankets and even clock radios.

The first thing I did after getting settled was to take a walk on the grounds, with a visit to the Watch Tower overlooking the coast. The Tower was built in the days when smugglers were active.

I was tempted to continue on the footpaths that lead in all directions, many with magnificent views of the sea.

All of this vigorous outdoor activity, on top of the ferry trip, made for a very healthy appetite, and after a consultation with Mr. Silver I placed an order for pork cutlets. Everything is cooked to order and the sauce for the cutlets was simply marvelous.

I awakened in the morning to the wonderful sound of one of the fourteen cascades that musically assist a small brook as it twists, tunnels, and tumbles through the chine down to the sea below.

By all means take the time (at least two nights) to visit Luccombe Chine House on the Isle of Wight. There are dozens of things to amuse a visitor, including riding, swimming, tennis, saunas, and so forth, but there's also the wonderful sense of tranquility in just looking out over the sea.

LUCCOMBE CHINE HOUSE, Shanklin, Isle of Wight, PO37 6RH. Tel.: (098 386) Shanklin 2037. A 6-guestroom (private baths) country house hotel located in a quiet corner of the Isle of Wight, overlooking the sea. Breakfast and dinner served daily. Open all year. Conveniently located to enjoy all of the myriad diversions and recreations of the Isle of Wight. Great walking country. No facilities for children. Paul and Stella Silver, Hoteliers. (See Index for rates.)

Directions: If you are not planning to stay for more than two nights, don't bring a car to Luccombe Chine House. There are several different ways to get to Shanklin, including the train from Waterloo Station in London to Portsmouth, then the ferry to the Isle of Wight, and then another little train to the end of the line. For full information about car ferries, foot ferries, etc., call Mr. and Mrs. Silver for schedules.

Rates for a room for two people for one night with breakfast, except where noted, are included in the Index of this book. They are not to be considered firm quotations, but should be used as guidelines only.

CHEWTON GLEN HOTEL
New Milton, Hampshire

Chewton Glen has real style. I don't mean this in a fashion sense—although the hotel certainly could be called stylish. It's more than having beautiful rooms, lovely grounds, excellent cuisine, and an attentive staff. It's probably an inherent attitude. I think the key may lie in something Joe Simonini, Martin Skan's right-hand man, said to me over dinner. "I came here from Tuscany twenty years ago when Martin first bought Chewton Glen, and I fell in love with the place. We have worked hard to make it the best hotel in the country, and I believe it *is* the best." I saw that sense of dedication and pride in other staff members, some of whom have worked there almost as long as Joe. I have to congratulate Martin Skan, the owner, for inspiring such loyalty and a desire for excellence in his very able, friendly, and cheerful staff. Everything is done with such *style!*

Martin, who looks a bit like a mature Roddy McDowall, had been telling me about the changes he had made since my last visit, and I was really impressed with all the differences. From the moment I drove into the new courtyard, paved with York stone, encircled with plantings of tulips and pansies and other pretty flowers, with an antique bronze fountain in the center, I could see that Chewton Glen Hotel had a very new look.

Inside, I really had to gasp. The two lounges, called the Elphinstone Suite after some early owners, are simply delightful. Martin told me that the well-known designer Diane Prestwich was responsible for the blending of colors and textures of fabrics in draperies, swags, upholstery, cushions, and wall coverings, along with the wonderful comfortable, cozy feeling of these actually very spacious and elegant rooms. Nina Campbell did a smashing job in the Marryat Bar.

Since Martin had been called away, I enjoyed an excellent dinner with Joe. Fishermen bring their daily catch and, with the English Channel so close, there is a wide selection of fresh fish and other seafood on the menu. I chose salmon, broiled to perfection, with a sorrel sauce and a side dish of fat, tender, fresh asparagus. The chef sent us a tasty avocado pâté with his compliments. I just have to say that the meal, the wines, and the service couldn't have been more elegant. Joe is very proud of their wine cellar, which has received many accolades. A time-honored British tradition is the standing rib roast on a handsome silver trolley, wheeled deftly from table to table, and carved with great flair to the preference of each guest.

After dinner, Joe showed me a very fat loose-leaf binder, kept for their guests, that is packed with literally endless suggestions for diversion and recreation. Just about anything you could think of is in this book, including such information as time schedules for a sports center, nearby churches, and trains to and from London. There are maps for walks through the gardens and glen out to the sea, information on making arrangements for fishing, shooting, bicycling, horseback riding, boat cruises in the Channel, and helicopter rides. There are lists of antiques shops, jewelers, Laura Ashley, Benetton, home furnishings, and on and on.

Some of the more important sightseeing possibilities are Stonehenge, Salisbury Cathedral, Winchester Cathedral, and the famous Exbury Gardens of the Rothschild estate, boasting the most beautiful and extensive collection of azaleas, rhododendrons, camellias, and magnolias in the country. There are many stately homes in the area, including Broadlands, home of the Mountbattens; Wilton House, home of the Earl of Pembroke; Kingston Lacey House and gardens; Longleat House, which also offers a lion safari; and many more. Chewton Glen is just on the edge of the famous New Forest, and has an interesting history of its own, dating back to the early 1700s.

Actually, the hotel itself is on thirty acres of parks and grounds, with lovely old trees, beautiful flowering shrubs, terraces, a gorgeous swimming pool, tennis court, croquet lawn, and a 9-hole golf course, along with a pitch-and-putt course. There is a billiards room that has a wonderful clubby atmosphere, and the walls are covered with framed clippings of the many, many articles written about Chewton Glen and photographs, sketches, and cartoons, many by former guests.

Well, I could go on at great length about this superlative place. Needless to say, the guest rooms are all beautifully and individually decorated, with every sort of amenity. There are some two-story suites with their own private enclosed patios.

It would be a perfect overnight stay for voyagers arriving or departing on the *QE2*, being just a half-hour from Southampton, although a longer stay would enable you to enjoy more of the lovely surrounding countryside.

With all of this, what I liked best was the note that a pair of "Wellies" (Wellington boots) were available for guests, if needed. Now that's *style!*

CHEWTON GLEN HOTEL (Relais et Chateaux), New Milton, Hampshire BH25 6QS. Tel.: Highcliffe (04252) 5341. Telex: 41456. U.S. reservations: 800-223-5581. A 46-guestroom luxury resort-hotel 10 mi. from Bournemouth. Open all year. King size beds available. Breakfast, lunch, and dinner served to travelers. Reservations necessary. Tennis, 9-hole golf, putting, outdoor heated swimming pool, croquet lawn on grounds. Golf, riding, fishing, nature walks in the New Forest, and all manner of recreation and sightseeing nearby. Martin Skan, Proprietor. (See Index for rates.)

Directions: Chewton Glen is situated on the A337 between New Milton and Highcliffe. From London take the M3 to A33 to Southampton and turn left on M27. Leave M27 at A337, marked Lyndhurst, and then follow A35 to a sign marked New Milton on the left side of the road. IGNORE THIS SIGN. Proceed toward Bournemouth and turn left on the road marked Walkford and Highcliffe (opposite the Cat and Fiddle Public House). From this turning, drive 1.3 mi. through Walkford to second left turn, marked Chewton Farm Rd. Hotel entrance is on your right. (Ignore all signs to New Milton.)

THE NEW FOREST

The New Forest stretches over heath and woodland in a 145-mile-square area west of Southampton. It is one of England's most attractive and popular natural areas. There are free-roaming animals of all kinds, including pigs, cattle, and ponies, and motorists are required to drive with great caution.

Being British, the forest, naturally, has great walking areas and public footpaths, as well as some narrow gravel roads for automobiles. The flowers, trees, and bushes, beautiful in themselves, are inhabited by hundreds of species of birds.

It's been called the "New Forest" ever since William of Normandy chose this part of Hampshire for his royal hunting grounds, as it was convenient to his palace and castle at Winchester. However, the area has prehistoric burial mounds and earthworks showing earlier occupation.

King William II later imposed such outrageous laws on the New Forest that it is said his death during a hunting expedition might have been an assassination. Both King John, of Magna Carta fame, and Charles I have a close association with this wooded area.

Many of the ancient laws of the forest still exist, but I don't believe that poachers are beheaded any longer.

SUMMER LODGE
Evershot, Dorset

I had been able to join another solo traveler at dinner, and now we were both enjoying coffee and a delectable chocolate morsel in the drawing room, while our host, Nigel Corbett, gave my new-found friend all sorts of ideas where she might go to paint. Having been a painting teacher for many years, she was now on a painting holiday for herself. Nigel, a tall, curly-haired gentleman, was saying, "There's a spectacular view of the south coast from the cliff, and you could walk to Golden Cap, the highest point on the coast. On a clear day you can see for fifty miles, from Portland Bill to Start Point. Or you could walk over to Melbury Osmond, a very pretty little thatched village. There are literally miles of footpaths, several of which go through the deer park at Melbury House. And, of course, there is Tess of the D'Urbervilles cottage at the end of High Street, right here in the village."

I knew this was Thomas Hardy country, but hadn't realized that one of his characters actually lived in the village of Evershot. "Oh yes," Nigel told me, "Hardy called the village 'Evershead' in his novel. By the way,

Hardy drew the plans for this wing of the house. He was also an architect, you know."

Looking around appreciatively, I noted the nobly proportioned fire-place, the floor-to-ceiling windows, the high ceiling, the serene aspect of the room. "Yes," I said, "I can see a fine intellect behind the design of this room." The discreet colors of the comfortable furnishings, the soft glow of the lamps, the many interesting paintings, books, magazines, and fresh flowers all formed a most agreeable background for the various conversations Nigel carried on with his guests, as he moved around the room.

Summer Lodge feels very British. There is a certain reserved air about the English guests. Couples murmur quietly between themselves and scrupulously respect the privacy of others. Margaret Corbett told me that when Americans come here, they tend to stimulate more group conversations. "Actually," she says, "they sometimes make such good friends that they've arranged to meet here the following year."

Margaret took some time away from her little workroom behind the office, where she puts together all the beautiful flower arrangements I noticed throughout the house, to show me the guest rooms. They were all very pleasing, with Laura Ashley wallpapers, harmonizing curtains and bedspreads, and with welcome views of gardens, fields, sloping meadows, and the thatched roofs of the village. Much of the furniture is cane, and adds to the light, airy feeling of the rooms.

Summer Lodge, until ten years ago, was part of the estate of the Earl of Ilchester, whose main abode is Melbury House. It was the dower house where the Earl's heirs would live until it was time for them to take the title and move into the big house.

The house is surrounded by lawns and gardens and lovely old trees. In a little walled courtyard garden that leads through a gate right onto the main street of the village, the wisteria was bursting into beautiful lavender blooms.

Meals in the very pleasant, many-windowed dining room tend to be simple and good, served by cheerful and attentive young people. The night I was there, the main course was one of my favorites—steak and kidney pie, with a starter of smoked haddock roulade. The main course was followed by a fresh green salad and a choice of sweets, including a combination of lovely fresh fruits.

Dinner is included in the tariff, and some of the other menu offerings might be a starter of fresh local asparagus, mushroom and parsley soup, or smoked salmon and scrambled eggs. Some of the main courses are beef Wellington with béarnaise sauce, roast pheasant, chicken marinated in lime juice with hollandaise sauce, baked local rainbow trout, and roast sirloin of beef with Yorkshire pudding.

The next morning, after a good night's sleep and a hearty breakfast, as I said my goodbyes, I saw my painter friend, paint box under her arm and wearing a pair of Wellies, making off for a day in the lush Dorset countryside.

SUMMER LODGE COUNTRY HOUSE HOTEL, Evershot, Dorset DT2 OJR. Tel.: Evershot (093583) 424. A 19-guestroom (private baths) country house hotel and coach house deep in Thomas Hardy country, midway between Yeovil and Dorchester. Breakfast and dinner included in tariff. Lunch and dinner served to public; reservations necessary. Open mid-Jan. to mid-Dec.; weekend minimum of 2 nights. Swimming pool, grass tennis court, croquet lawn on grounds. Golf, horseback riding, fishing, 20 mi. of footpaths, including cliff walks, hunting, beaches, sailing in Lyme Bay nearby. Wheelchair access. Children over 8 accepted. Three dogs and three cats in residence. Nigel and Margaret Corbett, Proprietors. (See Index for rates.)

Directions: From London, take the M3 to A303, the A359 to Yeovil, and then the A37 from Yeovil, going toward Dorchester. Watch for sign to Evershot.

PLUMBER MANOR
Sturminster Newton, Dorset

As I drove down the fence-lined driveway toward Plumber Manor (an imposing Jacobean structure surrounded by old chestnut trees), three men on horseback, wearing traditional riding habits, approached in single file. This is hunting country, I remembered, and fall is when much of the excitement begins. I knew there was a full livery service nearby, and I'd been told that guests at Plumber Manor could be given free stabling (straw and water provided) on a do-it-yourself basis if they wanted to join any of the local hunting packs. These gentlemen, however, were obviously just out for a morning ride.

In the front hall, I discovered a relaxed black labrador. As I passed, it eyed me with a polite tolerance that seemed to say my arrival was too early. Indeed, it was. I knew I wasn't expected until afternoon—ahead of schedule for once. "Mr. Prudeaux-Brune has gone out for a morning ride," his assistant said. "However, you are welcome at any time."

Plumber Manor has been the home of the Prudeaux-Brune family from its inception in the 17th century. Since 1973, it has been open to the public as a hotel and restaurant. Richard Prudeaux-Brune, owner and proprietor, is on hand most of the time to welcome guests and offer any advice needed, whether for riding, hunting, shooting, playing croquet on the lawn, playing tennis on the hard courts, or walking about the countryside. His brother, Brian, a highly talented chef, is in charge of the restaurant, which occupies three connecting dining rooms and is open to the public for dinner.

All guest rooms are large and luxurious—six in the main house and six in the reconverted stone barn, the latter with window seats overlooking a stream and garden. The bar is well-stocked, and sitting room fireplaces are lit in cool weather.

At the top of the stairway is a gallery with paintings of family ancestors, among them a depiction of Plumber Manor as it looked in the 17th century. Now, nearly 400 years later, the house is just as striking. The subtle installation of modern conveniences have not changed its character, and the countryside around it has remained just as unspoiled.

PLUMBER MANOR, Hazelbury Bryan Road, Sturminster Newton, Dorset DT10 2AF. Tel.: Sturminister Newton (0258)72507. A 12-guestroom (private baths) Jacobean manor house hotel in the middle of Hardy's Dorset countryside. Croquet, tennis, riding, hunting, shooting available. Closed Feb. No children under 12. No pets. Breakfast included. Dinners available to nonresidents. Richard Prideaux-Brune, Proprietor. (See Index for rates.)

Directions: A30 from Salisbury to East Stour. Left on B3092 past Sturminister Newton, right on A357, then immediately left (by Red Lion) onto road toward Hazelbury Bryan. Second left road leads to Plumber Manor.

FIFEHEAD MANOR
Middle Wallop, Hampshire

The proprietress of Fifehead Manor, Margaret van Veelen, recently wrote me of her discovery that George Washington was a direct descendant of a 15th-century Lord of the Manor of Wallop Fifehead.

I liked the feel of Fifehead Manor almost as soon as I arrived, because it seemed to be a family place. Being a Sunday, there were several families from the local area, who had driven over for a Sunday dinner. Some well-dressed children were playing outdoors in the October sunshine, and several others had taken some games and puzzles from the shelves in the living room and were stretched out on the carpet enjoying themselves.

I soon discovered that Mrs. van Veelen is capable of carrying on an animated conversation not only in English, but also in French, German, and Dutch, and this rather modest manor had a decidedly international air, with several visitors from the Continent.

She was able to spare me a few moments from her supervisory duties to point out that during the bizarre history of this old manor house it has been a nunnery and, later, the home of the Earl of Godwin, whose wife at the time was Lady Godiva, the famous horsewoman of Coventry.

There have been so many additions to the oldest part of the house, dating from the 11th century, that it is a sort of architectural "Pictures at an Exhibition." For example, the center section has typically medieval stone mullioned windows, and the Victorian newer portion has gingerbread ornamentation. There were two fireplaces in the dining room, one Jacobean and the other Elizabethan.

Middle Wallop (wonderful name, isn't it?) is just a few miles from one of the most famous trout streams in all the world, the River Test. In fact, one of the specialties on the menu is fresh trout from the Test, prepared in several different ways. The menu also lists Dover sole, roast lamb, veal, and beef in various forms.

The rather large guest rooms in the main house have been augmented recently by the addition of attractive, modernized bedrooms in an old barn.

Because it is such a relatively short distance from Heathrow Airport, Fifehead Manor would make a most sensible place to stay for the first night or two after arriving in the U.K. It is very quiet and relaxed and only a short distance from Salisbury, Stonehenge, and Winchester.

"Our guests from North America often stay here to recover from their jet lag and then go west to Devon and Cornwall, or north to the Cotswolds," commented Mrs. van Veelen.

I can think of many an enthusiastic fisherman who would love to start a holiday wetting a line in the River Test!

FIFEHEAD MANOR, Middle Wallop, Stockbridge, Hampshire SO20 8EG. Tel.: (0264) Andover 781565. A 16-guestroom rural inn (all with private baths), 10 mi. east of Salisbury, convenient to the famous trout-fishing Test River, and Stonehenge. Open every day except 2 wks. at Christmas. Breakfast, lunch, tea, and dinner served to non-residents. Mrs. M. van Veelen, Resident Owner. (See Index for rates.)

Directions: Fifehead Manor is located on A343 at Middle Wallop. There are several different routes. It is best to locate Middle Wallop and work backwards to where you are (east of Salisbury).

A LAZY SUNDAY AFTERNOON

Stockbridge, England, and Stockbridge, Massachusetts, have one common denominator. They are villages with a long main street, although the Hampshire village's street is much longer than the one in New England. A dissimilarity is the fact that the English Stockbridge has fewer trees.

This is a very important fishing area, and there are two streams that literally run through the town. These were frequented, on a sunny Sunday afternoon, by resident ducks. There were a few guest houses, a number of B&Bs, and one rather large hotel. Several small restaurants served teas and light lunches.

From Stockbridge, I took the country road that runs beside the Test River through the village of Houghton, which, I understand, is one of the great fishing centers. I turned left over the river on a humpbacked bridge into another world. It was, to say the least, the most idyllic of all English scenes, worthy of a Constable.

A series of these small bridges spanned the river as it wound its way through the woodland copse. Overhead, the leaves were turning yellow and brown against the wonderful blue English sky. A flock of crows added their own particular chorus to the chirping of other small birds.

The water on one side of my bridge was so placid and clear that the vegetation on the bottom looked like cabbages and cauliflowers. I could easily see the trout. However, on the other side of the bridge, the surface changed as the water rushed out into a broad channel where the sun danced and sparkled. The eddies spun around and around before proceeding on their short journey to the sea. A few ducks fished for their Sunday dinner. Along the banks there were blackberries, plump and ready for the picking.

I drove on and came to a small village with a fascinating triangular village green. A group of people were sitting in the sun at the Crown Inn enjoying a bar lunch. Some of the village lads were leaning up against their cars. A sign announced that it was "Hampshire Weekend," and there were small stalls nearby where people returning from church stopped off and purchased various crafts and other country things on sale. A very British girl prevailed upon me to "have a go" at one of them.

I saw a poster announcing that a "country and western dance" would be held with music by the Rustlers. Admission would be one pound and twenty-five pence, including supper, but an additional note said "no leather jackets."

ESSEBORNE MANOR
Hurstbourne Tarrant, Andover, Hampshire

There were many tiny, picturesque old villages along the winding course I took through the lush lowlands of the Bourne Valley, but my very favorite one was Saint Mary Bourne. I've never seen so many beautiful thatched cottages in one village. I had wandered off the main road from Basingstoke onto B3048, on my way to Hurstbourne Tarrant. This is not a well-known tourist area, and it is blessedly peaceful and pastoral. One of the principal industries in Saint Mary Bourne is raising watercress. I think Esseborne Manor is a real find.

The menu, which changes seasonally, includes such items as saddle of venison, monkfish with stem ginger in a pastry case, partridge roasted with kumquats, port, and red currants, and calf's liver with plums and Madeira. I might as well tempt you with a recitation of some of her desserts, too: coconut ice cream with raspberry sauce, chocolate and brandy roulade with a coffee sauce, lemon and rosewater custard cups served with a compote of poached apple and lemon macaroons.

This white, rather austere-looking mid-Victorian house is encircled by a lawn with lovely beech and lime, or linden, trees, and gardens in the middle of farmlands where cattle graze. There is a tennis court on one side and a croquet lawn on the other. Strolling around outside, I was shown their herb garden.

They serve tea and snacks, when weather permits, in the kind of courtyard, where there is a fountain and a pond with fish in it.

The residents' lounge is light and cheerful, with many windows looking out across the lawn to the tennis court and beyond to a pasture with cattle. Creamy yellow walls, a comfortable sofa and chairs, bookshelves with lots of books, and a large Queen Anne table in the center, decorated with a huge poinsettia and covered with magazines of all sorts, create a wonderful, relaxed atmosphere. A backgammon table sits in a little bay window area.

The dining room is most pleasant and serene, done in soft grays, blues, and rose, with a pastoral wallpaper, mauve upholstered chairs, and white tablecloths. A little bar-lounge has a cozy feeling with a fireplace and casement windows looking out on the croquet lawn.

Arrangements must be made in advance for pheasant and grouse shooting and deer stalking. There is also trout fishing on the famous River Test nearby. I was amused to learn we weren't far from Watership Down, which really *is* stuffed with rabbits. For sightseeing, there are all sorts of historic landmarks and pretty little villages, not to mention the ancient and historic towns of Winchester and Salisbury.

The guest rooms are named for small towns and villages such as Lymington, Maddingly, Chichester, and Westholme. The Ferndown Room is their honeymoon suite, and it is a pretty thing, indeed. Decorated in shades of white, lavender, and lime green, it has a curtained four-poster bed, a lavender settee, french doors opening out onto an enclosed garden patio, and a bathroom with a whirlpool bathtub and a stall shower.

All of the guest rooms are different, and they are all most attractive and pleasant. They all have telephones, radios, color television, and many other amenities.

Oh, in case you were wondering, "bourne" means small stream, and there is one that meanders through this lovely valley.

ESSEBORNE MANOR, Hurstbourne Tarrant, Andover, Hampshire SP11 OER. Tel.: (026 476) 444. A 12-guestroom (private baths) delightful country house hotel in a pastoral setting in the Bourne Valley, midway between Andover and Newbury. Full English breakfast included in tariff. Restaurant open for lunch Mon.–Fri.; dinner Mon.–Sat. Reservations necessary. Closed for 2 wks. at Christmas. Tennis court and croquet lawn on grounds. Fishing, golf, country walks, horse racing at Newbury, Hawk Conservancy and Wildlife Park, and many historic and cultural attractions nearby. No children under 10. No pets. One cocker spaniel in residence. Michael and Fried Yeo, Owners. (See Index for rates.)

Directions: From London, take the M3 to the A303 toward Andover, and the A343 toward Hurstbourne Tarrant. Continue 1½ mi. north to Esseborne Manor.

It's not that the distances are very long in the British Isles, it's the many diversions along the way that sometimes make it impossible to estimate traveling and arrival times. Last order times for dinner are included in the Index so that you can see what time you must arrive in order not to find the kitchen door locked. If you are going to arrive later, call ahead—there isn't a hotel/inn listed here that will not make some provision to feed you if they know you can't make it before the kitchen closes.

In Britain, acceptance of a hotel booking by telephone or in writing is generally regarded as a legally binding contract. If it's necessary to cancel, advise the hotel immediately. If they are unable to re-let the room, the hotel may be entitled to claim compensation—usually two thirds of the agreed price—and any deposit would be included as part of this payment.

THE WEST COUNTRY
Counties of Wiltshire, Avon, Dorset, Devon, Somerset, and Cornwall

Wiltshire has pleasant lofty downlands with rivers and meandering streams. It is a place of prehistoric monuments, the most famous of which is Stonehenge on the Salisbury Plain. Among its great buildings are the Salisbury Cathedral, the Malmesbury Abbey, and Lacock Abbey.

Avon is a new county in England, created on the first of April 1974, and it includes part of Gloucestershire, North Somerset, and the city of Bristol.

Somerset is the home of cider and cheddar cheese. There are some fine beaches and open countryside. Christianity in England is said to have its earliest roots in Somerset. This is also the romantic land of Lorna Doone and where King Arthur held court at fabled Camelot and Alfred sought refuge at Athelney.

Devon is one of Britain's leading holiday counties. It has sandy beaches, high-banked lanes, lush green valleys, rolling hills, and a mild climate. There are also wide open spaces like Dartmoor and Exmoor.

Cornwall is at the far southwest end of Britain and has a 300-mile coastline. The mild climate and semi-tropical foliage of the south coast has earned it the title of "Cornish Riviera." There are picturesque harbors crowded with fishing boats, many unusual villages and small towns with cobbled lanes. This is a photographer's and artist's paradise. Cornwall, as well as Devon, is famous for creamed teas.

THE WEST COUNTRY

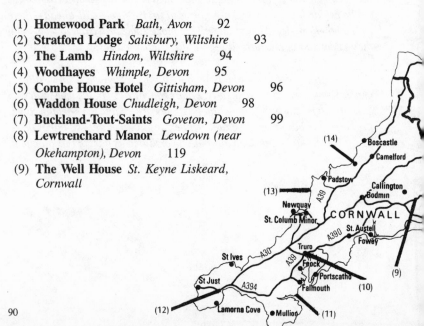

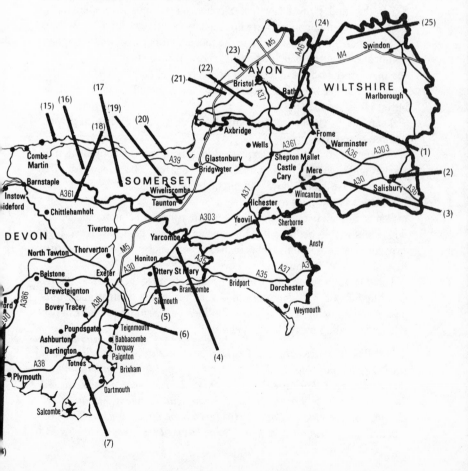

HOMEWOOD PARK
Hinton, Charterhouse, Bath, Avon

If the reader will take a moment to look on the page with the map of the West Country, he or she will note that distances are very short, and it's possible, using Bath as the hub, to visit points in Somerset, Avon, and Wiltshire. I would suggest staying in one place for two or three nights; they are all excellent and somewhat varied in price.

The Homewood Park Hotel, recommended by Richard and Annie Skipwith at the Old House Hotel in Wickham, is a short, pleasant drive from Bath to the east.

The first thing I saw was a croquet lawn bordered by extensive gardens. The main house is a very old building with the entrance through an attractive flower-bedecked patio.

The reception area and the other rooms on the first floor were bright and cheerful with a mixture of modern and traditional furnishings.

I had telephoned ahead and introduced myself as a friend of the Skipwiths, and I must say that Stephen and Penny Ross were most gracious, even though they were hosting a very large wedding party. I am sure I couldn't have chosen a more inopportune time; however, their good humor and excellent manners prevailed. As it turned out I was very glad to see this lovely family-run country house hotel at its brightest and most inviting, with the happy, celebrating guests all gathered around a fabulous buffet table.

There are fifteen bedrooms individually decorated, each with private bathroom and lovely view.

Stephen, who is the chef, explained that the menu is a combination of French and country cooking. "Mildly influenced," he added, "by the new style. We would never admit to being *cuisine nouvelle,* but our approach has the light touch."

Penny chimed in quickly, "I think we are running a country restaurant with comfortable bedrooms. Most people coming here have very high expectations, so we cannot relax in the kitchen when people are expecting to find the food interesting."

I could readily see that both of them had to attend to their guests and so I wandered about, both indoors and out, admiring the gardens and tennis court, and enjoying for a moment the idea of sharing in a real English country wedding party. It was delightful.

HOMEWOOD PARK, Hinton, Charterhouse, Bath, Avon BA3 6BB. Tel.: (022122) Limpley Stoke 3731. A 15-guestroom (private baths) country house hotel near Bath. Breakfast, lunch, and dinner served daily. Closed Dec. 24 to Jan. 5. Located near the American Museum and all of the delights of the city of Bath. Two nights booking on weekends. Good countryside walking and touring. Stephen and Penny Ross, Hoteliers.

*Directions: Follow A36 south from Bath for 5½ mi. Turn left for Sharp-
stone, then first left for Homewood.*

STRATFORD LODGE
4 Park Lane, Castle Road, Salisbury, Wiltshire
Stratford Lodge takes its name from a village near Salisbury and has no
relation to the town of Stratford-upon-Avon of Shakespeare fame. The
Lodge is actually a three-story guest house located on a quiet byway
overlooking a park. Don't let the unimpressive entrance to the building
put you off. It gets better inside. The house is filled with Victorian
antiques, including a fine collection of china. Each of the five guest rooms
has not only a private bath, rare for a home this size and age, but also a
special feature—one room contains a brass bed covered with an intricate
lace spread, while my room included a hand-carved antique bed with
cane insets. A nice touch is the immaculate drawn-tread linens that cover
the bedside tables.

What impressed me most, however, was the owner, Jill Bayly, who has
operated the establishment for eleven years. Not only is she an expert cook
in the French tradition, using fresh vegetables and herbs from her garden,
but she also darts about with a friendly personality, making certain her
guests have whatever they need.

"Come in, come in," she cried, when I peered into the large white
kitchen from which smells of roasting meat wafted. "We're having duck
with an orange sauce for dinner." Jill has taught cooking classes and still
gives demonstrations. She even gave me one, although I doubt if I could
reproduce such delicious duck.

*STRATFORD LODGE, 4 Park Lane, Castle Road, Salisbury, Wiltshire
SP1 3NP. Tel.: (0722)25177. A 5-guestroom (private baths) Victorian
house about 1 mi. from the central district, where Salisbury Cathedral is
located, and 8 mi. from Stonehenge. Breakfast included. Dinner available
for residents. Open all year except Christmas. Jill Bayly, Proprietor. (See
Index for rates.)*

*Directions: A303 to Amesbury, then south to Salisbury on A345 (Castle
Road). Turn right onto Park Lane by the store just before Victoria Park.*

*Rates for a room for two people for one night with breakfast, except
where noted, are included in the Index of this book. They are not to be
considered firm quotations, but should be used as guidelines only.*

THE LAMB
Hindon (near Salisbury), Wiltshire

Not far from Salisbury, in the small village of Hindon, is an inn that formerly served as a 17th-century coaching inn and posthouse. Alastair Morrison is the present proprietor, and he is gradually bringing the interior back to its former look while upgrading facilities in the rooms. All now have private bathrooms. Apart from the pub, there is a new, pleasant residents' lounge where fires are set and peace can be had. Although decor in a few guest rooms is still a bit spotty, plans are afoot to finish the work soon. Recently, the lobby and dining room have been refurbished, and the new hunter-green carpet and architectural prints greatly improve their appearance.

In the oldest section of the building, some of the upstairs floors are slanted. To me, this feeling of age beneath your feet is part of the charm of the inn. I even asked the day manager for a tour of the cellar, where wine bottles and beer kegs are kept, because I wanted to touch the 400-year-old foundation stones and original support beams, heavy timbers salvaged from wrecked sailing vessels in Portsmouth centuries ago.

"You can tell which ones are from the ships," he said. "In the old days they numbered the timbers."

During the recent remodelling, a brick-lined cavern well was discovered that once provided water for 300 horses. Although the well was resealed, a large old hand pump can still be seen in one of the courtyards.

Roast pheasant and grilled Avon trout almondine are frequently on the menu at the inn, as well as roast duckling and, of course, there is almost always lamb.

THE LAMB, Hindon (near Salisbury) Wiltshire SP3 6DP. Tel.: Hindon (074-789)573. A 15-guestroom (private baths) traditional village inn 16 mi. west of Salisbury. Open all year. Breakfast included. Lunch and dinner served to nonresidents. Convenient for Salisbury, Stonehenge, Stourhead House and Gardens. Riding, walking, fishing, and shooting available nearby. Alastair Morrison, Proprietor. (See Index for rates.)

Directions: From London take M3 to A303. Continue until 10 mi. past Stonehenge, then look for turning to left, signposted "Hindon."

WOODHAYES
Whimple (near Exeter), Devon

My first contact with Katherine Rendle, who with her husband Frank purchased Woodhayes in early 1988, was a phone call several weeks before I left the States for England.

"I'm so glad I caught you," the cheerful voice said. "Your letter was torn in route and I can't tell which day you're arriving."

I checked my calendar. "The afternoon of October sixth," said I.

"Lovely," said she. "Do come in time for tea."

When I met Katherine in person, red-headed and Irish, she proved to be as hospitable and enthusiastic as she had sounded over the phone. "Before this," she said, while we drank tea in one of her two attractive drawing rooms, "we were in the restaurant business in Hampshire for twenty-one years. I live and breathe cooking. Frank, on the other hand, lives to build."

A mason by trade, Frank has made remarkable improvements in Woodhayes. He found and unsealed an old fireplace hidden under tiles in the former kitchen, then turned the room into a snug bar complete with a built-in bench and stripped-pine tables. What used to be a ground floor bedroom and bath across the hall was turned into a new stainless steel kitchen where Katherine could work her wonders. Son Michael, now grown, has returned to take charge of the grounds, including a large vegetable garden.

Woodhayes, a Georgian house built for a country squire, is not an opulent manor, but the interior has understated elegance. Rooms are large, light, and decorated in pastels. As you can imagine, the food is given prime attention here. Lamb and beef are from the region as are fish, with the Devon north and south coasts not far away.

If I had my druthers, I would have preferred staying here for a week, to poke about in villages, to hike the country footpaths, to eat Katherine's food. Alas, I had to press on to Exmouth. The afternoon shadows already were too long.

WOODHAYES, Whimple (near Exeter), Devon EX5 2TD. Tel.: Whimple (0404)82237. A 6-guestroom (private baths) Georgian country house hotel in apple-orchard countryside. Park-like gardens with tennis, croquet. Open year round. Breakfast included. Lunch and dinner available. Frank, Katherine, and Michael Rendle, Proprietors. (See Index for rates.)

Directions: Whimple is a small village located to the north of A30. Look for signpost for Whimple a few miles west of Honiton.

COMBE HOUSE HOTEL
Gittisham (near Honiton), Devon

Dusk had fallen on the A30. A scant twenty minutes earlier I had left Exeter and was now anxiously looking for the signpost for Gittisham. Ah, there it was. I turned into a truly ancient village with cob and thatched cottages and a babbling brook. There was a parish church that enshrined 500 years of the community's history.

A gate at the end of the village led to a narrow road that wound its way through the meadows of an extensive country estate. I parked in front of a large three-story stone building with many towers and windows, surrounded by beautiful hedges and flowers.

In the impressive main hall I found no reception desk or porters in white jackets, but rather a large, imposing man, his face wreathed in smiles, who said, "Welcome to the Combe House Hotel."

This was my introduction to John Boswell, who, with his wife, Thérèse, is the proprietor of this remarkably well-preserved Elizabethan manor house, which possibly dates as far back as the 13th century. Standing at the head of a secluded valley, it commands extensive views over the hills where there are beautiful walks and a sublime serenity.

When the Boswells came to Combe in 1970, they found the old country house in a dilapidated condition. Since then, they have restored it completely and modernized all its facilities. "The gardens were in an almost hopeless condition," said John, a tall, charming fellow who converses easily with his guests, "and it pleases us now when people enjoy all the flowers. We also have an extensive kitchen garden, because my wife, Thérèse, insists that the vegetables in our restaurant be absolutely fresh."

Thérèse attended the Cordon Bleu School at Winkfield and lived in France for some time. She not only oversees the kitchen, but also, being an artist, is involved in the hotel's interior decoration, her delightful murals appearing in the halls and on the walls of several guest rooms.

John, whose early Scottish ancestors included the famous James

Boswell, author of *The Life of Samuel Johnson*, had worked for a shipping organization in the Far East before coming to Combe House. He has since developed an interest in race horses, and photos of the winning entries from his stables adorn the bar.

Around the manor house are fine antiques and relics of Combe's past owners. Especially interesting are the oil portraits, and John knows the history of each one. The Boswells have added their cherished pieces, including pictures from Auchinleck House in Scotland, the ancestral home of James Boswell.

Assisting in the hotel operation are the Boswells' two sons, Mark and Simon, both trained chefs. "This is a genuine country house hotel," John said, "and it is family-run, although additional staff is necessary. I want people to relax and enjoy themselves. Tell them we are not stuffed shirts here."

That evening I ate a wonderful dinner, starting with tomato and apple soup, followed by a whole roast partridge served with bread sauce and potatoes. Alongside was a dish of several kinds of vegetables lightly cooked. A trolley of tempting desserts was wheeled forward, but I bravely resisted, even though I heard the lady at the next table exclaim about the wonders of the fruit tart. I hastily retreated to the lounge for coffee, but, while there, lost my resolve when a tray of petits fours appeared, too tempting to resist.

COMBE HOUSE HOTEL, Gittisham (near Honiton), Devon EX14 OAD. Tel: Honiton (0404)42756/43560. Fax: Honiton (0404)46004. A 15-guestroom (private baths) Elizabethan country house hotel with sweeping views. Close to Exeter and Bath. Children served separately for supper. Fishing and croquet on grounds; tennis, swimming, squash, and riding nearby. For stable tour, advance arrangements should be made. Breakfast included. Lunch, tea, and dinner served daily. Closed mid-Jan. until late Feb., but office open during that period. John and Thérèse Boswell, Resident Proprietors. (See Index for rates.)

Directions: From Honiton take the A30 (Exeter road); after approx. 1 mi., turn left at the signpost for Gittisham. This road leads to Combe House.

WADDON HOUSE
Chudleigh (near Exeter), Devon

"I was just going to put on my Wellies and do a bit of gardening," said Sylvia Froud, her short red hair a halo for her face.

I had stopped the car in her driveway and asked if I could see her establishment.

"Come on in," she continued, setting down her trowel. "The garden is always here."

On the edge of Dartmoor, rolling hills and woodlands all around, stands Waddon House on three acres of landscaped gardens with over 100 species of trees and shrubs. The style of the building is Edwardian, a solid, traditionally English look—white, three-storied, gabled, beautiful oak floors throughout. The six charmingly decorated guest rooms (one with a brass bed owned by Lillie Langtry) share three en suite baths, unique with touches of whimsy, such as the large shower head that looks like a garden watering can. "I'm one of the few Brits," she said with a twinkle in her eyes, "who has a proper shower. It flows like Niagara Falls." I later learned that both of her daughters are married to Americans.

When Sylvia dashes about preparing four-course dinners for her guests—naturally using her own produce—or slips into her Wellington boots and plunges into gardening, she reminds me of an industrious little elf. If you like hedgerow lanes, groups of thatched cottages, gardens, gorgeous views, and miles of footpaths, come to Waddon House. In 1986, Sylvia won the Kellog Award for the Best Bed and Breakfast in the West Country. It's easy to see why.

WADDON HOUSE, Chudleigh (near Exeter), Devon TQ13 ODJ. Tel.: (0626)853216—"long ring, please." A 6-guestroom (en suite shared baths) house with large gardens and views of Dartmoor. Tennis court. Trout fishing 1 mi. Golf and riding nearby. Open all year. Breakfast included; dinner available. Prefer non-smokers. No children under 10. Suggest making reservations by noon to avoid disappointment. Sylvia Froud, Resident Proprietor. (See Index for rates.)

Directions: From A38, 10 mi. west of Exeter on Plymouth Rd., take Chudleigh Rd., B3344 (after Masons Garage, on left). Slow down 300 yds., then left turn signed Kerswell. Pass the Trout Farm on right, continue 1 mi. Waddon House is on right, over the cattle grid and down the drive.

BUCKLAND-TOUT-SAINTS
Goveton, Devon

Take a moment to look at the map of western England and you will note that at Exeter the main roads to Cornwall split, going around Dartmoor National Park to the north and south. There are roads through Dartmoor, principally B3212; however, the average visitors to Britain want to get to Cornwall as quickly as possible, so they usually opt for A30 to Okehampton or A38 going south toward Plymouth. It is to this second road that I would like to call your attention.

This peninsula, extending down into the sea and including Dartmouth, Salcombe, and Kingsbridge, is known as South Hams, so-called for the excellent quality of the native porkers. It is one of the holiday areas of the well-informed Briton.

Kingsbridge is a key turnoff for the village of Goveton, which I'm sure is only on the most specific of maps. I have been very specific about directions, but I'm certain that before you reach Buckland-Tout-Saints, just outside of Goveton, you will be convinced that you are totally lost. The sunken lanes are so deep and the hedges on top are so high that they are almost double the height of the car.

Regardless of whatever problems you may encounter, this exceptional Queen Anne mansion, part of which dates back to the 12th century, will be worth any motoring anxieties.

The hotel derives its name from the French-Norman family of Tout-sants, who held this manor after the Norman conquest of 1066. Today, it is a country house hotel of great dignity and grace in a delightful and remote park.

Ashburton marble fireplaces, 17th- and 18th-century molded plaster ceilings, intricate oak foliage scrollwork, and mahogany-and-gilt doors are just some of its characteristics. The main guest rooms are lofty and luxurious with tasteful furnishings and very choice views of the surrounding countryside. The gardens are exceptional and feature, among other things, a species of New Zealand fern that demands subtropical conditions, shelter from the winds, and constant attention.

There is an air of dignity at Buckland-Tout-Saints, in keeping with the formality of the manor house, which has been owned and operated by the Shepherd family for twenty years. David Shepherd, son of the owner, has recently taken over from his father, Victor, as manager and host. He is an authority on wine and cheese, dispensing them with great pride.

Chef Alastair Carter, in his fourth year here, presides over the newly-expanded, high-tech kitchen. He and his staff treat each dish as a work of art. Sauces are delicate. Meats are tender. All presentations are worthy of pictures. As an entree I had loin of veal with herb pasta and a lemon sage butter sauce. Superb.

BUCKLAND-TOUT-SAINTS, Govedon, Kingsbridge, Devon TQ7 2DS. Tel.: Kingsbridge (0548)3055. Telex: 42513 (Attn: BTS Hotel). Fax: (0548)6261. A 12-guestroom (private baths) country house hotel in 27 acres of parklane near the South Devon coast. Croquet lawn and putting green; golf, fishing, and horseback riding nearby. No children under 8. No pets. Breakfast included. Lunch and dinner served daily to nonresidents. Gentlemen are each requested to wear a jacket and tie for dinner. Closed Jan. Shepherd Family, Proprietors. (See Index for rates.)

Directions: From London take the M4 and M5 to Exeter; the A38 to Buckfastleigh. From there take A384 to Totnes, then A381 for Kingsbridge and look for hotel signs beyond Halwell. It is reached by a single passage road through the fields.

LEWTRENCHARD MANOR
Lewdown (near Okehampton), Devon

Lewtrenchard Manor, built in 1620, stands in the midst of 1,000 green acres like a gracious lady, welcoming all who come to visit her, and James and Sue Murray match the hospitable look of their home. They seem to belong here as much as the ancestors of the Baring-Gould family, who owned the house and whose paintings still grace its walls.

One of the paintings is of Margaret, an ancestor only by marriage, who inherited the estate in the 1700s along with tremendous debts. Because she loved the place so much, she spent the rest of her life fighting to save it. It is said her ghost benignly walks the upstairs rooms—several guests claim to have seen her.

Set in spectacular grounds that include walled gardens, lovely walks, a two-acre trout lake, and a sixty-foot waterfall, the estate extends out to include farms and woodlands.

"Originally it was the Lew House here," said Sue Murray, who, along with her husband James, is fascinated by the history of the area. "Then, in 1300, the Trenchard Family came and called it Lewtrenchard. It was recorded in the *Domesday Book*. The present house was built in 1626. Probably the most famous occupant was Sabine Baring-Gould, the composer of the hymn 'Onward Christian Soldiers.' Quite a Renaissance man, really. Not only a composer, but also an author, folklorist, traveler, and a compulsive collector." She pointed to the handsome wooden moldings in the ballroom. "He brought these from Bavaria. Probably, he was responsible for most of the carved ceilings and other architectural decoration throughout the house.

Certainly the house is full of baronial splendor—leaded windows in guest rooms, ornate fireplaces—but the Murrays, who sold their farm in Africa and came here to start a second career, have added informality, assisted by two children and an exhuberant labrador, Doma, that Susan laughingly says "lives in the house and considers it his own."

The Restaurant at Lewtrenchard features various treatments of fish, beef, and lamb. Two specialities are saddle of English lamb with Madeira, tarragon, and cream sauce, and Dutch veal in a light Stilton and basil sauce. It is known as one of the best places to dine in the West Country.

LEWTRENCHARD MANOR, Lewdown, (near Okehampton), Devon EX20 4PN. Tel.: (056683) 246 or 222. Fax: (056683) 332. For American reservations, free phone: 800-635-3608. An 8-guestroom (private baths) country house hotel in park-like grounds midway between Exeter and Plymouth. Can arrange horseback riding, golf, croquet, clay pigeon

shooting, rough shooting, and fishing. Open all year. Breakfast included.
Restaurant open daily for dinner and Sun. lunch. Reservations needed.
James and Sue Murray, Proprietors. (See Index for rates.)

Directions: Lewtrenchard is ¾ mi. from the village of Lewdown off the
A-30.

THE WELL HOUSE
St. Keyne, Liskeard, Cornwall

Tunnels of hazelnut trees arch over the narrow lane leading the last few miles to The Well House. The countryside here is mostly shades of green, brilliant in sunlight, suddenly black under cloud shadows, all colors constantly changing hue.

It was several years ago, in this corner of Cornwall, that Nicholas Wainford found a decaying stone house of classic proportions, built in 1894 by a tea planter with estates in Assam. "Maybe it was the cries of the rooks in the pines at the foot of the hill," he says, "or the constantly changing color of the valley below. Anyway, I felt the magic of the place."

Deftly, and with great care, he began the process of restoration, not only of the house but of the grounds. Today, you enter a doorway surrounded by sweet-smelling jasmine, pass through a hall with hand-painted Victorian tiles on the floor, and find large rooms that are decorated with a quiet beauty. On the walls are watercolors of grace and clarity. Seven bedrooms reflect the owner's impeccable taste.

The chef here makes everything from scratch, even the delicate tea biscuits and the hand-dipped chocolates. "Although his dishes reflect English traditions," Nick said, "they are adapted for the tastes of our age." I was especially impressed with the steamed breast of Aylesbury duck—crispy, pan-fried, and served with a passionfruit sauce.

Nick must have read my mind when he hastened to assure me the duck hadn't been taken from the ponds on the grounds. "Unfortunately, it is the foxes that have decimated our flock, not the chef," he said with a sigh. "Those are Call Ducks out there. Friendly little creatures, you'll find."

When I walked to the ponds to see for myself, a flotilla swam toward me. All around the garden and the new tennis courts, the ducks waddled after me, females quacking excitedly (males of the species make no sound). I couldn't tell if the flock was disgusted I hadn't brought bread crumbs or merely wanted company.

Later, I told Nick I planned to mention the ducks in my story. He looked heavenward and exclaimed, "I do hope by the time your readers come, the foxes haven't gotten them all."

THE WELL HOUSE, St. Keyne, Liskeard, Cornwall PL14 4RN. Tel.: (0579) 42001. An 8-guestroom (private baths) Victorian country manor in a spectacular setting. Swimming pool, hard tennis court, croquet; fishing, riding, walking, golf nearby. Coast minutes away. Continental breakfast included. Full breakfast; luncheon, tea, dinner available. Nicholas Wainford, Proprietor. (See Index for rates.)

Directions: From Liskeard take the B3254. Follow signs to St. Keyne (not St. Keyne Station). In the village, take the road to St. Keynewell, signed ½ mi. from the church.

ALVERTON MANOR
Tregolls Road, Truro, Cornwall

Alverton Manor, standing on a hill in the center of the town of Truro, is an impressive sight—massive sandstone walls, arched and mullioned windows, peaked Cornish Delabole slate roof, and tall-towered chapel.

"It was built for the Tweedy family about 150 years ago," said David Mead, the efficient and enthusiastic manager who showed me around. "In the late 1880's the Bishop of Truro acquired the property, then later the Sisters of Epiphany occupied it. I sometimes wonder what the sisters would think if they came back now to see its internal grandeur."

The present owners, the Costello family, must have spent a fortune here, I thought, as we toured one luxurious room after another. Besides creating a beautiful interior, they had to build a foundation for the whole structure, since originally it was built without one and had started to collapse and move toward the road. Now it is pinned solidly to bedrock, and every detail of restoration has been just as carefully thought out.

"The heavy mahogany doors were made locally," David said.

"There must be hundreds of them," I murmured, running my hand over the smooth finish. "Although you have only twenty-five guest rooms, the hotel's interior is so huge I could get lost."

David laughed and showed me into yet another public area, a delightful solarium with setees and numerous potted plants.

"We've made a hobby of trees," David said. "When we built the car park just above the hotel, we had to take out an orchard of two dozen apple trees. They were replanted on the grounds, and I'm proud to say we only lost one. The trees in here are some of the unusual, small ones we found on our six acres. They looked as if they needed nurturing, so we brought them inside."

At the time, I wondered if that was an indication of the care taken of guests. Apparently, it was, for Alverton Manor proved to be a courteous and well-serviced hotel. Although open for less than two years, it has become the highest rated hotel in Cornwall and has received top awards for its cuisine.

ALVERTON MANOR, Tregolls Road, Truro, Cornwall TR1 1XQ. Tel.: (0872) 76633. Fax: (0872) 222989. A 25-guestroom (private baths) luxury hotel in an old nunnery, secluded yet centrally located in the cathedral city of Truro. Accessible by train from London's Paddington Station. Good base for touring Cornwall. No children under 12. No pets. Continental breakfast included. Full breakfast, luncheon, afternoon tea, and dinner available. Alverton Manor Hotels, Ltd., Proprietor. David Mead, Manager. (See Index for rates.)

Directions: On A39, coming into Truro from the direction of St. Austell the hotel is located on the right side of the road.

NANSIDWELL COUNTRY HOUSE
Mawnan (near Falmouth), Cornwall

Clouds continually shifted across the sun as I drove along a lane between towering hedgerows. I went over a rise and the sun broke through, turning the Helford River below into silver. It was an early afternoon in late October, a slight chill in the air—not much, though. I've never found this part of England very cold. Even tropical plants can be grown in certain areas of South Cornwall.

Soon after I passed through the village of Mawnan Smith, I reached Nansidwell Country House, a large, steep-roofed stone building partially covered with wisteria, its many bay windows facing the green hills of National Trust Land and the sea beyond.

Felicity and Jamie Robertson, owners of Nansidwell, have five acres of splendid gardens. From the early days of February, when daffodils and camellias start to bloom, through the azaleas, rhododendrons, fuchsias, hydrangeas, mimosa and on and on into the fall colors of autumn now visable, the grounds are a delight to behold. There are even banana trees that bear fruit as late as the end of October, when Nansidwell closes for the season.

Over a cup of coffee in front of a fire, I chatted with Felicity and Jamie, who several years ago moved from London, where he ran a highly successful restaurant and she was an investment advisor. "We looked for a year before we found what we wanted," Felicity said. "It had been a hotel for fifty years, but it was terribly run down, so we immediately pitched in and remodelled, modernizing facilities, creating atmosphere. Rooms that are hospitable and relaxed—that's what we wanted for our guests."

And that's what they achieved with flowered chintz, squashy chairs, airy bedrooms, an interesting collection of plates on the dining room walls, lots of pillows, books, and magazines (the latest), and everywhere, a focus on views—the fantastic views.

Besides full dinners, there is an à la carte menu offered for those who wish lighter meals. "I insist on Cornish produce," Jamie said. "The fish is locally caught, and the game and meat are of highest quality. I carefully select my wines. But all this would mean little if we didn't have such a talented French chef."

To come in after a hike over the countryside, or a game of tennis, or a stroll through the garden, is not like coming into a hotel. It is more like returning to your own English manor.

NANSIDWELL COUNTRY HOUSE, Mawnan (near Falmouth), Cornwell TR11 5HU. Tel.: Falmouth (0326) 250340. A 13-room (private baths) country house hotel with extensive gardens and views of National Trust Land and the sea. Hard court tennis; nearby are 5 good golf courses (closest, 2 mi.), sea fishing, reservoir trout and coarse fishing, boating, and bowling. Breakfast included. Lunch, afternoon tea, and dinner available. Closed Nov. through Jan. Felicity and Jamie Robertson, Proprietors. (See Index for rates.)

Directions: Take A39 from Truro to Falmouth. Follow Falmouth Rd. about 7 mi. to mini roundabout at Treluswell crossroads. Take A394 Helston Rd. about 1 mi. to T-junction. Turn right, then immediately left up road signposted Mabe/Mawnan. Follow all signs for Mawnan. In about 3½ mi. you reach Mawnan Smith. At thatched inn (Red Lion), follow left fork to Nansidwell.

THE ABBEY HOTEL
Abbey Street, Penzance, Cornwall

The Abbey has been a hotel for forty years. "We came here quite a while ago as guests and fell in love with the place," said Jean Cox, who with her husband, Michael, now owns the Abbey. "In those days it was rather faded but charming, with some good things. Eccentric artists and poets came. It was a total time warp. Elderly residents lived here. There were three meals a day, only two bathrooms, and no heat, so they had to be a hardy lot."

Eleven years ago the couple bought the place and today there is central heat, bathrooms for each guest room, and nothing faded. Walls are newly papered and painted, fresh flowers are in all the rooms, and the decor is highly artistic, a reflection of the couple's own uniqueness.

Nooks abound with antiques. Art pieces from Thailand and the Sepik River of New Guinea intermingle with Persian miniatures and medieval tapestries. The guest rooms have bookcases loaded with novels you could spend weeks perusing.

You could walk for days through the quaint town of Penzance, from whence came the pirates, or tour nearby villages, or hike the famous Cornish coastal footpath, or take a boat trip to the spectacular island St. Michael's Mount or the Isles of Scilly.

And when you return to the hotel, exhausted, you might sit on one of the window seats and stare through arched panes at the picturesque harbor below. You might think you are back in 1680 when the main building was built. Perhaps you would prefer to be in 1820, when the drawing room was added. It might strike you as unusual that the outside of the building is Regency Gothic in style and painted blue. Again, the time warp.

However you want to pinpoint its place in time, the Abbey is a comfortable hotel with both an eclectic decor that seems just right and unpretentious food that tastes delicious. It manages to give its guests an education on how to relax and enjoy life by just being everything that it is.

THE ABBEY HOTEL, Abbey Street, Penzance, Cornwall TR18 4AR. Tel.: (0736) 66906. An 8-guestroom (private baths except for the 2-guestroom flat) hotel in a listed building overlooking the harbor of Penzance. Cornwall coast is full of interesting villages and footpaths. Breakfast included; dinner available. Open all year. Jean and Michael Cox, Proprietors. (See Index for rates.)

Directions: Take Sea Front road on entering Penzance. After about 300 yds., just before bridge, turn right. After about 10 yds., turn left. Drive up ramp. Abbey is at the top.

WATERBEACH HOTEL
Treyarnon Bay, Padstow, Cornwall

This part of Cornwall reminds me of Normandy, the same sort of pristine white buildings with steep gray slate roofs. From the Waterbeach Hotel, you have a view not only of these houses but of the countryside and the sea. It is like looking at a French painting.

The Waterbeach is a straightforward hotel with few frills, but everything is pleasant, comfortable, clean, and reasonably priced. Only steps away is a wide, sandy beach. Since it gets quite crowded in the summer, and the hotel is heavily booked by English tourists during that time, I suggest you come here for a stay in spring or fall.

This is truly a family-run hotel. Tony Etherington, a former publican, is either on the front desk or behind the bar and is always ready with a quick joke or a good story. Victoria, his wife, spends most of her time in the kitchen, preparing everything from scratch, including breads and jams. Then there is Charlie, Victoria's father, who wears a big smile and pitches in wherever needed, eager to lend a helping hand.

Let me dwell a minute on the food. It is unpretentious and delicious, with a different menu every day. A guest can have a five-course dinner, a three-course dinner, or just one course. And there is always an all-vegetable meal. Dinner is included in the price of the room, as is a full English breakfast (Tony usually cooks this to give his wife a rest).

What especially stands out in my mind, when I remember my stay at Waterbeach, is the family. They are warm, friendly people who are proud of the hotel they have operated for five years, and they work hard to give their guests an enjoyable stay.

WATERBEACH HOTEL, Treyarnon Bay, Padstow, Cornwall PL28 8JW. Tel.: (0841)520292. A 20-guestroom (13 private baths) unpretentious hotel by a sandy beach. Hard court tennis, large garden; nearby surfing, walking (the coastal footpath), golf (about 1 mi. away), boating, and fishing. No pets. Children welcome. Smoking not encouraged in dining room. Breakfast, dinner and afternoon tea included. Closed, Dec.–Feb. Tony and Vicky Etherington, Proprietors. (See Index for rates.)

Directions: A30 past Launceston, take North Cornwall Rte. to Wadebridge. Follow Padstow signpost until you see Newquay signs. Just past St. Merryn, follow signs to Treyarnon Bay.

THE WEST COUNTRY

The West Country could well be called a "Kingdom of Legends." Not only does it hold many of the great national legends of Britain that are a part of a centuries-old heritage—the Arthurian Legends, the search for the Holy Grail, and the Glastonbury stories—but it is full of stories of giants and saints, supernatural happenings, ghostly ships, holy places, wreckers and smugglers, pixies and witches in such a profusion as to give the whole of the area a touch of magic.

PORT GAVERNE HOTEL
Port Gaverne, Port Isaac, North Cornwall

"A chap by the name of Ken Duxbury, when he was writing a book about the area, found the signals, the number of lights they showed, to let the smugglers know if it was safe to come into Port Gaverne or if they had to go on to Boscastle with their contraband."

Fred Ross told me this as he showed me the little back room that was part of the original inn, built in 1608 with timbers and spars from ships that had wrecked on the rocky Cornish coast.

A few minutes earlier I had parked in a small area overlooking the narrow fishing cove across the street from the Port Gaverne Hotel and walked past an ice-cream stand toward a knot of people sitting in the sun around the front door, talking animatedly. A rather courtly gentleman detached himself from the rest and greeted me with an outstretched hand. It was Fred Ross, the owner of this interesting small hotel in the tiny fishing village of Port Gaverne, cheek by jowl with the larger 16th-century Port Isaac.

The hotel, with its cozy and interesting pub, is clearly a community gathering place for local folks and fishermen. But it betrays a more cosmopolitan character with the many, many paintings, watercolors, etchings, and fascinating artifacts collected by Fred and Midge Ross over their twenty years as proprietors here. Among other objects of interest were a beautiful early clock in a glass case, a 1628 John Speed map of North and South America, many antique ship and fishing implements, and some tiny dioramas of the original village of Port Gaverne and the cove, with models of sailing ships that brought in coal and limestone and took out the Delabole slate that has been quarried locally since time immemorial.

Mr. Ross took me all around the hotel, up and down twisty stairs, through corridors, and around corners, showing me room after attractive room, all pleasantly furnished and with nice, clean bathrooms. Some of

the rooms in the older section had original beamed ceilings; others in a more modern addition were off airy, white-painted, windowed corridors, decorated with plants and paintings. All the rooms had books and magazines, paintings, and TV, and looked most comfortable and agreeable. There are some brand-new suites across the road with completely equipped kitchens, and the residents' lounge and TV room are nicely furnished.

I was surprised to learn that Mr. Ross was originally from Cedar Rapids, Iowa. He met his English wife in New York, and in the mid-fifties took her back to England, where they have been living ever since. "Living in Port Gaverne is an Edwardian kind of life," he says. "The village makes its own entertainment. Everybody knows everybody."

He told me about the nearby Saint Enodoc golf course, on the grounds of which is a church where poet laureate Sir John Betjeman is buried. Tintagel Castle is just up the coast, and there is a coastal hiking path that runs for 300 miles.

The busy dining room of course features local fish, as well as locally grown beef, lamb, and fresh garden produce. The set menu changes daily, with a choice of three dishes for every course. The food is good, simple, home-style, with such local specialties as roast Cornish lamb stuffed with apricots and honey, grilled John Dory, and sautéed sliced duck breasts with green pepper sauce. A very nice feature for families is an early sitting for children, along with smaller portions and menus.

This is the sort of place where you can get a real sense of the daily life of a tiny fishing village, and at the same time enjoy the comforts and conveniences of a very attractive and interesting hotel.

PORT GAVERNE HOTEL, Port Gaverne, Port Isaac, North Cornwall PL29 3SQ. Tel.: Bodmin (0208) 880244. A 19-guestroom (private baths) village hotel on a fishing cove on Port Isaac Bay on the north Cornish coast, south of Tintagel and 6 mi. from the market town of Wadebridge. Restaurant serves breakfast, buffet lunch, and dinner. Open from March to mid-Jan. Offshore and deep-sea fishing, 300-mi. coastal path, swimming, surfing, sailing, golf, backpacking, bicycling, pony trekking nearby. One cat in residence. Fred and Midge Ross, Resident Proprietors. (See Index for rates.)

Directions: From A30 to Bodmin, continue to Wadebridge and follow signs to Port Isaac. From Port Isaac, continue on coastal road B3267, going down the hill to the right to Port Gaverne and the hotel.

For room rates and last time for dinner orders, see Index.

THE RISING SUN
Lynmouth, North Devon

The sky was clearing from an overnight rainstorm as I drove along the hogback cliffs on the last mile of coastal road before it dipped into the cove of Lynmouth. To my right, Foreland Point fingered into the Bristol Channel towards Wales, half hidden in clouds on the far side. To my left, sheep grazed on velvet green hills, divided into a patchwork by hedgerows and stone fences. What a wondrous part of Britain is this northern edge of Exmoor.

At the time of my arrival in Lynmouth, the tide was out and the sailboats and working boats were on their sides on the mud flats. The many buildings of the Rising Sun—in one of which, by the way, Shelley is supposed to have stayed—enjoy a splended view of the ever-changing harbor.

"We were just talking about you," said a tall, athletic gentleman who rose from behind the desk in a side office as I came through the front door of the inn.

His name is Hugo Jeune, and for nine years he has been the proprietor here. Beside him sat a young man who pored over menus.

"I wanted to make certain you met our chef," Hugo continued. "I believe you'll find he is awfully good in the kitchen."

That evening, in the low-ceilinged dining room I found out what a gem of a chef they had. His fillet of Exmoor venison, pan fried and served in a rich port wine sauce, was delicious, and the chocolate sauce on the delicate sponge pudding was sinfully good.

Because of the age of the building—parts of it go back 600 years— hallways and staircases in the inn are rather narrow and twisty, and some of the rooms might be described as snug, but all are comfortable and well furnished. A pleasant garden with many kinds of blooms is tucked up on the hill in back.

In the morning, the little harbor was again filled with water almost to the top of the wall, and the boats were bobbing merrily on the waves. The Devon cliffs and the town itself (which reminds me of Portofino, Italy) is very, very pleasant and the prospect of walking on the tops of the cliffs was most inviting. I learned that it is quite crowded in July, August, and September, so plan to visit during other months.

THE RISING SUN HOTEL, Harbourside, Lynmouth, Devon EX35 6EQ. Tel.: Lynton (0598)53223. A 16-guestroom (private baths) thatched-roof, smugglers' inn overlooking Lynmouth Harbor. Conveniently situated to explore Exmoor and Lorna Doone country. Sailing, fishing, horseback riding, and golf nearby. Breakfast included. Lunch and dinner served daily. No children under 5. No dogs. Closed Jan. Hugo F. Jeune, Proprietor. (See Index for rates.)

Directions: A39 is the main road traversing North Devon, occasionally providing wonderful glimpses of the Bristol Channel and Wales. Outside of Porlock, take the Toll Road, which rejoins A39 and continues on to Lynmouth and Lynton. Hotel is on the harbor.

SIMONSBATH HOUSE HOTEL
Simonsbath (near Minehead), Somerset

Mist hung in the air as I drove through a beech forest in Exmoor National Park. It was the sort of afternoon on which Lorna Doone's legendary family might be riding across the heather-clad moor just beyond. Around each bend in the road, I half expected to see something or someone mysterious. Exmoor does that to you, sets your imagination to work.

Another turn and I saw it—Simonsbath House—a long white building on a little hill above the road. Below stretched a green valley with the River Barle flowing through.

A blaze crackled in the library fireplace. Several groups of people drank tea and chatted amiably. Owner Mike Burns greeted me, saying, "Take off your coat and have a pot of tea."

Mike and Sue Burns purchased Simonsbath in December of 1985. Their intention: "To create a comfortable family-run hotel, retaining the attractive features of the 17th century manor house." Until 1815, this was the only dwelling in the forest area. Mike, a former surveyor who commuted into London, is relieved to be away from the traffic. "Exmoor is fantastic. We don't ever want to leave it."

Many guest rooms and baths have been redone in the last four years. All are now in top condition, with interesting color-coordinations of drapes, spreads, walls, and carpets, extending from the bedrooms into the large baths. The softly-lighted dining room is especially nice, with gilt-framed paintings on its pale green walls that match the carpet. The wainscoting, ceiling, and trim are painted white, and the round tables are covered with burgandy cloths topped by squares of white linen and candles, which are lit in the evening.

Sue does the cooking. "Her food isn't really French or English," Mike said. "The recipes come from her mind."

I experienced this for dinner when I had a wonderful pear and mushroom soup, dark brown and served piping hot. "I discovered this recipe several months ago," she told me, "when a friend gave us a box of pears and the lawn was covered with mushrooms." Exmoor really does set the imagination to work.

SIMONSBATH HOUSE HOTEL, Simonsbath (near Minehead), Somerset TA24 7SH. Tel.: (064-383)259. A 7-guestroom (private baths) hotel in Exmoor National Park with fine areas for walking and seeing wildlife and thatched cottages. Nearby horseback riding, fishing, and shooting. No pets. Breakfast included. Tea and dinner available. Closed Dec. and Jan. Sue and Mike Burns, Resident Proprietors. (See Index for rates.)

Directions: Situated in the center of Exmoor National Park on the B3223.

WHITECHAPEL MANOR
South Molton, North Devon

On a country lane in northwest Devon is an Elizabethan manor house close to the border of Exmoor National Park. I had heard good things about it and set off to take a look for myself, arriving in a downpour. From the car park, I ran up the steps to the front terrace, circled the ornamental stone pool, and rang the doorbell.

An attractive young lady let me in, and with a welcoming smile suggested I warm myself with tea and biscuits in front of the fire before going upstairs. I was rather startled, since I hadn't made an appointment here. How did she know who I was and that I wanted to tour the rooms? Before I could ask, she left to answer the telephone. Shortly thereafter a waitress arrived with a tray, and a young man poked his head through the doorway. With a Devonshire burr, he said, "Glad you're out of the storm. It's a bit bad out there right now."

Soon, I was thoroughly dry, relaxed, full of hot tea and lemon biscuits, and all by myself in the beautifully panelled drawing room. I wasn't sure what to do next.

As it turned out, it was Patricia Shapland who had let me in the door, thinking I was the American guest due to arrive that afternoon, and her husband, John, who had looked in on me, under the same illusion. We all had a good laugh about that.

The Shaplands, who previously owned a dairy farm in Devon, bought Whitechapel six years ago. Built in 1575, it is a Grade I listed building, which means any architectural changes have to be approved. For this reason several of the older downstairs rooms and stairways have a decided slant, attesting to their age. To straighten everything could destroy some of the fine interior details which make the building so fascinating. There is a long, intricately carved wooden screen, for example, made in 1650, which creates an entry hall by dividing one end of the drawing room, and in the bar, an ancient spanner beam. Upstairs, however, private baths and central heating have been allowed for each of the ten luxuriously decorated guest rooms.

The cuisine at Whitechapel—light, modern French with an English influence—won the Devon Country Restaurant of the Year Award for 1990 from the *Good Food Guide.* Only meat from naturally reared animals is used, and only produce from farms without chemicals. I wished I could have stayed to sample more than the tender, tasty lemon biscuits, but the storm was over, and I had another hotel to visit before nightfall.

WHITECHAPEL MANOR, South Molton, North Devon EX36 3EG. Tel.: (07695)3377. A 10-guestroom (private baths) Elizabethan country manor house hotel in scenic countryside near Exmoor. Shooting parties arranged. Croquet, stabling, horseback riding nearby. No children under 10. No smoking in dining room. Breakfast included. Lunch, afternoon tea, and dinner available. Open all year. John and Patricia Shapland, Proprietors. (See Index for rates.)

Directions: Exit 27 (Tiverton) from M5 motorway. Take the two lane road, following signs to Barnstaple (do not turn left to Tiverton). About 20 minutes after leaving the motorway, while on A361, you pass a services sign for Woodside Garage on the left. Almost immediately a Q8 garage on right. Take next right turn for ¾ mi. to Whitechapel.

THE ROYAL OAK INN
Winsford, Exmoor National Park

Every once in a while I get the longing to stay in a room under the eaves of a thatched-roof cottage, tucked away from the world. There's something comforting and cozy about it. It is even nicer when the building is old and beautiful, and I can look out the window and see other quaint, old cottages.

Recently I found such a place in the conservation village of Winsford on the edge of Exmoor National Park. It is the Royal Oak Inn, dating from the 12th century—yes, the 12th century. Hard to imagine anything that old. But it still has some of its original walls, hand-hewn beams, and open fireplaces. Facilities have been modernized, but very carefully, the owners always conscious of keeping an atmosphere of medieval England.

Charlie Steven and his wife Shelia have owned this establishment for eighteen years. Formerly, Charlie worked for an import/export company in Hong Kong. "The company was taken over by a conglomerate. I didn't want to get lost in it. When I heard about this place, I decided it was better to get lost in Exmoor than in a company filing cabinet."

A large, muscular man, Charlie plays a fierce game of hockey on the fields of Somerset. When he stands behind the bar of his inn, however, or greets guests in one of the two lounges, he has a smile and a friendly manner that would melt the frost on a mean man's heart.

As for his inn, completely run down when he bought it, everything is now in first-class shape, and the decor is wonderful. I could sit for hours in front of the fireplace in the cozy residents' lounge with the hunting mural on the walls. But the bar with its inglenook fireplace is even better. Or what about the dining room, where fine English-style food is prepared by Chef Martha Jones? (I cut two of her recipes out of a Gourmet magazine not long ago.) It is far better, though, to retreat to my bedroom under the thatched-roof eaves and fall asleep, dreaming I am back in ancient England.

THE ROYAL OAK INN. Winsford, Exmoor National Park, Somerset TA24 7JE. Tel.: (064-385)455. Telex: 46529 Ref: ROAK. A 14-guestroom (private baths) 12th century thatched-roof inn on the edge of Exmoor in a conservation village of thatched cottages. Nearby fishing, riding, and adventure walks. Shooting and hunting parties arranged. Open all year. Breakfast included. Lunch and dinner available. Shelia and Charles Steven, Proprietors. Mathew Shadbolt, Manager. (See Index for rates.)

Directions: Take A396 north from Tiverton. In Exmoor, Winsford is signposted to the left.

THE CASTLE HOTEL
Taunton, Somerset

The Castle has a fascinating history that is cloaked in the mists of time. The earliest written record indicates that there was a castle on the site in A.D. 710. There have been three castles since, the present building having stood for the past 300 years. But I leave you to discover the drama and romance surrounding this historic edifice. Be sure to see the 12th-century garden with its ancient moat wall and castle keep.

Tucked away in the center of a bustling market town, the Castle isn't easy to find. The town crowded in around it, seeming to want to huddle close to its protective walls. My first view as I drove around the corner on a narrow street was of the Green and indeed of a castle, with crenellated battlements and great stone turrets on either end. It formed an oasis of quiet in its busy surroundings. The facade was covered with magnificent wisteria blooms that I later found out were 150 years old. They obviously had to be pruned back around the many stone-mullioned windows.

Poring over the really impressive map that came in the Castle's very useful packet of information in my room, I was struck by the sheer wealth of historic places in the region. The Chapman family has put together an excellent map with careful annotations, which shows the locations of

ancient ruins, castles, cathedrals, wildlife preserves and parks, historic houses, and many other points of interest within easy driving distance.

I met Ian Flemming, the hotel manager, for tea in the Rose Room, which looked like a sitting room in a fine private home. I learned that it had been decorated by Mrs. Chapman. "For a long while, she did much of the interior decor," Ian told me. "However, Mr. and Mrs. Chapman are getting along in years, and although their son, Kit, is greatly interested in what goes on here, he's also involved in other projects. So recently they've given me a larger role in running the hotel."

While I consumed a tasty strawberry tart chosen from a variety of sweets on the tray and sipped the house blend of tea (many kinds were available), we discussed hotel policy.

"We aim to give friendly, unobtrusive, and professional service in that order of importance," Ian said. "The Chapmans still consider this a family business, and the family wishes to keep it that way."

A feeling for æsthetics is evident throughout the hotel. I very much enjoyed my room, with its high casement windows overlooking the town. There were all the amenities of a big-city hotel, with room service (extremely prompt and cheerful), remote-control color TV, towel warmer, huge wraparound bath towel, terry cloth robe, and all the attendant goods and services.

Ian gave me a tour of the guest rooms, and each is done differently, with great taste and very pleasing color schemes. There are canopied beds, brass beds, quilted beds; some rooms have a traditional feeling, while others have a more contemporary look. Some rooms have figured fabric wall coverings that match the draperies and bedspreads; some walls are covered with grass paper; others are painted in soft hues. Every room has comfortable chairs, pleasant lamps, handsome desks, paintings, plants, and fresh flowers. There is a new section of very luxurious suites overlooking the historic gardens.

As to the food at the Castle, lunch is traditionally English, moving in the evening toward a more classical style. To complement your meal, the splendid wine cellar gives you a choice from 550 different wines.

"Our chef is passionate about what he does," said Ian. "No English hotel has won more praise and more laurels more consistently." He went on to tell about some of the illustrious guests who had been entertained there, among them the Queen Mother, Princess Margaret, and the Duchess of Kent—not to mention a queen of another realm, Joan Collins.

For dinner I ordered the steamed fillet of turbot on a bed of green vegetables and wild mushrooms cooked in goose fat with ginger. It certainly was worthy of a top award, as was the hot chocolate soufflé with white chocolate ice cream served in special sauces.

A quote from Shakespeare that appears on one of the hotel's brochures sums up my experience here: "This castle hath a pleasant seat; the air nimbly and sweetly recommends itself unto our gentlest senses."

THE CASTLE HOTEL, Castle Green, Taunton, Somerset TA1 1NF. Tel.: (0823)272671. Telex: 46488. FAX (0823)336066. A 35-guestroom (private baths) luxury castle hotel with historic bow and garden in a busy market town in the Vale of Taunton Deane. Surrounded by points of interest. Continental breakfast included. Full breakfast, lunch, and dinner served daily. Open year-round. The Chapman Family, Proprietors. Ian Flemming, Manager. (See Index for rates.)

Directions: Follow signs to town center and continue toward Wellington and Exeter. Go straight through 2 sets of pedestrian lights and after about 150 yards, turn right immediately after the medieval municipal building signposted to the Castle Hotel. This will bring you to the Castle Green and the hotel on the right.

MEADOW HOUSE
Sea Lane, Kilve, Somerset

Just outside the village of Kilve, in the foothills of the Quantocks, is a narrow lane that leads to the sea. I drove along it between hedgerows, past thatched cottages, and under a group of graceful laburnum trees that hung over the lane like a canopy. In less than a mile I reached Meadow House. Beside it was a picturesque duck pond.

"Beautiful!" I exclaimed out the car window to a man who stood near the house with a lawn mower poised for attack on the grass. I pointed to the pond.

"Wasn't always." He leaned on the mower handle. "I helped excavate that a few years back. Did most of the work, in fact. As I remember, the pond was filled in during the war by the American Army. They drove tanks over it to get to their base."

"Oh. Sorry about that."

He grinned. "Well, tanks aren't boats, you know."

Sam Thorn, who has lived in the village of Kilve since his youth and been the gardener at Meadow House since its inception as a hotel four years ago, doffed his cap and charged forward, mower blades whirling up grass like confetti.

My arrival at the this lovely Georgian house, once the rectory for the church down the way, was unexpected. I knew the new owners, Alex and Tina Sampson, had done a lot of work in the last year. I had dropped in to see the results.

The Sampsons were off to town for supplies, but the housekeeper showed me around. A sunny conservatory has been added as a breakfast room. With garden and meadow views, it is quite an inviting place to start the morning. The other major work was in the old stone stable—turned into three charming suites, each accommodating a third person if necessary, as does the thatched-roof cottage converted by the previous owners. Also, the guest rooms in the main house have been redecorated with a country look—handmade quilts, pastel colors, fresh flowers.

From the study and the dining room, French doors open onto a terrace where drinks can be served in the summer. When the weather turns cool, guests can retreat inside and relax before log fires set in three lounge areas, including a billiards room.

Only minutes away is a fascinating beach with tidal pools and strange-shaped rocks, many containing prehistoric fossils. It was from here, as early as 1650, that rocks were taken to build some of the Meadow House walls.

MEADOW HOUSE, Sea Lane, Kilve, Somerset TA5 1EG. Tel.: (027-874)546. An 8-guestroom, including 4 suites (private baths) country house hotel with 8 acres of garden and meadows, in an area preserved by National Trust. Billiards, croquet, hiking; nearby horseback riding, Exmoor, and fossil beach. Breakfast included; dinner available. No smoking in dining room. No pets in main house. Open all year. Alec and Tina Sampson, Proprietors. (See Index for rates.)

Directions: From the M5 take the A39 toward Bridgwater and Minehead. Kilve is 12 mi. from Bridgwater. In the village, turn right on Sea Lane, just before the pub. Meadow House is ½ mi. on the left.

THORNBURY CASTLE
Thornbury (near Bristol), Avon

It is indeed a happy circumstance that Maurice Taylor and Thornbury Castle have found each other. Mr. Taylor, a distinguished-looking gentleman with a Van Dyke beard, is an art collector who has a fine appreciation for the history and character of this really superb Tudor castle. He is in the process of bringing into clearer focus the neo-Gothic origins of the castle, with his Renaissance tapestries, paintings, chandeliers, and other appointments. He has stonemasons working full time restoring the stonework in some of the towers.

While Mr. Taylor was engaged in an animated conversation with some guests, I read an inscription in a painted panel over the seven-foot-high fireplace in the Hall. It read in part: "This castle was built in the reign of King Henry VIII, A.D. 1514, by Edward Stafford, Duke of Buckingham, Earl of Stafford. . . ."

"Henry VIII might very well have stood right where you're standing now," Mr. Taylor said, returning from his duties as host. "He had appropriated the castle when the Duke was executed for treason. Public records in London show that he spent ten days here with Anne Boleyn in 1535. However, Mary Tudor, who lived here for some years, returned the castle to the Duke's descendants in 1554."

I noticed that the legend over the fireplace went on to declare that the interior of the castle had been restored in the reign of Queen Victoria, which accounted for the heavy Victorian dark wood paneling and other Victorian touches.

The Hall, which I would call the drawing room, has a two-story-high ceiling, colorful heraldic shields, and stained-glass windows, which are really unique. Mr. Taylor explained it to me while we were outside in the Privy Garden, where I could see the towerlike structure. "There are only two sets of windows like these in England, and the other one is in Windsor Castle. There are five banks with 704 curved panes of glass in the upper sections, and the lower windows are in a star-shaped structure."

The furnishings of the castle are luxurious, with deep, comfortable sofas, oriental rugs, fine antiques, beautiful fabrics and draperies, and many huge oil paintings. Mr. Taylor pointed out a portrait of Mary Tudor and a couple of other royal personages.

I liked the warm feeling of the cozy library with all the books, where soft music was playing and there were little nooks for reading.

Mr. Taylor led me up into a tower, going around and around on old stone steps, into the truly regal bedroom once occupied by Henry VIII and Anne Boleyn. The four-poster bed was canopied and curtained in a beautiful rose damask. The room is hexagonal with a carved wood crest in the ceiling and beams radiating out from the center. A settee is in front of the working fireplace, and a curtained and canopied standing wardrobe resembles a medieval tournament tent. This is a spectacular room, with stone mullioned windows and lovely views of surrounding farmlands and the hills of Wales.

Other guest rooms of various sizes in the tower and main section of the house are beautifully furnished. They are all replete with telephones, television, private bathrooms, and other amenities.

I had mentioned the Privy Garden, which was the Duke's private garden. It lies between the castle and the 14th-century Norman church next door. Protected by a high crenellated wall on the front, it's a place for peaceful contemplation, and I could imagine the Duke walking along the paths, enjoying the camellia tree and the ivy and wisteria climbing the castle walls, checking the flowering fruit trees, and perhaps pondering the outcome of his trial for treason. There are actually four enclosed formal gardens, with sculptured hedges, flowers, walks, a vineyard, and little shelters where one can sit and meditate.

I would be remiss not to mention the food. Some of the chef's dishes include calf's sweetbreads with a ginger wine sauce, salmon poached with saffron and sorrel, breast of free-range chicken stuffed with avocado and smoked bacon, and a vegetarian dish of cannelloni with a tomato, aubergine, and basil filling. I understand the wine cellar is extensive and first-rate.

When I asked Mr. Taylor what his aims for the castle were, he replied, "When people come to a castle, they expect a great deal, and I feel they will not be disappointed. It is a very unique place where they will feel at home and comfortable." I think he's being very modest.

THORNBURY CASTLE (Prestige Hotels), Thornbury, Bristol BS12 1HH. Tel.: Thornbury (0454) 418511 or 412647. U.S. reservations: 800-223-5581. A 14-guestroom (private baths) restored Tudor castle, in the Vale of Severn, 5 mi. from the Severn Bridge on the edge of the Cotswolds. Continental breakfast in room or full breakfast in dining room included in tariff. Lunch and dinner served daily. Closed Christmas week and 10 days in Jan. Croquet lawn on grounds. Clay pigeon shooting, fishing on private beat, horseback riding, ballooning, and many natural, cultural, and historic attractions in Bristol, the Cotswolds, Wye Valley, and South Wales nearby. No children under 12. No pets. No smoking in dining rooms. Maurice and Carol Taylor, Proprietors, Peter Strong, Manager.

Directions: From London, take the M4 to Exit 20. Go 3½ mi., turn left onto B4061 to High Street in Thornbury. Keep left at the village pump, going down a gentle hill. At the bottom a large gate beside the parish church leads to the castle.

STON EASTON PARK
Ston Easton, Chewton Mendip, Somerset

A Palladian mansion of great distinction, it contains some of the most exceptional architectural and decorative features to be found in Britain's West Country. The house was completed in 1791, and still retains the core of an earlier Tudor house and its Queen Anne additions within the present structure. For 400 years it was the home of the Hippisley family, and more recently it is the home of Peter and Christine Smedley.

On each of my visits I have been tremendously impressed with the 18th-century decorations and the appointments and furnishings of the guest rooms, all of which overlook the romantic parklands. Several rooms have four-poster beds of the Chippendale and Hepplewhite periods.

The menu is English and French.

STON EASTON PARK (Pride of Britain), Chewton Mendip, near Bath, Somerset BA3 4DF. Tel.: (076 121) Chewton Mendip 631. U.S. reservations: 800-323-3602. A distinguished 20 room (private baths) great house of Britain, now a country house hotel, 11 mi. from Bath and Bristol. Open year-round. Breakfast, lunch, and dinner served daily. Convenient to visit Bath, Wells, Stonehenge, Wilton, Castle Combe, Lacock, and Dyrham Park. One spaniel in residence. Peter and Christine Smedley, Proprietors. (See Index for rates.)

Directions: Ston Easton is on A37 between Bristol and Shepton Mallet, 6 mi. from Wells and 11 mi. from Bath and Bristol.

SOMERSET HOUSE
Bath, Avon

Once again, I was indebted to Bronwen Nixon for introducing me to some really lovely people who are the proprietors of a small hotel in Bath that can only be described as "super."

"Oh, you'll like Jean and Malcolm Seymour very much," Bronwen exclaimed. "They used to be restaurateurs in the Lake District, and now they have Somerset House, a lovely hotel in a quiet residential area of the city."

First, let me tell you about Somerset House. It is a classical Regency house, built in 1829, and because it is a listed building nothing has been allowed to harm its Georgian elegance. The rooms retain their original and comfortable dimensions, and by careful adaptation the Seymours have been able to provide all of the guest rooms with their own bathroom or shower. There are two lounges, a large, quiet garden that features an ancient Judas tree, and a car park within the grounds.

It is about a twelve-minute walk from Bath Abbey, the Pump Room, and Roman Baths.

Bed and breakfast are offered and dinner is on an optional basis, but I would suggest to everyone that they include dinner at the Somerset House during their stay. "If guests only take breakfast with us," Jean declared, "they cannot really appreciate the 'family house' atmosphere, and we don't get to know each other."

When I pressed Jean about the nature of some of the main dishes, she commented that because the standard of produce in the West Country is so superior, their menus have a great many homegrown items such as game, meat, fish, and farmhouse cheese and cream. "Just along the canal bank, we have our own allotment garden where we grow most of the fruits and vegetables served. In our kitchen we make everything that is possible to make. All cakes, pâtés, soups, ice cream, and yogurts are homemade, and almost all of the bread, using stone-ground flour from the mill at Priston."

Besides all of this, I think the special-interest and activity weekends, arranged autumn through spring, provide some fascinating reasons to visit Somerset House. I cannot list them all here, but let me give you a soupçon. There are opera weekends at various times, combining a stay in Bath with visits to the best of British opera outside London. There are Georgian Bath weekends and the opportunity to examine the architecture and see the city through the eyes of famous figures in Bath's past, including Beau Nash, Jane Austen, and John Wood. Visits are arranged to Stourhead Garden nearby and also include an escorted city sightseeing tour. There are other special-interest weekends as well, and I hope that readers will write for an excellent descriptive folder.

To me, Somerset House is a perfect complement to a visit to Bath and I urge everyone to plan ahead on at least a two-night stay, because to see the important points of Roman and Georgian Bath takes at least half a day. Also the cathedral cities of Wells, Salisbury, and Stonehenge, Tetbury and Cirencester, Castle Combe and Bradford-on-Avon are all within an hour's drive away.

I recently returned for a visit to Somerset House on a Saturday afternoon in October. Every Saturday night is special here. Malcolm and Jean were busy preparing another one of their theme dinners for their guests.

"This is the anniversary of the Battle of Hastings in 1066," announced Malcolm. "We're celebrating it with a Norman-style dinner."

Naturally, I had to celebrate along with them.

SOMERSET HOUSE, 35 Bathwick Hill, Bath, Avon BA2 6LD. Tel.: (0225) 66451. A 9-guestroom (private baths) beautiful classic Georgian house at the lower end of Bathwick Hill. Dinner, bed, and breakfast offered throughout the year. Special-interest weekends available. Especially suitable to enjoy all of the many attractions in the city of Bath and the surrounding countryside. Not suitable for children under 12. No smoking permitted. Jean and Malcolm Seymour, Proprietors. (See Index for rates.)

Directions: Once having arrived in Bath, locate Bathwick Hill on the southeast side of the city and drive about a quarter of the way to the top. Somerset House is at the corner of Bathwick Hill and Cleveland Walk and is readily identified by its garden, which is most unusual for a Georgian house.

EAGLE HOUSE
Church Street, Bathford, Avon

"Welcome. Would you like coffee?" asked my host, John Napier, as I entered Eagle House at ten o'clock one morning, having made an appointment to see the establishment.

"Certainly."

"Straight away. Make yourself at home." He gestured to the drawing room and hurried off to the kitchen.

His warm, hospitable greeting put me immediately at ease. I sat down on a comfortable couch in an impressive, octagonal room with a ceiling I judged to be about seventeen feet tall. Intricate moldings extended around the windows; a carved marble fireplace graced one side of the room.

John soon appeared with the tray. His wife Rosamund joined us, and we began to talk about the house.

"It's a listed Georgian," Rosamund said, "designed by John Wood the Elder, a famous Bath architect, and it was built on this hill to take advantage of the scenery."

I agreed that views from Eagle House were spectacular, not only of the countryside but of the quaint conservation village of Bathford. When I commented on this being a fine drawing room, John said, "You should have seen it when we came. Formerly, it was a home for young offenders, and a tide line of desolation rose up on the walls, as far as the boys could reach. I understand they would sharpen broom handles and hurl them into the ceiling where they would stick until a tall enough ladder was brought from afar."

Gazing at the immaculate cream and white walls, it was difficult to imagine how it must have looked before.

John gave me a tour of the eight bedrooms in the main house, each charmingly furnished and with a private bath, then took me outside to see the new addition being built in the walled garden area. I hadn't expected it to be quite so grand. There is a large central room, octagonal in shape (an echo of one in the main house), with a fireplace. Two bedrooms, baths en suite, open up on opposite sides. Excellent accommodations for two couples vacationing together. Completion date is April 1990.

EAGLE HOUSE, Church Street, Bathford, Avon BAJ 7RS. Tel.: Bath (0225)859946. An 8-guestroom (private baths) bed and breakfast 3 mi. from Bath in an area of outstanding beauty. Nearby National Trust houses,

Roman baths, golf, tennis, horseback riding, and boating. Closed mid-Dec. to early Jan. Prefer two nights stay on Sat. Continental breakfast included. Full breakfast available. John and Rosamund Napier, Resident Proprietors. (See Index for rates.)

Directions: Leave A4 ¼ mi. east of Batheaston on A363 to Bradford-on-Avon. After 150 yds., fork left up Bathford Hill. Turn first right into Church Street. Eagle House (not Eagle Lodge) is on right behind high stone wall and wrought iron gate.

CRUDWELL COURT HOTEL
Crudwell (near Malmesbury), Wiltshire

Several months before I left the States for England, I received a letter from Susan Howe, co-owner with husband, Brian, of Crudwell Court, a former vicarage of larger than usual proportions that a few years ago was turned into a country house hotel. It was a long letter—three pages, written with obvious enthusiasm, detailing the history of the building. Here are excerpts:

In case we forget to tell you when you come, the name Crudwell comes from St. Creoda's Well . . . Apparently, there are several records of pagans with particular eye diseases coming to perform pagan well worship rites in the churchyard. So please send any pagans with eye problems our way. . . .

When I finally did arrive at Crudwell Court and saw the lovely garden setting with a lily pond and fountain and the exquisite interior decoration of the hotel—special picture-pattern chintzes from Sandersons in London, basketwork chairs in the dining room, lifesized, hand-carved rabbits perched on the hallway buffets, as a few examples—I felt it would be a pity if anyone who came here had eye trouble. There is so much to see, so much that is beautiful.

Susan Howe is a lively, vivacious woman who extends a warm welcome to her guests. She loves to talk to people, find out their needs and interests, and help them enjoy their stay. Brian, who has always worked in the hotel and catering industry, and who formerly catered for Westminster Abbey, is in charge of the kitchen. The cuisine, traditional English dishes combined with those of a more European influence, has already attracted the attention of connoisseurs from all over England.

It is exciting to find a new, privately-owned hotel in the country that is not only a delight to see but also a delight to experience.

CRUDWELL COURT HOTEL, Crudwell (near Malmesbury), Wiltshire SN16 9EP. Tel.: Crudwell (06667)7194 or 7195. Fax: (06667)7853. A 15-guestroom (private baths) country house hotel in a 17th-century rectory with fine gardens and views. Close to Bath, stone villages, National Trust Properties, and the market town of Malmesbury. Breakfast included. Lunch and dinner available. Open all year. Susan and Brian Howe, Proprietors. (See Index for rates.)

Directions: Take exit 17 off the M4. Follow A429 past Malmesbury towards Cirencester. Crudwell village is 3 mi. after Malmesbury. At pub (Plough) on left, look for hotel to right across a small green. Train from London's Paddington Station takes 70 minutes to Kemble, 3 mi. from Crudwell.

It's not that the distances are very long in the British Isles, it's the many diversions along the way that sometimes make it impossible to estimate traveling and arrival times. Last order times for dinner are included in the Index so that you can see what time you must arrive in order not to find the kitchen door locked. If you are going to arrive later, call ahead—there isn't a hotel/inn listed here that will not make some provision to feed you if they know you can't make it before the kitchen closes.

In Britain, acceptance of a hotel booking by telephone or in writing is generally regarded as a legally binding contract. If it's necessary to cancel, advise the hotel immediately. If they are unable to re-let the room, the hotel may be entitled to claim compensation—usually two thirds of the agreed price—and any deposit would be included as part of this payment.

THE COTSWOLDS AND THE HEART OF ENGLAND
Counties of Gloucestershire, Hereford, Worcester, and Warwickshire

Sometimes known as the West Midlands, this area extends almost the full length of the Welsh border and spreads eastward to include the counties at the very heart of England.

Here is the land of Shakespeare, the Cotswolds, and the Shropshire Lakeland.

In Gloucestershire, which embraces the largest portion of the Cotswolds, are restful landscapes and gentle hills, clear rivers, shallow trout streams, and houses built of butter-colored limestone. It includes Cheltenham, Cirencester, Stroud, Chipping Campden, and Stow-on-the-Wold.

Herefordshire lies against the Welsh borders and has lush green meadows, apple orchards, hop fields, manor houses, castles, and an excellent collection of Elizabethan timber-framed buildings. This is excellent walking country.

The peaceful towns of Shropshire were once outposts on the grim frontier with Wales. Now ponies and grouse share the lonely heather-cloaked heights, and walkers carry A. E. Housman in their kit bags.

Stratford-upon-Avon, in Warwickshire, Shakespeare's birthplace, attracts thousands of visitors every year.

THE COTSWOLDS AND THE HEART OF ENGLAND

THE HUNDRED HOUSE HOTEL
Norton (near Shifnal), Shropshire

In the tiny village of Norton is a listed Georgian hostelry lovingly restored and furnished to a high standard by the Phillips family. Its name, Hundred House, is taken from the medieval division of England's shires into areas called hundreds, each with its own administrative court, which survived until the 1840s. This inn falls into the old Brimstree Hundred, and the 14th-century courthouse is part of the property.

The inn itself has a large Jacobean fireplace with cast-iron pots and utensils forged by local craftsmen. The atmosphere is of another time. Arrangements of dried herbs and flowers hang from the ceiling. Pumpkins and gourds decorate corners—all from Sylvia Phillips' elaborate garden, open to residents of the hotel. Her sweet-smelling potpourris are in every guest room, along with patchwork quilts, antique furniture, and, extending down from an oak beam in the bedrooms, a swing—yes, a real swing with a padded seat. "A bit of relaxation before retiring," commented son David, who helps run the inn. "An executive toy, so to speak."

Henry Phillips showed me the large new kitchen, which contained all manner of modern culinary conveniences. "We offer an à la carte menu at the inn," he said. "Everything from a simple ploughman's lunch to an elegant escalope of veal with marsala sauce garnished with wild rice."

I discovered Sylvia floating about the garden in a brilliantly flowered dress that looked like a recreation of the real blooms. "Henry and I have been in the inn business since 1976," she said, leaning down to inspect a row of thyme plants. "We had our own brewery business, which we plan to start again with David in charge."

She straightened up and smiled. "The history of this area fascinates us. That's why we're here. We wanted to preserve a part of it. It's taken exactly a year to fix the old inn up."

I looked across the street at the ancient wooden stocks that once held prisoners and at the 14th-century half-timbered and thatched-roof court-house, which now held the brewery equipment, soon to go into operation. Sylvia bent down to gather seeds from her French parsley plants to sow in next year's garden. This family-run establishment, I felt, was here to stay.

THE HUNDRED HOUSE HOTEL, Norton (near Shifnal), Shropshire TF11 9EE. Tel.: Norton (095-271)353. Fax: (095-271)353. A 9-guest-room (private baths) historical country inn. Close to golf and sports centers and many historical sites, such as Ironbridge Gorge Museums, Severn Valley attractions, and National Trust Properties, as well as beautiful country and villages. Breakfast included. Lunch and dinner available. Pets by arrangement. Open all year. Phillips Family, Proprietors. (See Index for rates.)

Directions: On the A442 between Bridgnorth and Telford.

THE OLD VICARAGE HOTEL
Worfield, Bridgnorth, Shropshire

Shropshire is largely undiscovered by tourists. They come for a night, see a few sights, and rush away. A shame, for there is great enjoyment to be had here, exploring the varied countryside—hills, dales, rocks, moors, pastures, and villages. Part of the land is wild and rugged; part is gentle, aptly described by the famous poet A.E. Houseman as "The country of easy living, the quietest under the sun."

Not only nature is varied here, but also the architecture of the past. Some of the finest half-timbered buildings in England are located in this shire. Also, there are ancient structures of sandstone, limestone, and especially brick.

An excellent example of a brick home from the Victorian period is The Old Vicarage in the conservation village of Worfield. Once the private home of Peter and Christine Iles, it became their hotel in 1981. It is secluded, comfortable, and well-appointed, decorated with Victorian-period pieces and paintings.

When I recently returned to the hotel, I discovered Peter working on a project in the garage and Christine by the front door, greeting newly arrived guests.

"We completed the reconstruction of the coach house," Peter told me as he closed up the garage and led me towards the new rooms. They looked perfectly integrated into the style of the main building. On the ground floor, there is a garden suite, twin-bedded and equipped for disabled guests. Also, non-smoking rooms are available for those who wish them. Such consideration is typical of the Iles's approach to running the hotel.

After a delicious dinner including tender breast of duckling, seasoned and glazed with honey and served with tarragon sauce, I had my coffee in the Edwardian-style conservatory where guests gathered around a crackling fire to listen to Peter discuss the birth of the industrial revolution in nearby Ironbridge. "Actually, the Severn Gorge was the scene of the remarkable breakthrough that led Britain to become the first industrial nation and workshop of the world," he declared. "Here the iron master Abraham Darby first smelted iron using coke as fuel. This paved the way for the first iron rails, iron bridges, iron boats, iron aqueducts, and iron-framed buildings. The museum itself has actually been created around a unique series of industrial monuments and spreads out over six square miles of the Gorge.

There is much to see and absorb in Shropshire. Stay for a few days at least.

THE OLD VICARAGE HOTEL, Worfield, Bridgnorth, Shropshire WV15 5JZ. Tel.: Worfield (07464)497 or 498. Telex: 35438 Telcom G. Fax:

(07464)552. A 15-guestroom (private baths) Victorian brick hotel in a secluded countryside location. Close to cultural, historical, and recreational attractions of the Severn Gorge, the Clee Hills, Shrewsbury, Ludlow, and Hereford. Convenient for a visit to Wales. Breakfast included. Dinner available. Children under 8 and pets discretionary. Open all year. Peter and Christine Iles, Proprietors. (See Index for rates.)

Directions: First locate Bridgnorth, west of Birmingham. Avoid going to Birmingham and Wolverhampton, and take the other roads to Bridgnorth. The hamlet of Worfield is north on A454, which runs between Bridgnorth and Wolverhampton; turn north at the Wheel Pub. Take the first left fork and go to top of hill.

CALCOT MANOR
(Near Tetbury), Gloucestershire

I turned off the hedgerow lane into a curved driveway, stone buildings rising around me: not the flat gray stone of London, smoothly finished and of equal size, but warm yellow stones that caught sunlight and shadows and made friendly patterned walls—ancient Cotswold stones, carefully built up and fitted under steeply-pitched roofs. It is these beautiful old buildings that keep pulling me back to this part of England.

At the end of the driveway stood a handsome structure with an inviting entry, firewood stacked to one side, and a cream-colored labrador in front, wagging its tail with an air of expectation. A tall, distinguished gentleman came forward to greet me. "Welcome to Calcot Manor."

It was Brian Ball, who, with his wife, Barbara, and their son, Richard, have for the last five years owned and managed one of the finest country house hotels in England. Originally a farm, most of the stone buildings date back to the 15th century, although there is a unique 14th century barn, among the oldest in Britain, and the area itself was once part of Kingswood Abbey, founded by the Cistercians in 1158.

"The whole family has worked on the place," Brian told me later as we sat in the drawing room in front of a fire. "It took us ten months to get Calcot into operation. Luckily, our daughter's husband was a builder. A new kitchen was built first with guest rooms above. Then, we converted the old stable into guest rooms."

Additions were constructed carefully so as to appear part of the original. Not only was this achieved by the design, but by using old stones found on the property from previous buildings. "Newly-cut stone doesn't have the same mellow color," Brian said.

Most of the interior decoration was done by Barbara, who coordinated bathroom colors with bedrooms in a delightful manner, with special touches such as fabric-covered sewing baskets and tissue boxes to match drapes and bedspreads. She also has a flair for flower arranging; her creations appear all over the house.

That night I ate a superb meal in their restaurant, one of the few outside London to receive a Michelin star. My main course was a delicate fish fillet of John Dory, on baby leeks and black grapes cooked in hazelnut oil and placed on a sauce flavored with smoked bacon—an unbelievably delicious combination.

CALCOT MANOR, (near Tetbury), Gloucestershire GL8 8YJ. Tel.: (0666-89)391. Fax (0666-89)394. A 13-guestroom (private baths) Cotswold stone country house hotel among rolling hills and hedgerows. Heated swimming pool, croquet; nearby fishing, golf, horseback riding, footpaths for walking. No children under 12. No pets. Closed 1st week in Jan. Breakfast included. Lunch and dinner available. The Ball Family, Proprietors. (See Index for rates.)

Directions: From M4 take Exit 28 onto A46 north toward Cheltenham. Take right toward Tetbury on A4135. Calcot on left.

BACKROADING IN THE COTSWOLDS

Some of the best English roads are not on the map, and don't even have numbers. These can be the most exciting, with surprises like pheasants in the fields, foxes—a blur of fur streaking across the road in front of the car—and flocks of birds swooping down to settle in the trees.

It's May in the Cotswolds, and on a sunny day the great rolling fields are separated by hedgerows and trees, and the greenness of the fields is blended with the blue-green of the sky. Ah, the skyline . . . sometimes a row of trees, sometimes a solitary tree . . . or the chimneys and roofs of an old Cotswold farmhouse.

Now, a family playing badminton without a net . . . a weekend mason mending his stone wall. . . . Here and there frequent picnickers.

At the crossroads there's always a pub, a B&B, and stopped automobiles with people bending over maps and peering at signposts. . . .

THE SWAN HOTEL
Bibury, Gloucestershire

Colin Morgan, a rather large man with a genial disposition to match, is the perfect picture of a debonair Cotswold innkeeper. He possesses a very

keen wit and is a man who laughs quite easily. I became acquainted with him under rather unusual circumstances.

I had driven to Bibury from Malmsbury on a Saturday morning and upon arrival in the village, I was immediately enchanted by the arched bridge over the Coln River. The Swan's handsome inn sign directed me to its vine-covered buildings and to innkeeper Morgan.

Introductions over, Colin explained that he was on his way to the market at Cheltenham, about three-quarters of an hour away, and suggested that I might enjoy the trip, which would give us a good opportunity to talk. So, off we went.

After about an hour or so of the attractions of Cheltenham on a pleasant Saturday morning, we returned to the Swan and Colin showed me through the hotel. Then we strolled in the garden across the road, talking about the joys of innkeeping in general.

"I think I'm a very fortunate person," he said. "I have an extremely comfortable inn in one of the beauty spots of Britain and the staff is friendly and courteous. It's like entertaining in my own home."

At this point, we were joined by Bob, a lovable English sheepdog, whose size made him a perfect companion for his master. "In addition to all that," he continued, patting Bob on his woolly head, "here I am situated on the bank of this lovely river in the center of one of Britain's prettiest villages. We are just a few miles of very pleasant driving from Cirencester, Chedworth, Cheltenham, and all of the picturesque villages of the Cotswolds."

Our stroll took us to one end of the gardens to a trout pool fed by a spring. We walked up to the very edge. "These are our own trout," he said. "The guests like to look at them because the water is so clear. Later, they appear on our menu either poached or grilled and served with a special cucumber sauce. I do hope that you'll come next time for our Sunday lunch, when we always have a large sirloin of beef that I carve at the table. It's the time when many residents from the surrounding area join us."

The public rooms and lodging facilities at the Swan are done in quiet good taste, and I could see that Colin has an appreciation for the prints of Hogarth and Thomas Rowlandson. The Swan is a beautifully mellowed old stone building set against a low hill with swaying trees. Most of the guest rooms look over the river and gardens to the adjacent wildlife refuge.

Yes, I quite agree with Colin Morgan. He is, indeed, a very fortunate man.

THE SWAN HOTEL, Bibury, Gloucestershire GL7 5NW. Tel.: (028 574) 204 or 277. A 24-guestroom Cotswold inn, 8 mi. from Cirencester. Breakfast, lunch, tea, and dinner served every day in the year. All of the many scenic and cultural attractions of the Cotswolds are within a short distance. Fishing on the grounds; golf and other sports available nearby. One sheep dog in residence. Colin Morgan, Innkeeper. (See Index for rates.)

Directions: From London take the M4 motorway to Exit 15 (Swindon). Follow A419 to Cirencester, then A433 to Bibury.

THE FOSSEBRIDGE INN
Fossebridge (near Cheltenham), Gloucestershire

"We're a cross between a country inn and a country inn hotel," said Hugh Roberts, the bearded proprietor. He adjusted his green bow tie—not the clip-on type. I found out he always wears bow ties because when he leans over a table in the restaurant, he doesn't want his tie "to dangle in the soup."

Fossebridge Inn is strategically situated on the banks of the River Coln at a place where the Fosseway, a long straight road built by the Romans, crosses the river. In the first century A.D., the Romans established a watering hole here, midway between Stow-on-the-Wold and Cirencester. In Tudor times, a coaching inn, the Bridge Bar, was built on the site; its yorkstone floors, limestone walls, large, arched inglenook fireplaces, and heavy, oak beams still remain. Then, in Regency times, a building was attached, which today houses the restaurant and the hotel.

One of the primary reasons for staying at the Fossebridge Inn, besides the comfortable rooms with their pleasant decor, is the choice a guest has of going from one atmosphere to another. In the pub section, a guest can have a light meal or a pint of ale and get the feeling of the lively local style of life. In the restaurant, where there is not only a traditional English dinner menu but also "a selection of plainly cooked dishes," a guest can find peace and quiet and gaze out five period windows that overlook lovely Fossebridge lake and lawned gardens where a gaggle of geese add to the picturesque scene.

Hugh Roberts has managed inns and pubs for thirteen years, while his wife, Suzanne, was born into the business. They bought this inn three years ago and set about refurbishing the rooms to a high standard. "Our aim," said Hugh, "is to ease weary backs and heads and give good food to sustain body and soul."

THE FOSSEBRIDGE INN, Fossebridge, (near Cheltenham), Gloucestershire GL54 3JS. Tel.: Fossebridge (028572)721. A 12-guestroom (private baths) historical country inn on the Roman Fosseway. Lake and garden; nearby Roman ruins, Manor Houses, Cotswold villages, museums, and wildlife and botany parks. Open all year. Breakfast included. Lunch and dinner available. Hugh and Suzanne Roberts, Proprietors. (See Index for rates.)

Directions: situated on A429 (Fosseway) between Cirencester and Northleach.

THE GREENWAY
Shurdington, Cheltenham, Gloucestershire

While I was sitting in the attractively furnished drawing room at the Greenway, looking out of the impressive floor-to-ceiling windows over a portion of the garden with its beautiful sculptured hedges, I happened upon an article in the British magazine Country Life dealing with the origins and perhaps some of the meanings of this manor house. The Greenway takes its name from the historic 4,000-year-old walkway running alongside the hotel up onto the Cotswolds. This walkway, the "Green Way," was the original drovers' road through the lowlands.

The house was built in 1584 as a private manor house by the Lawrence family. In the mid-17th century, William Lawrence created special gardens with statuary and decorative structures, all designed as a memorial to his recently deceased beloved wife and only son.

Today, the Greenway is expertly guided by Tony Elliott, who is among a growing number of hoteliers in Great Britain who are preserving the integrity and usefulness of former country manor houses by converting them into country house hotels.

Before relaxing in the drawing room, I had strolled around the extensive gardens in which, on this Easter weekend, some beautiful fruit trees were already in blossom and daffodils and other English spring flowers were in bloom. The extensive lawns and gardens are separated by a brick wall and some handsome hedges. On the front, the lawn stretches right out to the road, and many, many birds make their homes in literally dozens of beautiful old trees. There is a splendid old English oak that may date back to the early 1700s.

My bedroom was on the third floor with a marvelous view through the mullioned windows of the lily pond and the gardens. Each of the guest rooms is individually decorated and furnished with fine antiques, and also with the amenities that today's travelers have come to expect, including a bathroom en suite, direct dial telephone, and color television.

The coach house and stable block date from 1816 and, long before Tony's enthusiastic remodeling, had fallen into what he describes as "a totally derelict state." "We spent months and months restoring them, using all of the original beams, bricks, and so forth, and have created eight very, very large double bedrooms. They have a spectacular view over the walled garden and the hills."

Other innovations at the Greenway include a ride in an 8-seater 1934 Phantom II Rolls Royce and a two-hour trip around the Cotswolds in an open horse-drawn carriage, which, as Tony explains, "is a particularly delightful thing to do in the early part of the evening. The traffic on the roads has thinned out considerably."

The Greenway is a lovely place to stay for a holiday in the Cotswolds.

THE GREENWAY (Pride of Britain), Shurdington, Cheltenham, Gloucestershire GL51 5UG. Tel.: (0242) 862352. U.S. reservations: 800-543-4135. An 18-guestroom (private baths) former manor house in the Cotswolds. Lunch and dinner served daily. Restaurant closed for lunch Sat. and bank holidays; Sun. evenings available to residents only. Closed Dec. 28 to Jan. 11. Conveniently situated to enjoy the cultural, recreational, and historical attractions near Blenheim Palace, Stratford-upon-Avon, Broadway, Oxford, and the dozens of unspoiled Cotswolds villages. Golf and horseback riding nearby. Children over 7. Jackets required of gentlemen in public rooms after 7 p.m. No pets. Tony Elliott, Proprietor. (See Index for rates.)

Directions: From Heathrow take the M4 to Exit 15 (Swindon) and the A419 to Cirencester. Here, ignore the sign to Cheltenham and continue on A419 to Gloucester. At roundabout just beyond Bridlip, turn left at Air Balloon Pub down hill to A46. Turn right to Cheltenham. The Greenway is at Shurdington, 2½ mi. from roundabout on right-hand side.

For room rates and last time for dinner orders, see Index.

THE OLD NEW INN
Bourton-on-the-Water, Gloucestershire

Sixty years ago, Bo and Winifred Morris, while on their honeymoon, rode a tandem bicycle to Bourton-on-the-Water. They never left. Instead, they leased an old coaching inn and started a business. Winifred is still on duty, but the inn is now managed by her son, Peter, born here, and his wife, Maureen. Recently, their son began to work here, too. Three generations now run the inn with warmth, joviality, and consideration, alongside a dedicated staff. Polly Parrot number four dwells in a cage next to the inglenook fireplace. As part of its vast repertoire, the bird calls out, "Have a nice day," and, "I know my Redeemer liveth," to the delight of guests.

The story goes that years ago parrot number one accidentally flew into a kettle of soup and, although the horrified cook frantically bathed it in butter, never quite recovered. Parrot number two, which used to cry, "Come along, it's six o'clock" managed to fly completely away. Parrot number three "didn't like it here and stripped itself naked—we had to give it away." Parrot number four has been at the inn for eighteen years and is obviously quite happy to be there.

To give you an idea of the continuity of the place, the weekend before I arrived, by coincidence, two couples who didn't know each other returned to celebrate their silver wedding anniversaries. Besides meeting the same owner, the same clerk checked them in, the same waitress waited on them in the restaurant, and the same chambermaid serviced their rooms. "Just as it was twenty-five years ago," chirped the desk clerk, "except we're all older now."

The Old New Inn is a Queen Anne Hostel built in 1709 by Silas Wells of the same kind of yellow Cotswold stone that constructed the rest of beautiful Bourton-on-the-Water. The village lines both sides of the River Windrush, where flocks of ducks swim in the water, and stone bridges arch gracefully over it.

Inn guests can sample pints in three intimate bars while they play darts or spin yarns with the locals or peruse the memorabilia scattered about or the fine set of hunting prints on the restaurant walls. Residents have two private lounges, a TV room, and a garden across the way. Upstairs halls are narrow and most guest rooms small (quite a few with shared baths), but all is clean and cozy, and service is excellent.

THE OLD NEW INN, Bourton-on-the-Water, Gloucestershire GL54 2AF. Tel.: (0451)20467. A 24-guestroom (9 private baths) traditional coaching inn located in a beautiful village in the heart of the Cotswolds. Behind is a stone model of the village built ⅑ scale, constructed by Bo Morris and local craftsmen. Walking, cycling, touring nearby Cotswolds and historical houses and castles. Open all year. Breakfast included. Lunch and dinner available. Peter and Maureen Morris, Proprietors. (See Index for rates.)

Directions: Just off the A40 London-Wales Rd. on A429 between Cirencester and Stratford-upon-Avon.

OLD FARMHOUSE HOTEL
Lower Swell, Stow-on-the-Wold, Gloucestershire

In the center of Lower Swell (from Lady's Well), a peaceful village of honey-colored stone houses in which certain walls go back to Roman times, is a restored 16th-century farmhouse that until twenty years ago was a working farm. Since then, it has been an inn, today owned by a young Dutchman, Eric Burger, who previously owned two successful restaurants. "Six years ago," he said, "I came to England from Holland to learn English."

We were drinking coffee in the bar with its rough-hewn walls and friendly atmosphere. It was late morning, and the maids were bustling about with vacuum cleaners and dust cloths, getting ready for the arrival of the next set of guests.

"I married an English girl," he continued, "then decided I cared for the country, too."

The Burgers live across the courtyard from the hotel in a stone building adjacent to the reconverted stable, where there are six beautiful new guest rooms and a spacious residents' sitting room with a fireplace. Three main house guest rooms are on the ground floor near the car park for easy access. The remainder are upstairs in the main house. All are uniquely decorated, reflecting their 16th century farmhouse origins.

Behind the hotel is a stone-walled garden with numerous rose bushes and a wide lawn. Of particular interest is an old apple tree, grafted to bear both cooking and eating apples, and a fine herb garden that supplies the kitchen. "Our Table d'Hotel menu is fairly traditional," said Eric. "We also have an à la carte menu, which tends to be more on the adventurous side."

Old Farmhouse Hotel is a place to unwind, a base from which to tour the Cotswold villages and nearby manor house and museums. "We're informal here. No pretentions," said Eric, who manages the hotel with an all-female staff that does not include his wife—a baby has recently arrived, and "she has no time left over."

OLD FARMHOUSE HOTEL, Lower Swell, Stow-on-the-Wold, Gloucestershire GL54 1LF. Tel.: Cotswold (0451)30232. A 13-guestroom (private baths) 16th century hotel in a former farmhouse in an old

Cotswold village. Walled garden; nearby golf, squash, racing, hunts, Roman ruins, Cotswold villages, trout farm, and local brewery. Breakfast included. Dinner available daily; Sun. lunch. Pet restrictions. Open all year. Eric Burger, Proprietor. (See Index for rates.)

Directions: Take A429 (originally the Fosseway Roman Rd.), north toward Stratford-on-Avon. At Stow-on-the-Wold, turn left onto B4068 toward Cheltenham. One mile further is Lower Swell.

COLLIN HOUSE HOTEL
Broadway, Worcestershire

It was early afternoon on an autumn day when I returned for a stay at Collin House Hotel, a 300-year-old restored farmhouse in the Cotswolds. Near the entry I met a little red hen that stopped pecking at the ground and gave me a hard stare.

John and Judith Mills, proprietors of the hotel, shook their heads vigorously when I asked if the chicken was theirs.

"Heavens no!" exclaimed Judith. "That silly thing visits us every day from the neighboring farm."

John's face crinkled up in amusement, reminding me of one of those happy English faces on a Toby mug. I knew it meant a story was on its way.

"Quite mad, really," he said, rolling his eyes upward. "The bird thinks it owns the place. Runs home every night to be locked up with the rest of the flock. Next day it's back again. Hates our chef. Pecks him every chance it gets. One afternoon a dignified matron, who was dining at an outside table, marched into the bar with the hen under one arm. 'Please dispose of this creature,' she said. 'It is interferring with my lunch.'"

This is typical of the relaxed, jovial atmosphere that pervades Collin House Hotel. On cold days, fires are lit in the inglenook of the bar and in the fireplace of the lounge. Lunch and dinner specials are posted on blackboards in the manner of a pub. John, always the genial host, is adept at telling amusing tales and genuinely enjoys meeting people and giving suggestions on wines to accompany dinner or places to visit in the countryside.

Judith prefers to remain in the background, planning menus, obtaining the freshest produce, meat and fish, and making certain the kitchen runs smoothly. "I hope to achieve meals that are reasonably well balanced," she said. "Main courses not loaded with cream. I deliberately keep a fairly large selection of what I call 'light meals.'"

John has his serious side, too. I found this out shortly after I first met him, when I asked about a painting on an upstairs wall. Throughout the

house, even in the unique and comfortable guest rooms, numerous paintings have been hung, all selected from the family's extensive private collection. John loves to discuss them.

From the little red hen to the art collection, there is always something new, something unexpected at Collin House.

COLLIN HOUSE HOTEL, Broadway, Worcestershire WR12 7PB. Tel.: (0386)858354. A 7-guestroom (private baths) farmhouse-cum-inn in the heart of the Cotswolds. Breakfast, lunch, and dinner served except for Christmas and Boxing Day. Open all year. Swimming pool. Conveniently located to enjoy all of the scenic, literary, and recreational attractions of the Cotswolds. Many palaces, castles, and glorious countryside drives and walks nearby. Mr. and Mrs. John Mills, Proprietors. (See Index for rates.)

Directions: On A44, 1 mi. from Broadway toward Evesham. Turn right at signpost for Willersey. Entrance 300 yds. on right.

EASTNOR HOUSE HOTEL
Stratford-upon-Avon, Warwickshire

This is a small bed-and-breakfast hotel, modest and simple, but very clean and quite comfortable. The Everitts are most friendly and Graham Everitt is an obliging chap who is eager to help his guests find their way around Stratford. He directed me to the post office and showed me how to get to the Royal Shakespeare Theatre. He also gave me excellent directions on how to avoid the heavily traveled auto bridge and instead walk on a much more pleasant footbridge over the River Avon.

Dating from 1896, this fine Victorian town house, originally built by a draper, has been restored to provide excellent accommodations, with oak panelling, a central open staircase, a pleasant parlor, and large bedrooms—everything aimed toward giving guests a relaxing stay. And there is room to park your car on the property.

After a substantial English breakfast in the cheerful slate blue and cream dining room with red chairs, I felt fortified to tour Stratford, glad to be only a few minutes' walk away from the river, the theatres, and the center of town.

EASTNOR HOUSE HOTEL, 33 Shipston Road, Stratford-upon-Avon, Warwickshire CV37 7LN. Tel.: Stratford (0789)68115. A 9-guestroom (private baths) bed and breakfast hotel a stone's throw from the River Avon. English breakfast included. Open all year except 2 weeks in Jan. The Royal Shakespeare Theatre within walking distance. Margaret & Graham Everitt, Resident Proprietors.

Directions: From Oxford on the A34, continue to the intersection of Clopton Bridge. Eastnor House is on the left across from the Shell gas station on the south side of the river.

STRATFORD HOUSE
Sheep Street, Stratford-upon-Avon, Warwickshire

Just around the corner from the Royal Shakespeare Theatre, a little hotel nestles in a listed building from the George III period. Entrance is through a side archway into a narrow flower-filled courtyard with Virginia creeper vines partially covering brick walls.

It was a cool, dreary day in late fall as I hurried inside to check into the hotel. I peered into the homey lounge where a fire was lit. Sylvia Adcock, the perceptive hotel owner, immediately asked if I would like a pot of tea and a plate of biscuits.

"Just what I need," I replied and eased down into one of the pastel print chairs. Attractive paintings and china plates decorated pale pink walls, and through the large bay windows I could see people hurrying along the sidewalks of Sheep Street, where buildings were all of an ancient time. Somehow, the day had grown warmer and brighter.

Most of the guest rooms at Stratford House are fairly small, except for the large family suite, but all are well-appointed. Although there is no car park at the hotel itself, arrangements have been made for parking a few minutes away, where, for a nominal fee, cars can be kept. The staff is most helpful, assisting with theatre tickets or planning your day.

In the rear of the hotel is a beautiful conservatory-housed restaurant called Shepherd's Garden, which looks out onto an attractive courtyard. Groups of potted plants scattered around the restaurant make it seem like part of the garden beyond. In the summertime, additional chairs and tables are set up for outdoor eating. The menu is interesting and imaginative, the food good—one of the best restaurants in town.

Tucked away in the heart of this busy tourist mecca, Stratford House is indeed an oasis for the weary traveler.

STRATFORD HOUSE, Sheep Street, Stratford-upon-Avon, Warwickshire CV37 6EF. Tel.: Stratford-upon Avon (07891)68288. Telex: 311612. A 10-guestroom (private baths) private hotel 100 yds. from The Royal Shakespeare Theatre. Nearby golf, horse racing, Cotswold villages, cathedrals, historic houses, and castles. Breakfast included. Lunch and dinner available. No pets. Open all year. Sylvia Adcock, Proprietor. (See Index for rates.)

Directions: On the A422 road from Banbury, cross the Clopton Bridge into central Stratford and continue 2 more blocks. At that roundabout, turn left onto High St. and left again onto Sheep St.

WHITE LION HOTEL
High Street, Bidford-on-Avon, Warwickshire

According to legend, Shakespeare once came to the village of Bidford-on-Avon, close to Stratford, revelled with friends at a local inn, then slept under a crab-apple tree.

With a twinkle in her eyes, the young lady behind the front desk of the White Lion said, "Our rooms promise a much more comfortable night than that."

Situated on the banks of the Avon river with majestic views of the old eight-arched bridge and the Cotswold hills, the White Lion presents the opportunity of being very close to the Stratford scene, yet offers the peace of a quiet village. You might even bring along a fishing rod, since those rights belong to the hotel where it borders the river. Bidford itself is quaint, with shops worthy of exploration.

Ten luxurious bedrooms are available at the hotel, including a suite suitable for a family. The restaurant, with exposed beams and half-timbered walls, gives diners a feeling of Elizabethan times. Expertly cooked fresh local produce, meat, and fish are offered on either a set menu or à la carte basis. Should you wish an early dinner because of a theatre performance, this can easily be arranged, or you can have an afternoon snack in the Coffee Shop. Incidentally, there's a large car park in Stratford within walking distance of the theatres in case you drive there.

WHITE LION HOTEL, High Street, Bidford-on-Avon, Warwickshire B50 4BQ. Tel.: (0789)773-309. A 10-guestroom (private baths) country inn hotel on the Avon River about 15 minutes' drive from Stratford. Other Cotswold villages nearby, plus Vale of Evesham, and castles of Kenilworth and Warwick. Breakfast included. Lunch, snacks, and dinner available. Open all year. ???, Proprietor. (See Index for rates.)

Directions: On the A439 to Stratford-upon-Avon.

GRAFTON MANOR
Bromsgrove, Worcestershire

Little did I realize when I turned off the M5 to follow the byways and lanes to Bromsgrove that this manor house had such an extensive and exciting history.

Grafton Manor has been closely associated with many of the leading events in English history—Jack Cade's Rebellion, the War of the Roses, the Battle of Bosworth, the Gunpowder Plot, the expulsion of the Stuarts, and the establishment of William of Orange.

Nestled in a hollow off the Bromsgrove–Droitwich Road, Grafton Manor was one of a parcel of estates in the heart of England doled out to members of his family by no less than William the Conqueror. A short, illuminating history of the house points out that the Grafton estate then extended to about 400 acres, every one of which "sheltered resentful tenants and Saxon serfs."

During the second half of the 17th century, there ensued a scandal and an encounter on the field of honor that would make popular American TV evening soap operas seem pallid indeed.

There's much more to all of this, but for further and absolutely entrancing details, I commend you to June and John Morris, or to their children, Stephen, Nicola, and Simon. The family has lived at Grafton Manor since 1945. Ten years ago, they all pitched in to transform it into a small, stylish, country house hotel. Set in twenty-six acres of Worcestershire countryside, the manor offers a peaceful experience in the heart of England.

This architecturally splendid house has been painstakingly restored and furnished in a traditional and elegant style. The guest rooms are complete with such modern comforts as private bathrooms, color television, clock radios, and telephones. Some have their own open fires.

Beautiful scenery abounds, including six acres of well-tended gardens and a tranquil water garden bordering the lake. The large, formal herb garden has been laid out in a decorative chessboard pattern with over one hundred herbs, which are in regular use in the restaurant kitchen.

At the moment, I can't think of any other country house hotel in England where five members of the family run the establishment. June and John continue to direct the planning, while Stephen handles most of the administrative work and greets the guests. Nicola and Simon have replaced their father, the former chef extraordinaire. They have been carefully trained by him in the culinary arts and take a personal interest in the herbs and vegetables grown in the garden. Following in their father's footsteps, they use many of the original dishes and lighter sauces he developed, such as the gravlax salmon, served in a mild mustard sauce, and marinated leg of lamb, cooked on charcoal and served with lemon butter. A whiskey steamed pudding is always on the menu.

The family represents a true spirit of British hospitality, in preserving not only the history of this truly impressive manor house but also its many beautiful architectural features, yet unobtrusively introducing modern facilities for comfort and adding their own warm personalities to the atmosphere, they offer their guests some of the best of England, both past and present.

GRAFTON MANOR, Grafton Lane, Bromsgrove, Worcestershire B61 7HA. Tel.: Bromsgrove (0527)579-007. Telex: 254461. Fax: (0527)575-221. A 9-guestroom (private baths) country house hotel in the Cotswolds. Fishing and croquet on grounds; nearby stone villages and many other recreational, historical, and cultural activities, including the Royal Shakespeare Theatre in Stratford. Open year round. Breakfast included. Lunch and dinner served daily. No children under 5. The Morris Family, Proprietors. Stephen Morris, Manager. (See Index for rates.)

Directions: Going north on M5, take exit #5, and turn left at the roundabout towards Stoke Heath. Left again at Grafton Lane.

Rates for a room for two people for one night with breakfast, except where noted, are included in the Index of this book. They are not to be considered firm quotations, but should be used as guidelines only.

DERBYSHIRE

My interest in Derbyshire centered around the Peak District, comprising all of the North Derbyshire uplands. The Peak District National Park makes grand walking-and-touring country, easily explored from centers such as Buxton, Bakewell, Melbourne, and Ashbourne.

The region is characterized by many small villages with limestone houses and tiny greens. It is also the home of one of the great houses in England: Chatsworth, the home of the Dukes of Devonshire, which stands in the wide valley of the Derwent River. I think the best way really to enjoy the Peak District is to settle at one of the places I have suggested in the following text. The distances are not very far and the rewards are many. You might find it interesting to stay in one place for two nights or more and take lunch or dinner at the others.

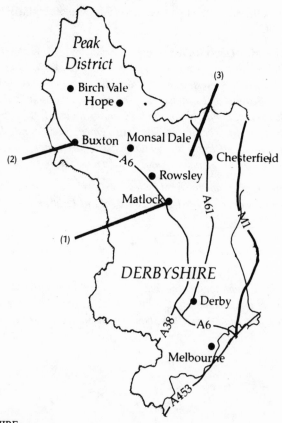

DERBYSHIRE

RIBER HALL
Matlock, Derbyshire

Riber Hall, on the borders of the Peak District, has many things to recommend it. Not necessarily in order of importance are the really auspicious views of the valleys and high, flat moors ending in dramatic cliffs, called "edges." There is also the house itself, dating to Elizabethan times, and so ancient that in 1668 seven generations of the same family had inhabited it. The latest addition (before 1970) was in 1661.

Certainly near the top of the list of its virtues is the wonderful walled garden, dominated by a great copper beech tree. In this garden I was allowing myself to be carried away with the entire Riber Hall atmosphere—being carried away was very easy with the wonderful English blue sky and fleecy clouds, the flittings of white-feathered birds, the green lawns, and beautiful flowers. The phlox and other spring blooms had made the garden their very own, and I can well imagine that some most romantic scenes have been played here ever since the 1400s.

The entrance area is through what was once a dovecote, and the little passages where the doves would fly in and alight are still visible. Beyond the reception area, dominated by flowers, the way leads down some well-worn stone steps into a cozy lounge area, where there was a nice fire burning on the second day of June. I could see out over the valley through a little courtyard. It is obvious that this is a favorite gathering place for Riber Hall guests in the late afternoon and evening.

The dining room is especially interesting, with decor that reflects different periods in the history of Riber Hall and is enhanced by fine period furniture and fireplaces.

There is one guest room in the Hall itself, and the staircase leading to it is lined with some diverting photographs and prints, along with several examples of stitchery.

Most of the guest rooms have been created in one of the stone outbuildings, just a few paces from the main hall. The building is of heavy wall construction and the low ceilings have exposed timbers. There are four-poster beds in most of the guest rooms, and the furnishings would make an antique collector green with envy. Several of the private bathrooms have whirlpool baths.

I arrived just after lunch had been served, but I studied the evening menu with care and noted that among other offerings were medallion of lamb with a port and orange sauce, fillet of turbot served in a light citrus sauce, as well as pork fillets served in a lemon-butter sauce.

Over and above the view, the integrity of the old house, and the enticement of the menu, I think I remember Riber Hall most of all for that truly impressive walled garden. It has a wonderful tranquility and the opportunity for introspection so dear to the hearts of Britishers everywhere.

RIBER HALL (Pride of Britain), Matlock, Derbyshire DE4 5JU. Tel.: (0629) 2795. U.S. reservations: 800-323-7308. An 11-guestroom (private baths) Elizabethan country house hotel on a high hill in the Peak District. Breakfast, lunch, afternoon tea, and dinner. Open all year. All-weather tennis court on grounds. Adjacent to Riber Castle. Conveniently located to enjoy all of the recreational, cultural, and scenic attractions in the Peak District. Alex Biggin, Proprietor. (See Index for rates.)

Directions: Leave the M1 at Exit 28 and continue to A38 toward Matlock for 3 mi. Turn off on A615, signposted Matlock, for 7 mi., at the end of which you come to a very long hill into the village of Tansley. Continue to bottom of hill and about 20 yds. on your left there is a UK filling station. The road to Riber runs on the near side of the filling station on your left-hand side. Continue on 1 mi. to the top of the hill.

THORN HEYES
Buxton, Derbyshire

If, by some chance, you have not heard of the Peak District, much less visited it, I can assure you that in the process of traveling throughout the U.K. I have met many Britons who have yet to visit it.

I have explained the virtues of Derbyshire elsewhere, but a visit should be made to the spa town of Buxton, which was discovered by the Romans. It nestles in a natural bowl surrounded by high moors at a thousand feet above sea level.

The town has many interesting buildings, including the famous Crescent; the Old Hall, where Mary Queen of Scots stayed; and the restored Opera House, the focal point, with the Pavilion Gardens, for the annual festival, held during July and August each year.

Built in 1860 of local stone, Thorn Heyes was a gentleman's residence, and its architecture is quite in harmony with the Victorian elegance of the town.

It is a very quiet, rather conservative accommodation, where the traveler would be more likely to meet Britons than visitors from other countries. There are several other so-called private hotels in Buxton of the same size and demeanor, but I found the rather low-keyed atmosphere maintained by David and Pat Green quite appealing.

They offer bed, breakfast, and the evening meal on request. The dining room looks out over the very pleasant garden, as do many of the bedrooms.

The dishes at the evening meal feature home-cooked soups, pâtés, meat pies, lamb, and desserts. A vegetarian meal is also available. As Pat Green explains, "We try to be friendly, clean, and give good value at the table."

THORN HEYES, 137 London Rd., Buxton, Derbyshire SK17 9NW. Tel.: (0298) 3539. A conservative 7-guestroom (private baths) private hotel on the outskirts of Buxton. Twin and double beds available. Open every day. Breakfast is included in the room rate. An optional evening meal is also served. Quite conveniently located to enjoy all of the many recreational, cultural, and scenic attractions of the Peak District. Three cats, one dog, and a fishbowl are in residence. Pat and David Green, Resident Proprietors. (See Index for rates.)

Directions: Locate Buxton on your map; note that it is about 45 min. from the M1, M6, and Ringway Airport (Manchester). Thorn Heyes is on A515 coming from Ashbourne.

CAVENDISH HOTEL
Baslow, Derbyshire

The British have a wonderful expression: "Good value for the money." I think that describes the many virtues of the Cavendish Hotel.

In the heart of the Peak District National Park, it is set in the Chatsworth Estate, owned by the Duke and Duchess of Devonshire. The Cavendish Hotel is actually within a very short walk of Chatsworth, one

of England's most beautiful and best-loved "great houses" and one of the many reasons to visit the Peak District.

A very imposing, two-story stone building with extensive lawns, gardens, and terraces, the Cavendish is situated so that all of the public rooms, dining rooms, and bedrooms overlook the valley of the Derwent River.

The furnishings, some of which enjoyed an earlier career at Chatsworth House, are entirely in keeping with the subdued yet casual atmosphere, and great taste and care are evident throughout the hotel. There are open fires, oak beams, fresh flowers, lovely views, and a friendly staff.

It is my understanding that originally there was an inn, called the Peacock, here for so long it is uncertain when it was built. The Peacock was the property of the Duke of Rutland and served the turnpike between Chesterfield and the spa town of Buxton. It became the Duke of Devonshire's property about 1830, and in the early 1970s was rebuilt as the Cavendish, with decor and furnishings selected by the Duchess herself.

The hotel has all of the amenities the British are very fond of, including breakfast any time in the morning; lunch served either formally in the Paxton Room or in the bar or gardens or even as a picnic; dinner is served very late (until 10 p.m.).

The menu for both lunch and dinner is lavish, much larger than I can cover here. For lunch I enjoyed the roast partridge with grape and Burgundy sauce.

Golfers will enjoy the putting greens and golf driving net, and fishermen will find the waters well stocked.

The Cavendish is a most unique experience—"Good value for the money."

CAVENDISH HOTEL, Baslow, Bakewell, Derbyshire DE4 1SP. Tel.: (024-688) 2311. A 23-guestroom (private baths) country house hotel in the heart of the Peak District. Open every day of the year. Breakfast, lunch, dinner, and tea served. A few moments from Chatsworth, one of England's most beautiful stately homes, with private art collections, state apartments, gardens, cascades, and fountains (open Mar. 27 to Oct. 30). Cavendish is ideally situated to enjoy all of the recreational, cultural, and scenic attractions of the Peak District. The Duke and Duchess of Devonshire, Owners; Eric Marsh, Manager (and tenant). (See Index for rates.)

Directions: From M1, use Exit 29 near Chesterfield; 2½ hrs. from London.

It's not that the distances are very long in the British Isles, it's the many diversions along the way that sometimes make it impossible to estimate traveling and arrival times. Last order times for dinner are included in the Index so that you can see what time you must arrive in order not to find the kitchen door locked. If you are going to arrive later, call ahead—there isn't a hotel/inn listed here that will not make some provision to feed you if they know you can't make it before the kitchen closes.

LANCASHIRE
County of Lancashire

Lancashire is one of the most diversified areas in England. Along the coast are invigorating holiday resorts, such as Blackpool and Morecambe. It is a region of vast and beautiful estuaries, old-world villages, and wide recreational areas.

A great deal of my interest was centered in the fell country to the northeast of Preston, near the town of Clitheroe.

LANCASHIRE

HARROP FOLD COUNTRY FARMHOUSE HOTEL
Bolton-by-Bowland, Clitheroe, Lancashire

Let me share a portion of a letter I recently received from Victoria Wood, who, with her husband, Peter, and their two sons, is the proprietor of Harrop Fold.

"Harrop looks really lovely now—everything is at its best. The hawthorne blossoms are magnificent, weighing the branches down on the trees. Swallows and swifts are darting to and fro catching flies for their young. The hedgerows and fields are full of wild flowers, their growth has been encouraged by the wet spring, and now the warmth. Farming-wise we are waiting for the grass to thicken in leaf, and in about another ten days Daniel will be ready to reap. Before then he will start to clip the sheep—all 200 of them! We have had a good lambing time in spite of the weather, due largely to Daniel's expert shepherding—what a difference it has made to Peter to have him at home.

"The garden is looking super too—Andrew's patient care is paying dividends. His attentions have extended to keeping the common well under control (at great expense, I may add). Harrop has become home for a second-hand Montfield tractor that makes light work of grass cutting.

"However, Andrew has become our full-time chef, and his creativity in the kitchen has been warmly praised. He bakes all of our bread, quite a mammoth task, and it is so good. He has finally settled on a granary recipe and is swapping bread-rising stories with all the whole-food enthusiasts."

The farmhouse accommodations are rustic-elegant. They all have private bathrooms, very comfortable, firm mattresses, and such fetching names as Meadow Sweet, Forget-me-not, and Buttercup.

The old farmhouse lounge is comfortable and easy to relax in with the original oak beams and meat hooks and a mellow pine cupboard with brasses and interesting pieces. A log fire burns merrily in the evenings in the stone fireplace.

If all this sounds rather intriguing, may I suggest you write to Victoria Wood for a brochure about the farm.

HARROP FOLD COUNTRY FARMHOUSE HOTEL, Bolton-by-Bowland, Clitheroe, Lancashire BB7 4PJ. Tel.: (02007) 600. A 7-guestroom (all have private baths) guest house in the lovely farming country of Lancashire. Open all year. Breakfast and afternoon tea included in tariff. Evening meal available on request. Conveniently located to enjoy excursions into the Lancashire and Yorkshire Dales. Private trout and salmon fishing on the Hodder and Ribble rivers. Peter and Victoria Wood, Proprietors. (See Index for rates.)

Directions: Clitheroe, which is reached by taking Exit 31 from the M6 and continuing on A59, is the key to locating Harrop Fold. When you get to Clitheroe, telephone the farm for directions into the rural countryside.

PARROCK HEAD FARM
Slaidburn, Clitheroe, Lancashire

The coffee was hot and the cream was thick. Richard and Vicky Umbers, the proprietors of this guest house, and I were enjoying the marvelous euphoria that follows a satisfying dinner. It was quite natural for the conversation to turn to regional British cooking. Richard was unstinting in his praise of their kitchen, "We make the best roast beef and Yorkshire pudding I've ever had, and I'll put our Lancashire hot pot up against anybody's! Here on the farm we serve lots of local roast lamb with mint sauce, and also cheese and onion pie."

They were full of enthusiasm over what fun it is to keep a small country hotel and how they meet people from all over the world. "We try to keep our farm as natural as possible," explained Vicky, passing me another helping of a tasty tart. "Almost everything we have on the table is raised right here on the property. I love to cook and this makes it all the more fun. We keep our kitchen door open to the guests and many of them come out to visit with us while we're mashing the potatoes or basting the lamb."

Parrock Head Farm offers dinner as well as bed and breakfast. The guest lounge has a whole wall of books, a table with many maps and suggestions about all the things to be enjoyed in this part of Lancashire and nearby Yorkshire.

There are several combinations of suites and guest rooms, all with private baths.

Even as we talked, the sun went down behind the fells and the wonderful countryside was bathed in a golden light.

During the recent Christmas season I was delighted to receive a beautiful full-color "Lancashire Life" calendar. Among the photographs of the Lancashire Fells area there was one of a farm in the Trough of Bowland, not far from Parrock Head.

PARROCK HEAD FARM, Slaidburn (near Clitheroe), Lancashire BB7 3AH. Tel.: (02006) Slaidburn 614. A 9-guestroom (private baths) small country hotel, 8 mi. from Clitheroe and about 1 mi. from Slaidburn, in the Bowland Fells area. Double and twin beds available. Breakfast, lunch, and dinner served to houseguests. Open all year except Dec. and Jan. Conveniently situated for walking and driving trips in the Lancashire countryside. Golf and fishing nearby. Located just 30 mi. from the coastline, 35 mi. from the Lake District, and 35 mi. from the Yorkshire Dales. Richard and Vicky Umbers, Proprietors.

Directions: Leave motorway M6 at Junction 31. Follow A59 to Clitheroe, 15 mi. Turn left at Clitheroe roundabout to B6478. Continue to Waddington, Newton, and Slaidburn. Turn left at Slaidburn and after 1 mi., Parrock Head Farm is on the left-hand side and plainly marked.

A LANCASHIRE IDYLL

Some people take their dogs for a walk; I take my tape recorder. Such was the case in late May when I arose early and went for a walk in the Lancashire countryside. Here are a few of my impressions as I dictated them into my recorder:

"Beautiful stone walls on each side of the road leading past ancient farmhouses . . . Rippling waters of the brook mingling with the sound of early morning crows and the animals at the watering troughs . . . Milk already out on the platform waiting for the pickup . . . Trees getting well armed for their full leaf . . . The sheep ever placid, ever grazing, to be seen in all directions, and always turning to watch me as I pass by. I think they can hear me talking to the tape recorder. Here's a public footpath . . . continuing down into the meadow and over the rise into the forest . . . More black-faced sheep with lambs still at the nursing stage, and as the mothers move away from me their young charges plainly show their annoyance.

In front of me a rabbit disappears into the underbrush . . . down in the meadow, white birds dot the lush green grass . . . Now, near the crest of a hill, a bench with a small medallion that says simply: "Elizabeth, 1953." This is the simple country way of recognizing the Queen's coronation . . . A wooden bench has been placed on a concrete slab and is ideal for sitting and looking over the fells and the peaceful countryside, down into the village of Slaidburn.

. . . Now along the side of the road, a huge oak whose center section has been torn away by the elements—its two side branches still remain—looking for all the world like some gigantic figure with its arms raised imploringly to heaven . . .

Here, a herd of cows moving toward the barn . . . overhead, two birds shrilly signal to each other . . . in the middle distance, a sheepdog running through the fields . . .

Reluctantly turning back to the village . . . my presence is being announced by feathery watchers calling back and forth . . . different calls and different greetings to the morning . . .

Two or three errant sheep on the road, finding grass on the outside of the fence sweeter than on the inside . . . there are always a few who seem to find their way out of the enclosures. Across the valley, a man walking in the field, approaching a herd of sheep . . . he seems to be searching for something. I know not what.

Most of all, it is a refreshingly complete natural quietness, with the pastoral accompaniment of the sounds of nature wafting up from the valley—the occasional baa-ing of the sheep and the moo of the cattle. These are the sounds that inspired the poets of the English countryside . . .

Returning to town on the quiet road . . . the small garden area over-looking the Ribble River . . . a wonderful view of its three arches. On one of the benches, a small plaque, saying "Presented by the Ribble Valley Borough Counsel to Slaidburn, the Best Decorated Village in the Queen's Silver Jubilee Year, 1977."

THE INN AT WHITEWELL
Forest of Bowland, Clitheroe, Lancashire

"Typically English"—how blithely we Americans use that term, and yet as I went back over my notes on the visit to the Inn at Whitewell those two words kept coming to the front of my mind. It is a real country-cum-village hotel in a section of England that really has not yet been discovered by the North American traveler. I think this inn is difficult to find, and if it were not for the good offices of the innkeepers at Parrock Head Farm in nearby Slaidburn, I never would have discovered it at all.

As soon as I saw the Inn at Whitewell one beautiful Saturday morning, I knew it would be a special place. It was indeed a rather bustling hotel, as evidenced by the numbers of English couples who were making use of the reception room and lounge on a weekend holiday. Meanwhile, more guests were coming in for that great English tradition, morning coffee, which has become almost as important as afternoon tea.

I was given a very courteous tour of all of the guest rooms, many of which look out over the Hodder river. The view is of the valley with the fells on each side. The large dining room has a big bow window that also overlooks the river. I was amused to see some interesting and colorful prints by Thomas Rowlandson.

The evening meal has four courses, including duckling, lamb, pork, and halibut as the main dishes.

Mention should be made of the parish church of Saint Michael, immediately adjacent, with a history dating back many centuries. Walking through the graveyard and into the church itself reminded me that my good friend, Rev. Robert Whitman in Lenox, Massachusetts, a fellow Anglophile, would indeed find it interesting and worthwhile. At the back of the church there was a reproduction of the list of disbursements made for the repair of the chapel in the year 1666, which came to 37 pounds 2 pence. I dropped a donation in the milk churn, which had been placed at the gate of the church; the coins bounced around on the bottom with a hollow, tinny sound. A recent note from Richard Bowman reports that he has added a gallery, which features contemporary artworks and some early sporting prints.

Visit Whitewell and stay overnight at the inn, or at least enjoy a bar lunch or dinner. I promise you'll never forget it.

THE INN AT WHITEWELL, Forest of Bowland, Clitheroe, Lancashire BB7 3AT. Tel.: (02008) Dunsop Bridge 222. A 10-guestroom (6 have private baths) traditional country inn situated in a most pleasant hamlet in the valley of the Hodder River in rural Lancashire. Breakfast, lunch, dinner, and bar supper served. Open all year. Most conveniently located for pleasant walks or drives into the Lancashire and nearby Yorkshire countryside. Richard Bowman, Innkeeper. (See Index for rates.)

Directions: The key once again is the town of Clitheroe, which is on A59 between Preston and Skipton. Once in Clitheroe, telephone the inn for further directions.

YORKSHIRE

Yorkshire is England's largest county, comprising two national parks, one hundred miles of coastline, and many attractive fishing villages. The county is centered around the ancient city of York with its four great gates, old streets, and world-famous York Minster, a church that contains over half the medieval stained glass left in England. The castle museum is another principal attraction with recreations of complete Victorian and Edwardian streets and old crafts workshops.

Yorkshire is divided into sections called "Ridings," a Scandinavian term meaning one-third. The North Riding is famous for its national park, its popularity with walkers, and its lavish display of heather. The West Riding contains the Yorkshire Dales National Park and is one of the most peaceful and unspoiled regions in Britain.

West Yorkshire is the land of the Brontë sisters, Charlotte and Emily. Many people make a literary pilgrimage to the village of Haworth, located in typical brooding Brontë country among the rolling moors and dark purple hills. It is situated between Leeds and Blackburn, south of Keighly. The Brontë parsonage has been reproduced to look as it did when the sisters lived there with their father.

YORKSHIRE

OLD SILENT INN
Stanbury (near Haworth), West Yorkshire

There are now two reasons to visit this part of Yorkshire; the first is to experience the Brontë presence and the other is to visit the Old Silent Inn.

The Brontë presence is experienced by visiting the Parsonage in Haworth; once the home of the Brontë family, it is now an intimate museum cared for by the Brontë Society. The rooms of this small Georgian parsonage are furnished as in the Brontës' day, with displays of their personal treasures, pictures, books, and manuscripts. Visitors can see where the writers of *Jane Eyre* and *Wuthering Heights* lived.

Now to the Old Silent Inn, a few miles out in the West Yorkshire countryside, which would be a curiosity no matter where it was located. As the story goes, Bonnie Prince Charlie, in his flight from Scotland, took refuge here, and because everyone kept silent about his presence, the inn was named "Old Silent."

It is jammed from top to bottom with knickknacks and photos and prints of the royal family, including the Queen and Duke of Edinburgh and the Prince and Princess of Wales. Around the inside of one of the dining rooms are display cabinets with wonderful collections of silver, while the walls are covered with handpainted dishes.

The guest rooms are traditional pub-inn rooms, all with private baths, telephone, television, and videotapes.

The menu is extensive, with everything from bar snacks to a full à la carte dinner, including soup, country pâté, individual dishes of home-made steak and kidney pie and chicken pie. There is also the Plowman's Brunch, with two cheeses, potatoes, a hard-boiled egg with pickles, lettuce, and tomatoes. And much, much more.

Children are welcome, and children's portions are available.

OLD SILENT INN, Stanbury (near Haworth), West Yorkshire BD22 8DR. Tel.: (0535) 42503. A 12-guestroom (private baths) country pub-inn in the heart of Brontë country in West Yorkshire. Breakfast included in room rate. Light lunches and evening meals also served. Closed from 3:00 to 6:30 p.m. Make arrangements ahead if checking in between these times. Conveniently located to enjoy all of the recreational, cultural, and scenic attractions of this section of Yorkshire, including a visit to the famous Brontë Parsonage. One dog in residence. Open year-round. Adrian Beevers, owner-host. (See Index for rates.)

Directions: From London take the M1 north and M62 west to Bradford, then M606 to Bradford city center. Follow signs for Keighley. Haworth is signposted from Keighley. Follow main road to Stanbury.

WOODLANDS
The Mains, Giggleswick, North Yorkshire

Afternoon teatime at Woodlands. I was enjoying a splendid solitary moment on the terrace, allowing my eye to play the game of following the course of the seemingly endless stone walls that wind their way down into the valley of the Ribble River and continue on up the green, rugged countryside, now joining other walls and finally disappearing over the top of the fell into some kind of Yorkshire eternity.

A little earlier, coming from the Lake District, I turned off A65 and found my way to the top of the hill for my first glimpse of this Georgian-style country house, serenely master of all it surveys. The view is of wooded slopes and grassy fields dotted with sheep, the Ribble River rushing over pebble and rock, and the Dale itself dotted with stone houses and barns.

The house, built of local stone, was originally designed as a private estate around the turn of the century. The bedrooms and public rooms are well appointed and many helpful amenities, such as television, radio, and electric blankets, are provided by Roger and Margaret Callan, the hosts. Almost every bedroom shares this marvelous view.

There are many different plans available for the traveler, but by all means do arrange to have dinner at Woodlands. You must make your table reservations by noon that same day.

Woodlands is within easy driving distance of the Lake District, James Herriott country, Haworth (home of the Brontë family), and the city of York. The footpaths wind up the famous limestone fells and along the bank of the Ribble. The unspoiled Yorkshire Dales provide ample diversions for a two- or three-night stay.

WOODLANDS, The Mains, Giggleswick, Settle, North Yorkshire BD24 OAX. Tel.: (072 92) Settle 2576. An 8-guestroom (3 private bathrooms) Georgian-style country house in the Yorkshire Dales district. Open all year except Christmas and New Year. Bed and breakfast; dinner also available. Most conveniently located for walking and automobile tours of this section of Yorkshire. Many castles, abbeys, halls, and distinguished houses nearby, as well as the Yorkshire Dales National Park. Margaret and Roger Callan, Proprietors. (See Index for rates.)

Directions: The A65 runs from Skipton northwest to the edge of Cumbria. Woodlands is actually located in the village of Giggleswick, next to the larger town of Settle. Once in Giggleswick, look for the signpost for the Mains. Continue to the top of the rise for Woodlands.

THREE TUNS HOTEL
Thirsk, North Yorkshire

The more I traveled in Yorkshire, the more fascinated I became, and the more I realized just how many different faces Yorkshire presents to the world.

I originally journeyed to the town of Thirsk in hopes of getting a glimpse or even a word with James Herriot, the author of *All Creatures Great and Small* and several other books on his life in Yorkshire. I am a tremendous fan of the TV series, which has been playing on public television in North America for the last few years and have even seen some episodes three times, laughing and even crying at the same episodes more than once.

It was through my good friend Lou Satz that I actually received an introduction to Mr. Herriot and also learned about the Three Tuns. I think that even if James Herriot were not in Thirsk, the town and the small hotel would be worth a visit.

It sits in one corner of this traditional North Yorkshire market town. On market day the village becomes a blend of the past, the present, and the future as everyone gathers from miles around to buy and sell.

The Three Tuns belongs in just such an atmosphere. It was built in 1698 as a dower house for the Bell family of Thirsk. It started its public life in 1740, when it was converted into a coaching house. It has undergone several changes through the many decades, but still retains some of its original features and cozy atmosphere.

I could hear the ticking of the large, old clock from Paterson & Son hanging on one wall. It was obvious that the lobby was also a meeting place for townsfolk, because there were many tables and chairs, suggesting congenial gatherings of coffee or tea drinkers.

Glancing at the menu, I noticed that for the most part the Three Tuns serves traditional English food, including beef and roast duckling and the like. There were a few Continental dishes as well, because this part of Yorkshire also has quite a few visitors from the Continent.

I found the Three Tuns a very warm and generous experience, and Thirsk, a Yorkshire town with a natural, unaffected feeling.

Now a word or two about James Herriot. Ordinarily, he is quite willing to see visitors at his Surgery, and if you arrive between 2:30 and 2:45 on either Wednesdays or Fridays, he's happy to have a word with you and perhaps autograph one of his books. I was fortunate to be there at the appointed time. We did have a very splendid, short talk as he explained, "I cannot guarantee that I am going to be here on those two days and I hope that no one makes a special trip. However, if I am here, I'm delighted to meet anyone. You see, I'm still very much a country veterinarian."

The Surgery is located on the little road off the square next to the Royal British Legion Club and the signs says, "Sinclair & Wight."

THREE TUNS HOTEL, Market Place, Thirsk, North Yorkshire Y07 1LH. Tel.: (0845) No. Thirsk 23124. A 12-guestroom (7 with private baths) traditional town hotel overlooking the square. Serving breakfast, lunch, and dinner 365 days a year. An ideal center for touring the Yorkshire Dales, the North Yorkshire Moors National Park, and the city of York. Pony-trekking, gliding, fishing, golfing nearby. Market days are Mon. and Sat. Within walking distance of Dr. James Herriot's surgery. B. Coates, Manager.(See Index for rates.)

Directions: From south, take M1 and A1 to Dishforth; turn right on A168 to Thirsk. From York, take A19 direct to Thirsk. From north on A1, turn left on A61 at the Ripon/Thirsk intersection. Nearest railway station— Thirsk 1½ mi. Phone hotel to arrange transport.

MALLYAN SPOUT HOTEL
Goathland, Whitby, North Yorkshire

"Cozy" and "bustling" are two good words to describe the Mallyan Spout Hotel, in the heart of the Yorkshire moors. The note of coziness is underscored by the decoration and furnishings of all of the three spacious lounges that have welcome fires most evenings and wide windows overlooking the spectacular moorland.

I arrived at the end of a rather stormy day and was immediately taken in hand by Judy Heslop. She ensconced me in a room at the top of the house with an impressive view of the countryside, and after a welcome tub and a bit of rest, I joined her in the main lounge before dinner.

Again I was struck with the thought that inns and pubs in England

provide an opportunity really to get acquainted with the people of the surrounding area. All around me were the sounds of distinctive Yorkshire accents and faces that seemed to be crinkled up in good humor much of the time. The hotel is an ivy-clad stone building that in some ways typifies British solidarity.

Because this part of Yorkshire is really not on the main tourist route, Judy pointed out that Americans are not readily apt to find their way here. "We love to see them," she said, "because there is so much to do out-of-doors here that appeals to the American 'get-up-and-go' spirit. Besides the moors, there's tennis, golf, horseback riding, and also some good trout and salmon fishing in the River Esk."

For dinner, I ordered grilled Whitby plaice, a local fish garnished with sliced bananas and served with a special sauce. Other dishes included Goathland broth, another local tradition, and moorland trout, of which I had two bites from Judy's plate. Super.

Judy told me that Castle Howard, where "Brideshead Revisited" was filmed, is just a short distance away.

I was up early the next morning for a brisk walk in the freshly washed moors, which today gave promise of being blessed with sunshine. Filled with American "get-up-and-go," I would have enjoyed several days at the Mallyan Spout.

MALLYAN SPOUT HOTEL, Goathland, Whitby, North Yorkshire YO2 2AN. Tel.: (094786) 206. A 24-guestroom (most with private bath-shower) traditional country inn, 35 mi. from York. Open all year. Breakfast, lunch, tea, dinner served to non-residents. Horse riding, golf, walking the York-shire moors, all within a convenient distance. Judith Peter Heslop, Owner/ host. (See Index for rates.)

Directions: From York take A64 to Malton Bypass. At Malton take A169, signposted Pickering/Whitby. After passing Flying-Dales radar station, take first turning to Goathland. It is 3 mi. to hotel.

MORNING ON THE MOORS

I'm always an early riser and sometimes that's the very best time to take walks. On this Sunday morning I found myself wandering through a parish churchyard, considerably in advance of the eight o'clock service. It was located right across the road from the Mallyan Spout Hotel in a small triangular park where several roads all came together. Among the headstones in that churchyard was one marked 1695.

A signpost by the road said thirteen-and-a-half miles to Pickering and four miles to Egton Bridge, where the Roman Road is. Still another sign said nine miles to Whitby-on-the-Sea.

Dominating everything and stretching out into all distances are the low fells of the North York Moors, where the heather will bloom madly at the height of the season.

Carefully making my way among a flock of sheep, I climbed to the top of one of the fells, where I could see the splendid farms tucked into their own fields, now serenely verdant. I could imagine what it would be like here in January and February with the snow swirling, and the winds off the moors rattling the windowpanes and shaking the buildings—a time for sitting-by-the-fire.

These are not the dramatically deserted heaths of Northumbria, nor the gentler hills of Lancashire. Here, the earth is convoluted with twists and folds. Above a certain line, the shrubs are low, and the grazing meager.

The sun climbed higher and shone brightly off the wet surface of the road. I stopped to look at a plaque on a big chestnut tree behind a stone wall that announced "His Majesty's Manor of Goathland commemorates the Silver Jubilee of His Majesty King George V." The tree was planted by Captain Smalass on the sixth day of May in 1935. The fence around the tree kept the sheep from getting inside. I couldn't help but wonder what happened to the good Captain . . . did he see action at Dunkirk, or perhaps in the jungles of Burma? The peaceful years between wars were all too short.

On my way back, I passed in front of the Mallyan Spout Hotel and two young lads lying on a bench at the bus stop. I asked them if they were waiting for the first bus to Whidbey, and they said no, they were resting— they had been up all night at a party.

WHITWELL HALL COUNTRY HOUSE HOTEL
Whitwell on the Hill, York

I'd been told that Whitwell Hall was very impressive, but I never expected anything like this. It was almost as if some genii had rubbed his magic lamp and suddenly created a gracious and expansive country house hosted by a former Naval type and his beautiful wife. It was worthy of a motion picture setting.

Set in its own park at the end of a curving gravel drive, the front entry to the hall is made through a stately porte cochere and into a center hall with a cantilevered staircase and balcony framed by an elegant wrought iron balustrade. It is two-and-a-half stories high with a skylight that creates a gentle even glow. It all reminded me somewhat of Inverlochy Castle in Scotland.

Lieutenant Commander Peter Milner, formerly of the Royal Navy, turned out to be a very entertaining, voluble man with a keen interest in many different areas. He joined the Navy when he was seventeen and went to Dartmouth School, which also provided Prince Philip's naval training.

Both the Lt. Commdr. and Mrs. Milner obviously share a great interest in art, because the hotel is enhanced by many oil paintings, some quite heroic in dimension.

The furniture and decorations in the graceful, spacious drawing room have been chosen with care to blend with the numerous works of art.

"We actually like to feel that this is a real house party," he said, as we strolled through the gardens and grounds. "We have eighteen acres of grounds here, and if I do say so myself, we keep the gardens in fairly good condition. It is not easy, because at one time there were half a dozen gardeners; now we get along with just one. The Americans who come here enjoy our tennis court, indoor swimming pool, and sauna, as well as fishing and bicycling. Croquet is something we feel rather serious about, too."

Whitwell Hall is quite convenient to many of the beautiful natural attractions of Yorkshire, as well as being only twelve miles from the city of York. In fact, the famous tower of the Minister is visible from the terrace. In the adjacent woodland areas there are beeches, sycamores, and yews, and delightful walks overlooking the Vale of York. Close by are the River Derwent and Kirkham Abbey.

All the guest rooms have their own bath or shower, color TV, radio alarm, and direct telephone, and all overlook the gardens and spacious lawns.

For years I've been looking for the perfect place where I can stride into the drawing room in my white flannels and utter that inimitable line, "Tennis anyone?" I believe Whitwell Hall is the place.

WHITWELL HALL COUNTRY HOUSE HOTEL, Whitwell on the Hill, Yorkshire YO6 7JJ. Tel.: (065 381) 551. A 23-guestroom (private bath/ shower) country house hotel, 12 mi. from York. Open every day of the year. Breakfast, lunch, tea, dinner served to non-residents. (Please ring in advance.) Castle Howard ("Brideshead Revisited"), York, North Yorkshire Moors neaby. Tennis, indoor swimming pool, sauna, bicycles, croquet, and garden walks in grounds. Not suitable for children under 12. Two cats and two dogs in residence. Lt. Commdr. and Mrs. P.F.M. Milner, Resident Owners. (See Index for rates.)

Directions: Exit A1 for York. Follow A64 bypass signposted "Scarborough." Leave A64 and turn into village of Whitwell on the Hill. Turn left in village at telephone box.

THE NATIONAL PARKS OF BRITAIN

It was while crossing the North York Moors and the Yorkshire Dales that I became aware of the National Park System, established in the 1950s by what is now the Countryside Commission and administered by local planning authorities who have the double duty of conserving the fine landscape and then ensuring that people can get there to enjoy it.

Fortunately, these parks will preserve some of the remaining forest lands of Britain, which over the past five centuries were all but decimated for the building of ships and for fuel.

In my journeys for this book, I have traveled in Dartmoor Park in Devon, the biggest area of elevated moorland and wilderness remaining in southern England; in Exmoor, with its wild red deer in Somerset; Brecon Beacons in Wales; Snowdonia, an unusually large park in North Wales containing high bleak passes and valleys that were scoured by glaciers; the Lake District, which contains England's highest mountains; and the North York Moors and the Yorkshire Dales.

There are National Park Information Centres throughout Britain. Extensive and valuable literature on each park is available.

CUMBRIA
The County of Cumbria

Cumbria, which includes all of the English Lake District, is one of the most sought-after tourist objectives in the U.K., although some of the roads through the fells and passes are narrow and quite steep. There are switch-back roads and tranquil lakes interspersed with majestic mountains and sweeping views.

Nearly every town or village in Cumbria has a literary association. The great Lake Country poet William Wordsworth was born in Cockermouth, went to school in Hawkshead, lived in Grasmere at Dove Cottage, now the Wordsworth museum, and then moved to Rydal Mount. He is buried in the churchyard in Grasmere. Matthew Arnold lived for a time in Ambleside, and Charlotte Brontë stayed there for a week visiting the Arnold family. Coleridge found a house in Keswick with a magnificent view and was in frequent contact with Wordsworth. Charles Lamb and Robert Southey also visited Coleridge. Coniston contains the Charles Ruskin Museum with a collection of drawings and letters. Nab Farm, on the shores of Rydal Water, provided a setting for a series of rather bizarre relationships involving Thomas DeQuincey (Confessions of an English Opium Eater*) and the Wordsworth family. It's worth investigating.*

I'm indebted to Bronwen Nixon, the proprietress of Rothay Manor, for an unusual overview of all the activities in the English Lake District. There are national parks, museums, forest, market days in various villages (usually Wednesdays and Saturdays), castles, gardens, festivals, sheep dog trials, boating, cycling, pony trekking, twenty-three different golf courses, crafts workshops, and all manner of Wordsworth memorabilia. There is summer theater, a wildlife center, and of course, that great Lake Country diversion, fell walking.

June, October, and November, are excellent months to visit, but please make reservations well in advance.

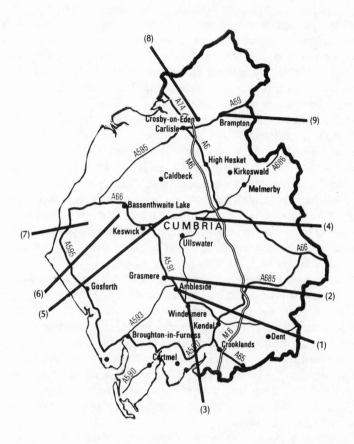

CUMBRIA

ROTHAY MANOR
Ambleside, Cumbria

Many of my most pleasant memories of this handsome country house hotel are centered around the very early morning walks that I took with Bronwen Nixon. We didn't stray too far and because the morning dew was always pretty heavy we stuck to the designated footpaths and country roads. Her dog, Hootie, was our advance guard and every once in a while he would scamper back, bark a little as much as to say, "Why are you lagging, there are so many wonderful things to see!"

On one occasion she shared some of her deep love of the Lake Country. "We move to a different rhythm than the world outside. To enjoy one's self it is sufficient to be here, anything else you may choose to do is a bonus. Walking is of course a natural choice. There is golf at Windermere, which is a very attractive and challenging course. There is a first-class stable nearby if you care to ride horseback. We have fishing here, both river and lake. There is the literary heritage of the lakes to explore as well as our 'industrial past.' You can enjoy a day of pure nostalgia, taking a motor launch down the lake and from the southern tip take a steam train to Haverthwaite and back."

"Looking after" is a wonderful English term that goes a long way in describing just how guests are treated at Rothay. There are separate dimmer switches and good reading lamps, bedside control of all other lamps in the room, bedside telephone, a hair dryer, a handsome wash basin set into a dressing table with plenty of space for cosmetics, shaving kits and the like, a bowl of fruit with a sharp knife for assuaging hunger before bedtime. The bathrooms are, as the British would say, "first rate." And, besides towel warmers, there is a rack folding out from the wall over the bathtub to provide a quick, ready method of drying those small items that may have to be washed.

Decorated in shades of brown with beige accents and with candles on each table, the dining room has a wonderful feeling of relaxed elegance. The menu includes an interesting combination of British and Continental cuisine. In addition to roast mallard, pheasant, venison, lamb and pork, there are gourmet dinners in the winter, each of which has a special theme, including cuisine from various regions of France.

Bronwen passed on over two years ago, but whenever I return to Rothay I go out for the early morning walks and can still hear some of her comments as she pointed out the many features of this gorgeous landscape. Under her sons Stephen and Nigel's direction, Rothay Manor continues.

ROTHAY MANOR, Ambleside, Cumbria LA22 OEH. Tel.: Ambleside (05394) 33605. U.S. reservations: 800-323-5463. An 18-guestroom (pri-

vate baths) country house hotel in the heart of English Lake District, 46 mi. from Carlisle. Open mid-Feb. to early Jan. Lunch, afternoon tea, dinner served to non-residents. Ambleside is in the center of the national park famous for its mountains, lakes, and rivers. The sea is 20 mi. away. Carlisle and Hadrian's Roman Wall, 45 mi. Wordsworth's Dove Cottage and museum, 4 mi. Rydal Mount, 2 mi. The Lake Country abounds in theater, museums, and galleries. Croquet on grounds, mountain and fell walking, pony trekking, sailing, boating, fishing, and golf nearby. The Nixon Family, Proprietors. (See Index for rates.)

Directions: From London leave M6 to Exit 36. Follow A591, 16 mi. Fork left on A593, signposted "Coniston and Langdales"; ½ mi. beyond, there's a black and white Georgian house. Follow Coniston signs again to get to front entrance.

WHITE MOSS HOUSE
Grasmere, Cumbria

"Yes, the house was once owned by Wordsworth, and that lake out there is called Rydal Water. Actually, we're midway between two other Wordsworth houses: Dove Cottage at Grasmere and Rydal Mount. It's possible to walk to either one of those."

Sue and Peter Dixon were telling me about the joys of innkeeping at the White Moss House, deep in the Lakelands District of England.

"Things have changed relatively little as far as the hotel is concerned since your first visit with my mother and father, Jean and Arthur Butterworth," Sue remarked. "We still have five bedrooms and Brockstone, an

old Lakeland cottage. My mother and father furnished and decorated White Moss and, as you see, it has some lovely English touches, with fresh flowers, gay curtains and bedspreads."

"I think the highlight of any day is dinner," Peter declared. "I do all the cooking, and we are essentially English. Each meal is designed as a whole, so that the flavors and textures balance and complement each other. There is also a set menu for the soup, starter, and main course, and for dessert there is always a choice, including a 'proper' old-fashioned hot pudding. Of course we have lots of fine English cheeses."

"Peter's rack of lamb" Sue added, "with gooseberry mint sauce, as well as his crispy roast Lakeland mallard with sage and onion stuffing, are two of our most popular main dishes. The *London Times* described our meals as 'the best English food in the country.' As well as being a warm, hospitable, caring inn, we are also a top restaurant—perhaps the top 'English restaurant' in the country."

Now Arthur and Jean Butterworth have retired, and Susan and Peter are on hand to meet people, and to help out and make suggestions about Lakeland walks and drives. The atmosphere and the house are the same as they were on my first visit in the mid-seventies, with general redecoration and refurnishing.

Fishing permits are available for guests to fish on the river or on Rydal Water, and the Dixons have walked all over the Lake District mountains many times and can offer expert help and advice. Each room has, among other things, copies of eight different walks that begin and end at the house.

Advance bookings at the White Moss are normally taken for a minimum of three nights or, when mutually acceptable, one or two nights may be taken. In such cases, there is a small surcharge per night. I would suggest that an overseas telephone call directly to the White Moss is well worth the effort.

White Moss was one of the first inns that I visited in the Lake District, almost fifteen years ago. I am sure that Jean and Arthur Butterworth, who worked so diligently and sincerely to make it an outstanding experience, are very pleased with what Susan and Peter Dixon have done during the last few years.

WHITE MOSS HOUSE, Rydal Water, Grasmere, Cumbria LA22 9SE. Tel.: (096 65) Grasmere 295. A 6-guestroom country house hotel in the midst of the beautiful English Lake Country, approx. 14 mi. from Kendal. Modified American plan. Resident guests are served full English breakfast, and dinner promptly at 8:00 every night. Dinner served to nonresident guests by reservation only. Within easy driving distance of every point in the Lake District, including museums, historical and literary landmarks, and Wordsworth's cottage. Excellent center for some marvelous fell walks; fishing nearby. Commissions are not paid to travel agents. No children under 10. No pets. Susan and Peter Dixon, Owners. (See Index for rates.)

Directions: From the south: leave the M6 at Exit 36. Follow A591 through Ambleside. The hotel is at the head of Rydal Lake, 2 mi. north of Ambleside on the right side. From the north: leave M6 at Exit 40, follow A66 to Keswick, turn left on small country lane B5322. Turn left at A591 for 7 or 8 mi. Arrive at the Swan Hotel, Grasmere; carry on a mile farther. White Moss House is on the left at the head of Rydal Lake.

MILLER HOWE
Windermere, Cumbria

As far as Miller Howe is concerned, frankly, I don't know whether to talk about the fabulous view of the English Lakes from the bedrooms and the terrace, the highly acclaimed cuisine, or the Master of the House himself, John Tovey.

Let's take a few lines to discuss John Tovey, because it is his ideas and innovations that have gained such an excellent reputation in England and beyond.

He was in the British Colonial Service and then in the theater for ten years before acquiring Miller Howe in 1971. I first visited him two or three years later. As the owner-chef, he has ample opportunity to create original new dishes, many of which he demonstrates on television and has shared in his cookbooks. He visits the United States frequently, and has given English country house dinners and breakfasts in many places.

Since the evening meal (there is no lunch served, although a boxed lunch is available) plays an important role in any guest's stay at Miller Howe, it might be well to share a small inventory of some of his main dishes. These include Windermere Char with horseradish cream, turkey breasts with Cumberland sauce, cold leeks with sour cream, Scottish salmon, and, of course, Lakeland lamb.

John is particularly well known for desserts and sweets, including his apple and orange farmhouse pie, chocolate butterscotch shortbread tart, and homemade pistachio cream ice.

Guests gather for dinner at 8:30 in the bilevel dining room overlooking Lake Windermere. Everyone eats each course at the same time. There are no choices for the main course, but an alternative can be arranged. It is John's belief that since he serves just one meal a day it's got to be super.

All of the guest rooms have undergone what John refers to as "major surgery" and now have, along with the normal things, stereo sets with a selection of tapes, hair dryers, trouser presses, clove/orange sachets in the closets, and other amenities, including handmade shoehorns, umbrellas for all the guests, and binoculars strategically placed in the front bedrooms.

Each arriving guest is presented with a small booklet, especially inscribed with his name, which contains a diamond mine of information to enhance a three-day stay (the minimum according to the tariff sheet). It contains a complete description of each of the meals served and a list of the attractions in the Lake District, including cinema, public gardens, art galleries, libraries, all of the outdoor recreational facilities, guided walks, and a generous dollop of interesting Lake District statistics about mountain heights and lake dimensions.

The setting is superb. As I stood on the terrace watching a solitary, silent sailboat beating its way across the lake, I overheard a conversation between two other guests, wherein one guest said, "I'm going to spend the entire day on the balcony of our room. I'm settling down with a chair and a book and just let the lake, the hills, and the sky envelop me. It's no wonder that Wordsworth felt such a lift from this countryside."

MILLER HOWE, Windermere, Cumbria LA23 1EY. Tel.: (09662) 2536. A 13-guestroom country house hotel in the English Lake Country, 1 mi. from Windermere. Modified American plan. Breakfast, tea, dinner served to non-residents. (Dinner by reservation only.) Open early March to Dec. Located within convenient distance of all of the scenic, cultural, and recreational attractions of the English Lake District. Not particularly suitable for children. John Tovey, Resident Owner. (See Index for rates.)

Directions: From the south use Exit 36 from M6. Follow A591 to Windermere, then take A592 to Bowness.

OVER KIRKSTONE PASS

It had been three years since I had taken the Kirkstone Pass road from Ambleside to Ullswater, and once again I was blessed with a fairly clear day. "Fairly clear," in England means that it's not raining at the moment. Once again I had to pause on the upward climb to allow for sheep on the road. With each twist of the road, I could look back down into the valley at the village of Ambleside and its lakes.

On each side the grassy fells changed to bare rock near the top, and every so often I could see the silhouette of an adventuresome sheep along the skyline.

The public house at the crest of the paths was still there. I headed down the steep grade to the north, shifting into second gear and hugging the stone wall on the left side of the road as closely as I could to accommodate the buses on their way up. Soon, I was on the floor of the valley, which was brilliantly lit by sunlight through the pass. It was late May and there were very few other cars on the road, although there was a bank holiday weekend coming up and I was sure that this section would be much traveled. (It is always best to allow for bank holidays, if possible, when planning a vacation in Britain. All Britons love to go "on holiday" then.)

At numerous small parking areas along the road, a few people had left their cars taking to the nearby footpaths over the fells. They wore heavy boots and knickers, carried raingear, and usually wore wool caps. I noted a few vacancies at the B&Bs, but it was still early in the day and the season was not really under way. Even so, these would be filled before noon, as people from the city arrived in the Lake Country for the holidays.

The road continued on through Patterdale and Glenridding, the latter located on the shores of Lake Ullswater. The road was occasionally overhung by precipitous granite cliffs, reminding me of the lake country in northern Italy. Some mergansers and mallards were making tiny ripples in the otherwise glasslike surface of the lake, which faithfully reflected the mountains on each side. Here and there was a beach with coarse sand.

One of the sights that continually amazed me in this country, as well as in the Lancashire Fells, was seeing the stone walls that march right up one side of the mountains and down the other. They are formidable barriers placed, no doubt, to establish boundaries and to keep sheep under control. They are kept in extremely good repair. I understand that it is the custom here, just as it is in rural New England, for people to walk along each side of the walls together, replacing the stones that have been disrupted by frost and weather.

This time, I turned left on the A5901 to the west and went through and over the mountains, once again past several fields of sheep. It's such a wondrous sight to see the care and affection that exists between the mother lamb and her lambkins. Such complete innocent trusting, care, and love.

SHARROW BAY COUNTRY HOUSE HOTEL
Lake Ullswater (near Pooley Bridge), Cumbria

For forty years paeans of praise have been heaped upon Sharrow Bay by travel writers and food critics alike. The first group extolled the lake and mountain scenery. (The view from the main drawing room overlooking the lake and the mountains won an award as being the best in Great Britain a few years ago.)

Food guide writers are expansive in their description of chef Francis Coulson's true gourmet offerings. They have rhapsodized over the roast loin of English lamb Doria cooked on a bed of cucumbers and shallots and served with a red currant and orange sauce; the roast sirloin of Scotch beef served with Yorkshire pudding and horseradish cream sauce; and the choux pastry with a filling of partridge, duck, chicken, and herbs and served with bacon. When it comes to the sweets, even my masters in this field, the food guide writers, are humbled before the white peaches with grated apple, orange juice and cream; the chocolate brandy cake; and the famous sticky-toffee sponge cake served with cream. I would dearly love to introduce my good friend and *chef extraordinaire,* John Ashby Conway of the Farmhouse Restaurant in Port Townsend, Washington, to both Francis Coulson and Brian Sack, and then just sit back and listen to their conversation.

Sharrow Bay is situated on the northeast edge of Lake Ullswater in the English Lake District. It is owned and operated by two men whose interests seem to have blended beautifully. Francis Coulson does all the cooking and his partner, Brian Sack, handles the myriad details that are connected with the rooms and the "front of the house." The real beneficiaries of this partnership are the Sharrow Bay guests.

The main house sits on twelve acres of garden and woodlands, and there's about a half-mile of lakeshore for all the guests to enjoy. In addition to the twelve rooms in the main house, there are other accommodations available, including a converted farmhouse about one mile up the lake, where long-staying guests may enjoy the peace and solitude.

On my most recent visit, both Brian and Francis reminded me that a few years ago I had skipped the main course at lunch and had decided on three "starters" and a dessert. In fact, Francis remembered that I had had the French peasant vegetable soup and the purée of carrots and oranges, the supreme specialty of the house. "I'm sure," he added, "I also served you some chicken livers in a pastry shell."

Talk to anyone who has ever visited Sharrow Bay, and it seems that they inevitably sigh and say, "Ah, yes."

SHARROW BAY COUNTRY HOUSE HOTEL, Lake Ullswater (near Pooley Bridge), Cumbria CA10 2LZ. Tel.: (08536) Pooley Bridge 301. A 28-guestroom (24 with private baths/showers) country house hotel on the edge of Lake Ullswater. Open from early Mar. to early Dec. Breakfast, lunch, tea, dinner served to non-residents (please reserve). Minimum booking for overnight guests includes bed, breakfast, and dinner. All of the scenic, cultural, and recreational attractions of the Lake Country within a short distance. No credit cards. Not suitable for younger children. Francis Coulson, Brian Sack, Proprietors. (See Index for rates.)

Directions: Use Exit 40 from M6 and follow A66 for ½ mi. Go through the roundabout and turn left on A592 to Ullswater. Turn left at the lake, pass through village of Pooley Bridge, then right at small church and signpost, "Howtown and Martindale." After 100 yds., turn right at crossroads signposted, "Howtown and Martindale." Sharrow Bay is 2 mi. along this road.

THE MILL
Mungrisdale, Penrith, Cumbria

I have been trying to think of an inn included in the North American edition of *Country Inns and Back Roads* that would most closely resemble the Mill, which is located at the foot of the mountains in northern Cumbria.

I think the Seven Pines Lodge in Lewis, Wisconsin, the Inverary Inn in Baddeck, Nova Scotia, and the Jordon Hollow Farm in Virginia would be fairly close, but because all of these inns are highly individual, I guess we could only borrow a few features of each of the three mentioned.

Richard and Eleanor Quinlan purchased the Mill from Pam and David Wood in 1985. Both of them had experience in the hospitality field, and they were delighted with the opportunity to have their own place.

As Richard explained it to me, "Eleanor does the cooking. She is most particular about her homemade soups and sweets, and she serves quite a few regional dishes from Cumbria. Tonight, she is doing a curry and she decorates the dish with at least a dozen tidbits. Sometimes people don't know whether to wear them or eat them. We think that dinner is the height of any guest's stay here at the Mill and I think that most of our guests share our enthusiasm."

In the main house there are seven guest rooms, four with private baths. The original "Old Mill" has been converted into a suite of rooms (two doubles, spacious lounge, and a private bathroom). They retain all of the Old World look, with their original heavy oak beams. There is a wonderful view over the river which flows through the grounds.

Mungrisdale is an unspoiled Lakeland village comprising a 16th-century inn and church together with a cluster of farms and shady sycamores against a background of blue-gray crags and soft mountain slopes.

As Richard wrote in the very colorful and useful brochure about the Mill: "From the seclusion of our little-known beauty spot, the whole of the Lake District can be easily explored and many other areas are accessible for day trips, such as the Solway Coast, the Scottish border country, Hadrian's Wall, the Yorkshire Dales, and the Penninnes."

Eleanor was quick to point out that within the immediate vicinity there are a wildlife park and a great many places of historic interest, as well as a wide range of activities available, including fell walking, rock climbing, pony trekking, bird watching, sailing, fishing, hang gliding, and golf.

With quite a few country house hotels in Cumbria, I was delighted to find this snug little guest house, which incidentally is now the possessor of a recommendation from the British Tourist Authority.

Reader Comment: "My husband and I had the pleasure of staying one week at the Mill, which was not long enough. The owners were wonderful attentive hosts. In our experience this was the most hospitable establishment we have ever visited. It was personal and yet afforded privacy. The food was excellent, the rooms were attractive and comfortable with attention to details; it has fresh flowers, tea service and cookies."

THE MILL, Mungrisdale, Penrith, Cumbria CA11 OXR. Tel.: (059 683) Threlkeld 659. A 9-guestroom guest house located about 20 mi. from Carlisle in the English Lake Country. Bed, breakfast, and the evening meal included. Open every day from March 1 to Oct. 31. No credit cards. Richard and Eleanor Quinlan, Proprietors. (See Index for rates.)

Directions: Leave the M6 Motorway at Penrith (Junction 40) and take the A66 road for Keswick. The Mill is 2 mi. north; watch for signpost midway between Penrith and Keswick.

THE PHEASANT INN
Bassenthwaite Lake, Cockermouth, Cumbria

"I think that we are best described as being a residential English country pub." I readily agreed with innkeeper Barrington Wilson's evaluation of the Pheasant Inn.

This welcoming inn is set in the countryside at the head of Bassenthwaite Lake with Thornwaite Forest behind. The 16th-century L-shaped building is white with black trim, and there is a very pleasant lawn and extensive gardens in the rear. When I visited, the poppies were out in great numbers, as well as some of the other early summer flowers.

Over the rather rustic entrance are some mounted birds of the region, including several pheasants. There are several other references to this noble bird, including a handsome painting against a background of lakes and mountains. The snug conviviality of the interior is emphasized by low, beamed ceilings, patterned curtains, and comfortable lounges with chintz-covered furniture, log fires, and fresh flowers.

Over the years, apparently both Mr. and Mrs. Barrington Wilson and previous owners had collected a number of Lake Country memorabilia, including a mounted fish with a notice that it was caught in 1921 by one of the hotel guests. I was also interested in a novel collection of prints of old British inns that were at one time included in cigarette packages.

There are twenty spotless, comfortable guest rooms at the Pheasant, all of which have private bathrooms.

The innkeeper thoughtfully provides his guests with an excellent map of Keswick ("Kezz-ik"), which shows hotels and pubs in the area serving bar lunches and snacks. This is particularly important, because it's possible to motor all over the Lake District, as well as walk on the fells (hills), and it is good to know where there is a friendly pub. A hearty bar lunch usually includes some specialty of the house such as meat pies and salads, and many of these smaller places have a house pâté of which they are very proud.

After a day of motoring and walking in the Lake Country, it is most pleasant to return to the Pheasant and settle down in the lounge where

there is a view of the blue mountain peaks and the dark green fir trees. There are many good American and British magazines scattered about.

The dinner menu consists principally of good English cooking, including braised ox tongue, roast turkey with bread sauce, roast capon with bacon and bread, and rhubarb and ginger pie served with cream.

Sailing, boating, fishing, walking, pony trekking, fox hunting (on foot), exhibitions, festivals, visiting the Roman Wall, and touring the Lake Country by car, are just a few of the many things enjoyed by Pheasant Inn guests.

This part of the Lake District is particularly beautiful in spring and autumn when the trees are at their loveliest.

THE PHEASANT INN, Bassenthwaite Lake, Cockermouth, Cumbria. Tel.: (059 681) Bassenthwaite Lake 234. A 20-guestroom traditional residential English country pub (inn) in the English Lake District. Open Jan. to Dec. All Lake Country scenic and recreational attractions nearby. No credit cards. W. E. Barrington Wilson, Resident Director. (See Index for rates.)

Directions: From Keswick, follow A66, 7 mi. on west side of Bassenthwaite Lake.

NORTHERN CUMBRIA

This part of Cumbria closely resembles Scotland with its narrow-passage roads and steep fells, and also Norway, which, in places, has much the same scenery. I decided to go to Scale Hill by way of Keswick and was delighted to find that the road, actually the long way around, was alpine in nature but completely safe. Although it was a Sunday afternoon, the high season had passed and there was a paucity of traffic.

The road winds and twists alongside a lake, continues up over a pass, and drops down into the dales with a descent that is breathtaking. Low gear is the word for both going up and coming down, but it is worth every great inch of it. This is one of those roads where British courtesy is to be commended. Many cars pull off in the lay-bys to let others pass. I only regret I was unaccompanied and there was no one to share this really wonderful adventure.

The clouds put on a remarkable show. The mist at the top of the fells would shift unexpectedly and let in a little ray of sunshine and a patch of blue sky.

Most spectacular were the great profiles created by the mountain skyline. My mind played tricks as I read various shapes into all of them.

The valley widened out and I could see several swift-flowing streams tumbling down from the tops of the hills. It reminded me of just such sights while cruising the Norwegian fjords. Now, after a very pleasant journey I could see the unmistakable outline of Scale Hill Hotel in the distance.

SCALE HILL HOTEL
Loweswater, Cumbria

Much to my delight, Scale Hill turned out to be a small hotel quite resembling the Pheasant at Cockermouth, ten miles to the north. It is a two-story white building with impressive views out over the meadows toward the fells. There is a pleasant garden in the rear, with many benches permitting visitors to quietly enjoy the spectacular scenery. The view from the front is a little more threatening, as the fells seem to be much higher and, under a leaden sky on the day of my visit, more ominous.

However, there was nothing ominous about the tempting Saturday afternoon tea being served by a very pert miss to the many people who happened by to enjoy the warm coal fire, the cups of tea, and the enticing scones with whipped cream and jam.

As is the case with most inns of this type, there is a residents' lounge separated from the main lobby. It was occupied by a black cat with white paws, who was curled up contentedly by the fire.

Upstairs, the hallways have many photographs, sporting prints, and the unmistakable air of an old British inn. The guest rooms look clean and comfortable and, once again, enjoy the marvelous view.

There is a tiny bar, which was not open during the time of my visit, but I peeked through the window and could well imagine that it provided a pleasant atmosphere for locals and visitors alike.

Innkeepers Michael and Sheila Thompson provide a hearty menu with four courses. Some of the main dishes include shoulder of lamb, local trout, Solway salmon, roast turkey, and roast duck with applesauce.

A modified American plan that includes dinner is available. Picnic lunches are provided for guests who either walk the fells or motor through the countryside.

Michael Thompson explained that there's been an inn here since 1633. The property was originally a farm, and because it was located at the top of the hill, it became customary for the stage drivers to stop and give the horses a rest and for the farm to provide some hearty bread and cheese for the travelers. This quite naturally led to the establishment of the inn, or to what would be known then as a pub.

SCALE HILL HOTEL, Loweswater, English Lakeland, Cumbria. Tel.: (090085) Lorton 232. A 17-guestroom (mostly private baths) traditional country inn in the northern Lake District. Dinner, bed, and breakfast served to houseguests. Dinners served to non-residents. Advance reservations are accepted for a minimum of 2 nights. Open year-round, although an inquiry would be in order during the deep winter months. Most conveniently located to enjoy all of the English Lake scenery and attractions. Walking, fishing, bird watching, golfing, horseback riding, and many other recreational advantages nearby. Three cats in residence. Michael and Sheila Thompson, Resident Proprietors. (See Index for rates.)

Directions: M6 to Penrith, A66 to Keswick to Braithwaite; turn left over Whinlatter Pass to High Lorton and on to Scale Hill.

CROSBY LODGE
Crosby-on-Eden, Carlisle, Cumbria

"This is, indeed, the Border Country," said Patricia Sedgwick, as we were enjoying a cup of tea in the sunny dining room of the Crosby Lodge Hotel. (I realize that this book sounds as if I subsist on tea, but it is the marvelous British way of expressing hospitality and I've enjoyed dozens of cups of tea and cakes with hoteliers and innkeepers from Inverness to Mousehole and from County Galway to Norfolk.)

"Hadrian's Wall, which is just a few miles away, was constructed by the Romans to keep the raiding Scottish tribes from marauding the lands to the south. We are within a day trip of Edinburgh, both the east and west coasts, the Cumberland and Northumberland country, and the Scottish lowlands. The Lake District is a few miles away to the west."

Until 1970, Patricia and her husband, Michael, lived in nearby Carlisle where they operated a restaurant. "Michael is an expert chef," she said proudly, "trained in both London and Switzerland. I was born in Carlisle, and I've never moved away.

"In the years we've had Crosby Lodge we've gradually upgraded it. You'd be surprised how run-down it was when we first saw it in October, 1970. Now we've done all the bedrooms over and added further guest rooms in the stable block. I guess you'd call us a country house hotel and restaurant. Our prices for rooms include a full English breakfast. We have a nice walled garden that is available to our guests. Most of the people who stay here spend the days touring about and return in time for dinner."

It was obvious that the Sedgwicks had done much to improve both the interior and exterior of this country house, built around 1805. The two towers in front are connected by a crenelated battlement that, of course, has never seen any sieges.

Many trees grace the spacious lawn, and meadows are abloom with flowers.

As I made a reluctant departure after a pleasant tour of the house and grounds, Patricia extended a friendly invitation to return in the future.

CROSBY LODGE, Crosby-on-Eden, Carlisle, Cumbria CA6 4QZ. Tel.: (022873) Crosby-on-Eden 618. An 11-guestroom (private baths) manor house hotel, 4½ mi. east of Carlisle in the lush Cumbria countryside. Open mid-Jan. to Dec. 23. Breakfast, lunch, dinner served to non-residents. Restaurant closed Sun. evenings. Convenient for tours through the English Lake District, the Scottish lowlands. Hadrian's Wall, Carlisle Castle, Rosehill Theatre, and other scenic and cultural attractions nearby. Mrs. and Mrs. G. M. Sedgwick, Resident Owners. (See Index for rates.)

Directions: From M6 use Exit 44. Follow B6264 approx. 2 mi. Turn left at crossroads, still following B6264 sign. Approx. 2 mi. to hotel, just through Crosby village. Crosby Lodge stands on right at the top of the hill.

FARLAM HALL HOTEL
Brampton, Cumbria

"There are other Bramptons in Britain," explained Alan Quinion, "but we're the one near Carlisle. That's why it's necessary to be very careful about fully identifying some of the villages and towns." Alan and I were enjoying a relaxing chat in front of the crackling fire in the residents' lounge in Farlam Hall.

He was telling me the fascinating story about the long search he and his wife and daughter, Helen, and son, Barry, had made, looking for a country house to convert into a hotel. "We had looked for at least two years, and even as tired and run-down as this place was when we saw it, we knew that the location and situation were exactly perfect for us. The house had the right feeling . . . the 'vibes' were right, and we just ached to bring it to life."

And bring it to life is exactly what the Quinion family has done since they moved to Farlam Hall in 1975. The departments of the hotel are divided almost equally, with Barry, the chef, being responsible for the kitchen and the food. "He has worked in some excellent restaurants," said his father, "and is very well trained. We're building our strength on his foundations. If the food and genuine comfort are good enough, people will seek you out."

Daughter Helen and her husband, Alastair, are mainly responsible for the reception and running of the dining room.

"Mrs. Quinion takes the responsibility for the decor, the furnishings, the housekeeping, and generally looks after all of us," he smiled. "And I believe we need some looking after. I handle the accounts, supervise the gardens and outside developing, and run the bar."

At dinner, I had ample opportunity to sample some of Barry's cuisine. The starter was avocado mousse, the main course was beef Wellington served in a very crisp pastry jacket, and the cheese selection was one of the most extensive I'd ever seen.

In a moment of complete madness, I accepted Mrs. Quinion's suggestion that I try both a small helping of the raspberry mousse, which was decorated with whipped cream, and the chocolate gateau. Heavenly.

Farlam Hall started life as a 17th-century farmhouse and was enlarged in stages. It subsequently became the elegant Victorian manor house it is today, set in its own gardens with an ornamental lake and stream.

FARLAM HALL, Brampton, Cumbria CA8 2NG. Tel.: (069-76) Hall-bankgate 234. A 13-guestroom (private baths) country house hotel, 11 mi. from Carlisle in the vicinity of the Roman Wall. Open Mar. to Jan. Dinner served to non-residents. Color TV in guest rooms. Ample Lake Country and Northumbria recreation and sightseeing nearby, including the Roman Wall and three golf courses. Quinion and Stevenson Families, Proprietors. (See Index for rates.)

Directions: Leave M6 at Carlisle, Exit 43; follow A69 (Newcastle Rd.) to Brampton. Leaving Brampton, take right fork (A689) to Hallbankgate and Alston. Hotel is 2½ mi. along this road on left.

NORTHUMBERLAND

There is a marvelous system of very fast roads in the United Kingdom; those running from London, north, can be divided into two basic roads. The M6 goes as far north as Carlisle and then breaks up into a series of good routes to both coasts, as well as to Glasgow or Edinburgh. The M1, when it is not a Motorway, becomes the A1. The A1 continues north through York, Durham, Newcastle-upon-Tyne, and into Edinburgh by way of Berwick-upon-Tweed. Of the two roads, the M1 (A1) is the least used north of Newcastle. In Northumberland it provides one of the most scenic routes in Britain. In this edition I have provided some accommodation suggestions on and just off the A1 that would be ideal for an overnight visit and even longer, as there are literally hundreds of castles, beaches, and nature preserves along the Northumberland coast.

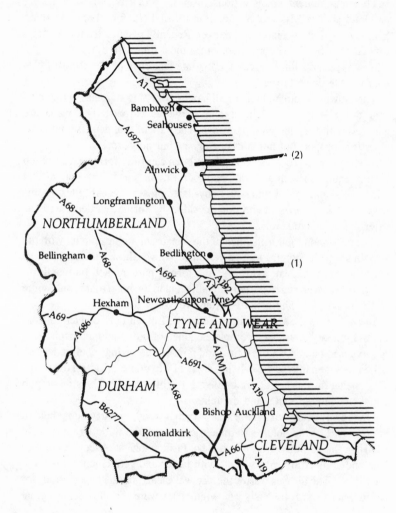

NORTHUMBERLAND

LINDEN HALL HOTEL
Longhorsley, Northumberland

This magnificent country house, set in 300 acres of breathtaking parkland and woods, was originally built in 1812 for Charles William Bigge, a local industrialist and banker. Recently rescued from ignominy, Linden Hall has been converted into a most impressive hotel.

Newly planted linden trees flank some stretches of the almost-mile-long private drive to the hotel.

The drawing room and inner hall have a sweeping staircase, a magnificent dome, huge chandeliers, and gorgeous carpets. The walls are adorned with very large oil paintings. The aura of grandeur is unmistakable. It is proper, but not stuffy; elegant, but not formal.

The various-sized guest rooms have been carefully furnished and each is fully equipped with a private bathroom, color television, a direct-dial telephone—and, of all things, a baby-listening service. All guest rooms have unbroken views of the countryside, the formal gardens, and the extensive woodland walks.

The decor and the furnishings of the restaurant are in keeping with the remainder of the hotel. Floor-to-ceiling windows allow panoramic views over the croquet lawn, as well as the formal gardens and parklands.

There are large vegetable gardens adjacent to the hotel that supply some of the provender. The menu is extensive to say the least.

In contrast to the Georgian opulence, the Linden Pub, converted from the old granary, conveys a complete change of mood and atmosphere. It has exposed beams, an open fire, and a most interesting inner gallery. A collection of enameled advertising signs of a bygone age adorn the walls. The sheltered courtyard has barbecue facilities and such outdoor pub games as quoits, boule, and draughts.

On the day of my visit there was a formal wedding party being held in another part of the hotel, and male members of the wedding party were wearing the famous grey top hat so fashionable at Ascot. This was England at its 20th-century best, with ladies and gentlemen "dressed to the nines." The air was warm, the sky was clear, and the expectations for the marriage were obviously very high. They were certainly off to a great start.

LINDEN HALL HOTEL, Longhorsley, Morpeth, Northumberland. Tel.: (0670) 56611. Telex: 538224. U.S. reservations: 800-223-5581. A 45-guestroom (private baths) luxurious country house hotel in a former 1812 Georgian mansion, set in 300 acres of parkland and woods. Breakfast, lunch, and dinner. Open year-round. Billiards, table tennis, outdoor tennis, and croquet on grounds. Many museums, stately homes, foot paths and backroading nearby. All modern amenities. Jon Moore, Manager. (See Index for rates.)

Directions: Take A1 north out of Newcastle-upon-Tyne an' turn onto A697 just above Morpeth. Linden Hall is just a short distance north of the village of Longhorsley.

MARINE HOUSE PRIVATE HOTEL
Alnmouth, Northumberland

Continuing on the A1, my next stop was Alnmouth, an attractive small seaside village that was once a small seaport not particularly noted for its righteousness. These matters, I am told, have receded into the past and the village is now a very popular resort.

The Marine House Hotel is a large, comfortable stone house, built on the edge of the village golf links, with fine views of Alnmouth Bay. The seaside sands are of a very fine consistency and bathing, boating, sea and river angling, and pony trekking are much favored.

I think the real point about stopping off here is that it is a very natural small hotel that would be quite popular with the British because of its location and because of its relatively reasonable tariffs. It isn't the kind of place that the visitor to England would be likely to find, because it is a little out of the way. It affords an opportunity for an English seaside hotel experience with very friendly and affable proprietors. Four of the guest rooms face the sea and there is a little terrace and a garden, which also share this pleasant view.

Proprietress Sheila Inkster does all of the cooking, and this includes roast beef, Yorkshire pudding, roast turkey, and creamed potatoes.

If the reader stays here, please send me a card with your impressions. It had an appeal for me.

MARINE HOUSE PRIVATE HOTEL, Alnmouth, Northumberland NE66 2RW. Tel.: (0665) 830-349. A 10-guestroom traditional small seaside hotel (some shared baths). Open all year. Breakfast and dinner served daily. Overlooking a 9-hole seaside golf course. Seabathing, yachting, pony trekking nearby. Sheila and Gordon Inkster, Proprietors. (See Index for rates.)

Directions: Alnmouth is on the Northumbrian coast between Berwick and Newcastle, and east of Alnwick, off the A1. Can be reached by London-Edinburgh railway, 1 mi. away.

Wales

Wales is utterly fascinating and to me quite mind-boggling. The people are friendly and accommodating, the scenery runs the gamut from beaches to great mountain peaks, the numerous castles are all history-laden, and the varied opportunities for a holiday are literally uncountable.

Wales has three impressive national parks, including Snowdonia Park, the haunt of intrepid mountain climbers and holiday seekers. Brecon Beacons Park is perfect for pony trekking and walking.

Llangollen is the home of the world-famous International Musical Eisteddfod in July. "The great little trains" in Wales afford several opportunities for amusement.

Just a word about the Welsh language: Unbelievable. I say that to give encouragement to anyone who has tried to pronounce the "lls," "ffs," and a few of the totally unfamiliar combinations of consonants. Fortunately, the Welsh people have a good sense of humor and are probably adjusted to the mangling of their native tongue. Give it a try, it's part of the fun, and the Welsh give "A" for effort.

List of common Welsh words and some meanings in English:

> *aber—mouth of a river*
> *bryn—hill*
> *plas—mansion*
> *coed—woods*
> *llyn—lake*
> *eglwys—church*
> *caer—fort*
> *newydd—new*
> *bedd—grave*

From the mountains, lakes, and seacoasts of Wales have come such notables as David Lloyd George, Sir Henry Morton Stanley (of Stanley and Livingston fame), Dylan Thomas, Richard Burton, and Merlin, King Arthur's wizard.

Wales is filled with stories of bards, poets, and heroes. No one can possibly understand and fully appreciate Wales in just one visit.

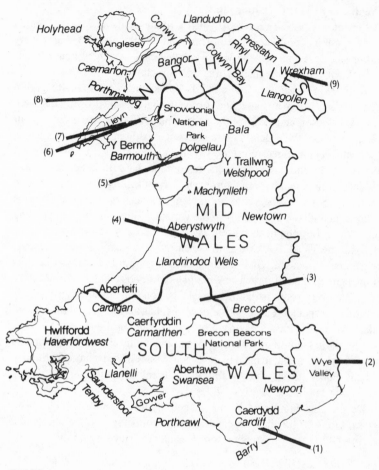

WALES

EGERTON GREY
Porthkerry, South Glamorgan

"Egerton Grey," I repeated, "such a romantic name."

"My parents and I found it in some old documents," Manager Amy Adler said. "It sounded the way we envisioned a country house hotel, though for most of its history this was a rectory."

Amy and her parents, Bart and Iris Zuzik, know a lot about Egerton Grey for a family who came here from Chicago. Iris was originally from Wales, however, and many of the handsome antiques you see throughout the inn crossed the Atlantic more than once. Although the Zuziks began their innkeeping career not far away in Cardiff, it was the discovery of Egerton Grey and its need for total restoration that fulfilled their dreams.

The house is set on more than seven acres of rolling land in the Vale of Glamorgan and looks out to an ancient viaduct and the sea. There is croquet and all-weather tennis in the garden; riding, fishing, and sailing are arranged by the hosts on request. Sightseeing is a town and country delight: the Welsh Folk Museum is nearby, as is Cardiff with its shops, museums, and castle. On a blustery day, fires burn in the Egerton Grey drawing room and library. There are plenty of books and magazines, too.

While every room is distinctive, at Egerton Grey even the bathrooms are worth a special tour. One, for example, has an Edwardian tub shaped like a keyhole with a glass cage over it containing the shower.

The skylighted dining room is open to the public and serves a wonderful six- or seven-course meal in the evening as well as an elaborate Sunday lunch. House guests enjoy a full Welsh breakfast, and there is always afternoon tea in the loggia.

Despite the handsome formal panelling, oil paintings, and leaded glass, Egerton Grey has a special warmth. You know you are guests of a caring family who lives here, too. I wanted to stay on and on.

EGERTON GREY, Porthkerry, South Glamorgan C56 9BZ. Tel.: (0446)71666. Fax: (0446) 71690. An 11-room (private baths) country house hotel on an 8-acre estate in South Wales. Double and twin beds. Tennis and croquet on grounds. Fine restaurant. Open all year. Major credit cards accepted. Special values for two-day breaks. Bart and Iris Zuzik, Proprietors. Amy Zuzik Adler, Manager. (See Index for rates.)

Directions: From M4 motorway, exit 33, and follow Cardiff Airport signs for 10 mi. Take A4226 towards Porthkerry and after 1/5 mi. turn onto lane between 4 thatched cottages.

Rates for a room for two people for one night with breakfast, except where noted, are included in the Index of this book. They are not to be considered firm quotations, but should be used as guidelines only.

THE CROWN AT WHITEBROOK
Whitebrook, near Monmouth, Gwent

I was in the Wye River Valley traveling south on A466, the road from Monmouth to Chepstow. On the east bank, it's Gloucestershire, England, and on the west, it's Gwent in Wales.

At the river crossing, there was a signpost clearly marked Whitebrook, the village where the Crown is located. The road doubled back on the west side of the river for a short distance and then became a single passage route. I began to feel somewhat tentative about the expedition when the road passed through some barnyards and twisted its way around huge boulders; however, I pressed on and was rewarded with the sight of the village.

The Crown proved to be a very jolly place, a traditional village inn (as opposed to a country house hotel), which probably dates back to 1680. The rooms have been modernized with intercommunications systems, direct-dial telephones, and built-in radios. The Manor Room has a four-poster bed and a whirlpool bath.

The Crown is situated in the hills next to a brook flowing into the Wye through the steep wooded valley, on the edge of Tintern Forest. It reminds me a great deal of parts of New England and North Carolina. There are many roses, rhododendrons, irises, pansies, and other flowers, as well as oak, ash, and beech trees, which provide homes for nightingales, owls, and magpies.

For many travelers, the Crown may provide an introduction to Wales, and I'm sure the Bates family will make it a cordial stay.

Reader Comment: "This was our second visit and we'll return every year. Wonderful food! Typical bedrooms—smallish but comfortable."

THE CROWN AT WHITEBROOK (near Monmouth), Gwent NP5 4TX. Tel.: (0600) Monmouth 860254. A 12-guestroom (private baths) village inn in the true inn tradition, located approx. 4 mi. from Monmouth and about 2½ hrs. from London. Breakfast, lunch, tea, and dinner served every day. Walking in the Tintern Forest, fishing for salmon in the River Wye, and golf on the three local courses provide interesting recreation. One dog in residence. Roger and Sandra Bates, Owners/hosts. (See Index for rates.)

Directions: Traveling west on M4, take the first exit after crossing the Severn Bridge, follow signs for Monmouth (A466) through Tintern and Llandogo. At Bigsweir Bridge, turn left for Whitebrook. The Crown is 2 mi. up a narrow country lane.

TŶ MAWR COUNTRY HOUSE HOTEL
Brechfa, Dyfed

Except for the distinctive Welsh signposts, I might well have been in Vermont. The road and surroundings—the rushing brook, the boulders, and the fir trees—reminded me of the back way between Wells and Cambridge Springs, Vermont. This area is right on the border of the Cambrian Mountains, some of the most remote upland country in southern Wales. There are large tracts with no roads crossing them.

Now, following the simple directions, I arrived at the village of Brechfa, hidden in the valley and steep rolling hills surrounding the River Cothi. I spotted Tŷ Mawr almost immediately—a restored 16th-century house standing on the banks of the Marlais, a smaller stream.

My feeling of being in Vermont was heightened even more when I stepped inside the front door. Except for the very old building, I might well have been in a Vermont ski lodge. The interior walls were of stone and heavy supporting beams, brightened by a generous use of colorful draperies and wall hangings. It had a modern contemporary look, but at the same time, I sensed a keen appreciation of the past.

Three of the walls in the attractive residents' lounge were done in massive stone, and a fire crackled merrily in the fireplace. The combination of the old and new was highlighted by the contemporary furniture and the colorful prints on the walls. I noted quite a few familiar-looking American and British magazines.

There are five double bedrooms at Tŷ Mawr, one with twin beds, and all with private bathrooms. They are furnished, as is the rest of the house, with an eye toward blending the furniture and draperies with the stone walls and oak beams.

Brechfa is a truly rural Welsh-speaking area, and throughout the year there are always local farming and social events, such as sheep shearing, horse sales, haymaking, pony racing and trotting, village fêtes, and the Eisteddfodau. It is really quite natural.

The sea is within a half-hour's drive, and there are many beaches along the Pembroke and Cardigan coasts which are just a short distance away. There are lots of ancient castles to explore, as well as the Roman gold mines, the woolen mills, and Brecon Beacons National Park. There's lots of good fishing as well as golf courses in the area and horseback riding or pony trekking.

Brechfa is a reasonable drive to Fishguard, the place to catch the ferries to Rosslare and Cork in Ireland.

A bit of Vermont in Wales. This is a sort of reverse exchange, because years ago a great many Welshmen and their families immigrated to Vermont's slate-quarrying hills and valleys near Wells and Poultney. The choirs in Vermont's small country churches are swelled with the rich Welsh voices. There are still strong connections with the rugged Welsh homeland.

TŶ MAWR COUNTRY HOUSE HOTEL, Brechfa (near Carmarthen), Dyfed. Tel.: (026 789) Brechfa 332. A small 5-guestroom country house hotel and restaurant 12 mi. from Carmarthen and 30 min. from beaches on the Pembroke and Cardigan coasts. Double and twin beds available. Closed last 2 wks. in Feb. Ruined castles, Roman gold mines, woolen mills, picnic areas, Brecon Beacons National Park, and nature reserves nearby. Fishing and horse riding on the grounds. Rough shooting, golf, walking nearby. One cat in residence. Flaherty Family, Proprietors. (See Index for rates.)

Directions: Follow A40 from Llandeilo to Carmarthen. Watch for B4310 on the right and follow 6 mi. to Brechfa.

TRAVELING IN WALES

The roads are all paved, even those that look like little single yellow or blue lines on the map. Even the roads marked in red with three numbers, such as A485, are inclined to be narrow; four-number roads can become single passageways every so often, but not the three-number variety. I found the four-numbered roads basically more fun.

On checking the routes, I discovered that the center of the town was a key point. This is where the signposts are located, and once out in the country there are very few reassuring route numbers until the next crossroads. The villages all have Welsh names and this can be confusing,

especially with a two-worded village name where none of the letters are
vowels. I gave up trying to pronounce them, because I realized I was trying
to associate them with English sounds and not with Welsh sounds.

I found the best way to go from point to point was to stop at the
crossroads and check the signposts, even though I might not be able to do
anything except look at the name of the village. People of whom I inquired
directions were most accommodating, and in some cases I had to go into
the pub with the map, rather than trust myself for any pronunciation. My
approach was, "Oh pardon me, sir, can you show me where we are on this
map?"

Counties are not mentioned as much in Wales as they are in England,
but people are very proud to be from North Wales or from Mid-Wales or
South Wales.

Just as April is an ideal time to be in the south of England, May is an
excellent time for traveling in Wales. School is still in session and there
aren't as many travelers on the road, especially in caravans (known as
trailers or mobile homes in North America).

Whenever I asked someone in Britain about the length of time it takes to
get from point to point, I found that it was a good idea to double the
estimate. Britons drive much faster than North Americans, besides which
they are used to the narrow-passage roads.

Quite frequently I found myself on the top of a hill in a brief shower
looking down into the valley or hill beyond, which was bathed in sunshine.

Instead of wearing traditional blue jeans or something similar, Welsh
farmers running tractors in the fields generally wear suit coats, and
sometimes a shirt and a tie. Men wear a variety of hats and caps here. A
deerstalker hat is quite popular with many different men. There are also
wool caps of varied designs. On Sundays, gentlemen are turned out in very
good sport jackets with either grey or fawn-colored trousers and suede
shoes.

LLWYNDERW HOTEL
Abergwesyn, Powys

"It takes a few days before people realize why they have come here," Michael Yates remarked as we relaxed in the library after dinner. "They want to 'go' and 'do' instead of 'be.' At first it does not occur to them how wonderful it is to take a walk; to listen to birdsong. Then suddenly they come upon a flower they have never seen before or a fox darts across their path, and they understand."

Llwynderw (the name means Oak Grove), a Georgian manor house with early 18th-century origins, stands on a tract of wild moorland 1000 feet above sea level in central Wales. Mountains cradle its tranquility; sheep crop its doorstep meadows. Yet, for all its otherworldly isolation, we were not far from main roadways and were within easy driving to famous gardens and castles.

The inn is a delightful hodgepodge of connected wings, and it was a full day before I could find my room without backtracking down yet another panelled hall. Once there, I found the chintz-covered armchair so comfortable, the selection of books and magazines so entrancing, and the view (I could see for miles from my windows) so pleasant, it was tempting to stay put.

Dinner, however, was "promptly at eight," and I had been warned by other guests—many of whom had been coming here for years—that hot food was meant to be served hot and dilly-dallying was not tolerated. In fact, should you arrive at Llwynderw past the appointed hour, you just might not be given supper at all. Be advised: the lamb spiked with fresh herbs and served with mint and garden vegetables is far too good to miss.

LLWYNDERW HOTEL, Abergwesyn, Llanwrtyd Wells, Powys LD5 4TW. Tel.: (05913) 238. U.S. Reservations: 800-323-3602. A country house hotel on high moorland in north-central Wales. Open Mar. through Oct.; higher rates on Sat. and July 15–Sept. 30. Ten rooms (private baths); twin and double beds. Two night minimum. Dining room open only to guests. Demi-pension. Michael Yates, Proprietor. (See Index for rates.)

Directions: Follow A40 to Llandovery, bear north on A483, and turn off towards Aberwgesyn at Lanwrtyd Wells. The driveway of Llwynderw will be on your left.

Rates for a room for two people for one night with breakfast, except where noted, are included in the Index of this book. They are not to be considered firm quotations, but should be used as guidelines only.

BONTDDU HALL HOTEL
Bontddu (near Dolgellau), Gwynedd

I was enjoying what the British call a "good tea" in the Green Room at the Bontddu (pronounced "bont-thee" in Welsh) Hotel on an afternoon whose mood was alternately sunny and stormy. The magnificent view of the Mawddach Estuary and Cader Idris range of mountains are alternately spectacular and clear or quickly obscured by fog or a hailstorm. This view, which is above all else the distinguishing feature of the hotel, is an unforgettable blend of water, mountain, and wood—one of the most splendid in the highlands of Wales.

All of the drawing rooms and the dining room are situated on the view side of the hotel, as are most of the guest rooms.

The Bontddu Hall was the only three-star hotel that I visited in Wales, and it had all of the unmistakable accouterments of a luxury resort. There was a very impressive entrance hall, much wood paneling, and the high-ceilinged public rooms had rich-looking furniture and draperies. The cloistered entrance was decorated with a most unusual collection of shining cavalry helmets, resplendent with horsehair plumes.

There are twenty-six guest rooms, all with private bathrooms, and these include a newer section of a more modern design.

Although I could not stay for dinner, there was an obvious emphasis on food, since the dining room is called the Gourmet Room. This might be because *Gourmet Magazine* gave a most favorable review of the hotel's menu a number of years ago, making particular mention of the North Wales lamb, lobster, salmon, smoked trout, and pheasant.

This is really a most impressive area of Wales, quite convenient for a holiday of longer duration. Guests may play golf at several famous courses nearby, and there is fishing, walking, or swimming on the sandy beaches.

Incidentally, Bontddu has won the "Prettiest Village in Wales" title three times.

BONTDDU HALL HOTEL, Bontddu (near Dolgellau), Gwynedd. Tel.: (034149) Bontddu 661. A 22-guestroom luxury hotel 5 mi. from Dolgellau. The hotel has an inspiring view of the famous Mawddach Estuary and the Cader Idris range of mountains near some outstanding golf courses. Open from Easter to Christmas. Breakfast, lunch, tea, and dinner served to non-residents. May be reserved from U.S. by travel agents through Dial Britain. Tel.: 800-424-9822. One Irish setter in residence. D. J. Ball, Owner. (See Index for rates.)

Directions: Use Exit 12 from M6 and go left on A5 towards Shrewsbury. From Shrewsbury take A458 to Dinas Mawddwy, then follow A470 to Dolgellau and A496 toward Barmouth.

BWLCH-Y-FEDWEN COUNTRY HOUSE HOTEL
Penmorfa, Porthmadog, Gwynedd

I leaned against the door watching Gwyneth Bridge prepare my breakfast, cooking the eggs exactly as I ordered.

"This is a coaching inn dating back to 1664," she said, deftly sliding two sunnyside-up eggs onto a warm plate and then adding a rasher of bacon and a few small sausages. "Arthur and I have been here for ten years and I think we have finally gotten things in order." This selfsame Arthur Bridges, he of the ready smile and fierce beard, joined us in the kitchen at that precise moment.

"Good morning," he boomed. "I hope you slept well. I see that you were out early this morning on a walk and I am glad that we had some of our usual beautiful weather for you." His eyes twinkled as he picked up the waiting breakfast plates and disappeared into the dining room.

"Arthur is really awfully good with the guests," said Gwyneth, as she bustled about preparing still more breakfasts. "He's very well informed about Wales and has some of the greatest stories."

Bwlch-y-Fedwen is situated in the middle of Penmorfa village, two miles from Porthmadog, and one mile from Tremadog.

The hotel has now been fully modernized in a warm and homey manner, which, at the same time, retains its original character. Antique furniture, oak beams, stone walls, and huge open fireplaces and candlelight in the dining room and bar create a very friendly and warming atmosphere.

During a lull in the kitchen activities I asked Gwyneth about the evening meal. "Well, our local lamb is really our specialty." she replied. "And of course we have local salmon in season. Our guests all seem to enjoy my sweets, including the 'Queen of Puddings,' another of our specialties. I also enjoy making meringues."

My bedroom was most comfortably furnished, with a view of a little garden in the rear and then down across the valley to some of the North Wales mountains.

I must add a word about the spic-and-span appearance of the Bwlch-y-Fedwen. Cleanliness is one of the virtues highly prized by Britons everywhere, but this particular hotel has to get the lifetime "Mr. Clean Certificate" for neatness. Not only were the bedrooms and public rooms most tastefully decorated, but nothing, and I mean *nothing,* was out of place.

Gwyneth and Arthur . . . you're terrific!

BWLCH-Y-FEDWEN COUNTRY HOUSE HOTEL, Penmorfa, Porthmadog, Gwynedd LL49 9RY. Tel.: (0766) Porthmadog 2975. A 5-guest-

room hotel, approx. 70 mi. from Chester in North Wales. Open from Apr. to Oct. Meals are served to residents only. Twin and double beds available. Within a short distance of the mountains of Snowdonia National Park, and within an easy drive of the many castles, railways, and other attractions of North Wales. Walking, climbing, fishing, golf courses, and sailing available nearby. No credit cards. Mrs. Gwyneth Bridge, Proprietor. (See Index for rates.)

Directions: From Chester follow A55 to Mold, then Ruthin. Here, use A494 to Cerrigydrudion. Take A5 to Betsy-Y-Coed and Capel Curig. Turn left on A4086 and then A498 for Beddgelert to Tremadog. Follow A487 to Penmorfa. This road leads through some of the most spectacular mountain scenery in Wales. I also realize that these are most confusing directions. May I suggest that having a map of Wales in advance and tracing the road under more leisurely circumstances would be an excellent idea.

PLAS BODEGROES
Pwllheli, Gwynedd

When the prestigious British *Good Food Guide* named Plas Bodegroes "Newcomer of the Year," it was quite in keeping with the inn's self-definition as a "restaurant with rooms."

Of course the food is wonderful, but so is the Georgian manor house, the five acres of estate grounds, and, yes, the guest rooms, too.

"They're coming along," said Gunna Chown modestly. "We'll have a total of eight finished next year, and that will be all."

If remodeling is second to cookery, it is only because young owner/chef Christopher Chown is so enthusiastic about his craft. He studied in London and Zurich before deciding that some of the best natural ingredients in Europe are available right here on the Llyn Peninsula of North Wales. In fact, ninety-five percent of the ingredients used in the exceptional cuisine come from within thirty-five miles of the hotel.

The flower-filled sitting room was comfortable as well as beautiful, but we were soon tempted out to the terrace where we sipped our aperitifs while gazing across the meadows. A black and white cat was chasing moths through the bluebells, and "tranquil" seemed an understatement.

Our room had pale apricot-colored walls, a four-poster bed, and an eclectic blend of period furnishings and collectibles. In the divided bath, a Jacuzzi tub promised extra relaxation after our evening stroll down the avenue of beech trees that once marked the main drive to the manor.

Although Plas Bodegroes (literally, place of rose hips) appeared the ultimate faraway retreat, we found we were close to three castles, seven golf courses, excellent sailing, and numerous coves and beaches. Nearby is the yacht harbor and market town of Pwllheli, and from the pretty fishing village of Aberdaron at the end of the peninsula, you can take a boat to Bardsey Island, the westernmost point of Wales. Bardsey is now primarily a bird sanctuary, but once it was the "Isle of a Thousand Saints" with an abbey founded in 516 by St. Cadfan.

So much to see starting from a "restaurant with rooms."

PLAS BODEGROES, Pwllheli, Gwynedd LL53 5TH. Tel.: (0758) 612363. An 8-guestroom (private baths), Georgian country house hotel on the Llyn Peninsula in northwest Wales. Double or twin beds. Highly recommended restaurant. Tariff includes full breakfast, morning tea, dinner. Closed Jan. 2 thru Feb. 28. Christopher and Gunna Chown, Proprietors. (See Index for rates.)

Directions: Bodegroes is on the A497 Nefyn Rd., 1 mi. west of Pwllheli.

SYGUN FAWR COUNTRY HOUSE HOTEL
Beddgelert, Gwynedd

I well remember the day. I was absolutely exhilarated. I had spent the previous night at the Bwlch-y-Fedwen, at Penmorfa, and as a result of hearing about the beauty of the Mount Snowdon area had decided to drive into this section of Gwynedd in Northern Wales, although it was not on my original itinerary. The way led upward through some beautiful mountains to the village of Beddgelert. The morning was beautiful with the

sunlight sparkling on the river. Reaching the village center, I followed the A498 up the valley toward the pass of Llanberis.

On my way out of Beddgelert I saw the sign that pointed over the river and said, "Sygun Fawr Country House Hotel." I just couldn't resist it. And what a happy impulse that was. For one thing, it directed me to this very attractive 17th-century Welsh manor house with beautiful views of the Gwynant Valley and the Snowdon Range. It also introduced me to two very warm and hospitable proprietors, Norman and Peggy Wilson.

Norman is from Lancashire, and after all, anybody with the name Norman is bound to find a receptive audience in me. As we were touring the house, he explained that *sygun fawr* means "high bog"—literally, a high peat bog.

The rooms were very clean and comfortable with mountain views. Downstairs, in a little back bar, which is used mostly by diners and friends, Peggy came out of the kitchen and we all had a cup of lovely morning tea.

"We found a wonderful new way of life up here," Peggy said. "We aren't Welsh, but the people of the village have taken us in most heartily. I've learned how to cook many of the traditional Welsh dishes, as well as those from England. We have visitors from all over the world, but I must say that in spite of all of our efforts, we simply can't get Americans to walk!"

We all had a good laugh at this and I hope this book encourages Americans to try, rather than hurrying through Britain and attempting to see Wales in three days, to settle down and find a place like Sygun Fawr and stay for three or four days to "get the feel" of the land.

As we stepped outside in the morning sunshine, I remarked to Peggy and Norman that this part of Wales reminded me a great deal of Norway, and they said that many other guests had also made that observation, although it was not the Norway of the fjords. "It's the mountains and flowers, I think," said Norman. "You're headed toward Mount Snowdon now, and you'll see what I mean."

Yes, I, too, like the other Americans (not so much the Canadians), had to hurry on to get over the next hill and follow the river to the seaside and beyond. Someday, I'm going back to see Norman and Peggy and spend a week.

SYGUN FAWR COUNTRY HOUSE HOTEL, Beddgelert, Gwynedd LL55 4NE. Tel.: (076-686) Beddgelert 258. A 7-guestroom (private baths) somewhat secluded country house hotel. Twin and double beds available. Approx. 3 hrs. from Chester. Open all year. Dinner served to non-residents. Within an easy drive of all scenic points in North and Mid-Wales. Located in the scenic Snowdon area. No credit cards. Two cats and one dog in residence. Norman and Peggy Wilson, Owners/hosts. (See Index for rates.)

Directions: The A483 runs north and south along the imaginary boundary between Wales and England. There are several roads going west, including the A5, which can be followed west to Capel Curig, where 4086 goes southwest into A498 at Pen-y-Gwryd. The Snowdon area and Beddgelert are slightly to the south on A498. The hotel is just a few minutes from the center of Beddgelert over the brook on A498. Coming from farther south in England, after locating Beddgelert, using the above directions, work out your own way; it's really not difficult.

LLWYN ONN HALL
Wrexham, Clwyd

Should you get the massive Jacobean bed at Llwyn Onn Hall, you will be advised that Bonnie Prince Charlie most likely slept in it. "It was bought from a house where we know he stayed, and he would naturally have been given the finest bed. . . ."

If that room—number 7—is already taken, not to worry. I was more than comfortable in number 5, a sunny room with twin beds, a beam ceiling and furniture handpainted by a local artist. Each of the thirteen rooms in this hilltop country house hotel has its own charm and distinction. Should you plan to stay a week, you might consider a fully equipped apartment in Llwyn Knottia, a Georgian farmhouse with its own walled garden that is part of the larger estate.

Llwyn Onn Hall dates from the 1600s and belonged to the same family for four centuries. However, the house had become a derelict when bought and restored a few years ago by the Graham-Palmers, who already owned all the surrounding land.

The Hall is south of Wrexham town center and convenient to Chester, across the border in England, as well as to Chirk Castle and Erddig, the National Trust house. I arrived from the States at the Manchester International Airport and found it an easy drive.

Llwyn Onn (the name means Ash Grove) has a wood-panelled pub on the first floor and several pretty dining rooms, plus a verandah that overlooks a vast meadow complete with friendly cows. A sitting room for guests only is upstairs. The food is excellent, by the way, and breakfast includes such Welsh specialties as kedgeree and black pudding as well as bacon, eggs, porridge, juice, and fruit.

As Wrexham is an important industrial and market town, many of the guests are business people. For this reason there is a special weekend rate, which includes full breakfasts and evening meals at a great savings.

LLWYN ONN HALL, Cefn Road, Wrexham, Clwyd LL13 ONY. Tel.: (0978) 261225. A 13-guestroom (private baths) country house hotel in North Wales near the English border with double and twin beds; 1 family room; and 3 apartments in a separate farmhouse on the estate. Very good restaurant. Serves breakfast, lunch, afternoon tea, dinner. Open all year. Mr. and Mrs. Roger Graham-Palmer, Proprietors. (See Index for rates.)

Directions: From the A534 (Holt Rd.) turn south on Cefn Rd. Private road to Llwyn Onn Hall will be on your left and is marked.

It's not that the distances are very long in the British Isles, it's the many diversions along the way that sometimes make it impossible to estimate traveling and arrival times. Last order times for dinner are included in the Index so that you can see what time you must arrive in order not to find the kitchen door locked. If you are going to arrive later, call ahead—there isn't a hotel/inn listed here that will not make some provision to feed you if they know you can't make it before the kitchen closes.

In Britain, acceptance of a hotel booking by telephone or in writing is generally regarded as a legally binding contract. If it's necessary to cancel, advise the hotel immediately. If they are unable to re-let the room, the hotel may be entitled to claim compensation—usually two thirds of the agreed price—and any deposit would be included as part of this payment.

Scotland

Welcome to Scotland, or, as it is expressed in Gaelic, Ceud mile fáilte. *Translation: "a hundred thousand welcomes." (Try pronouncing it "cute mela falsha.")*

Scotland has some of the most beautiful and rugged scenery in the world—mountains, firths, glens, lochs, and islands. Scotland is tartans, haggis, oat cakes, pipes, kilts, trews, grouse on the wing, Highland games, hundreds of ruined castles and abbeys, golf, monsters, sheep on narrow roads, hidden fishing villages, and rich farmland.

Scotland is also history, a history intertwined with heroes and villains. One of the best ways to prepare for a trip to Scotland is to read the history and identify with some of the personalities: Robert the Bruce, Mary Queen of Scots, Rob Roy MacGregor, Flora Macdonald, and Bonnie Prince Charlie. Read about the Campbells, Macdonalds and Bloody Glencoe, the Glorious Revolution, Bannockburn, and Culloden.

Return to Sir Walter Scott's poems and novels. He perhaps unknowingly became Scotland's best press agent.

To further enrich a Scottish experience, dip into the poetry of Robert Burns, the novels of Robert Louis Stevenson, and the famous trip to Scotland by Doctor Samuel Johnson, described by his biographer, James Boswell, himself a canny Scot.

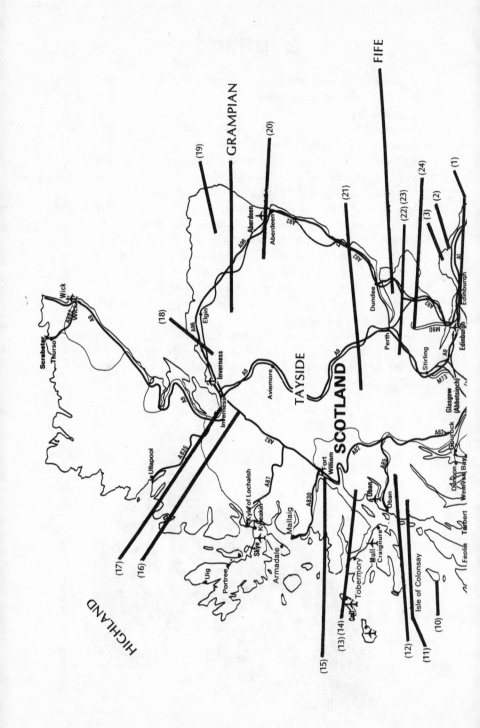

SCOTLAND

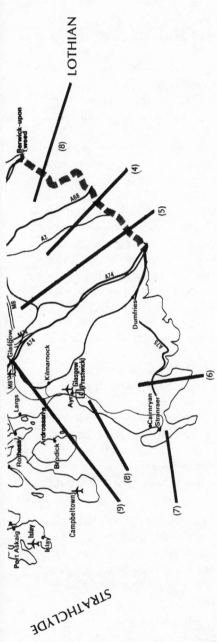

THE ALBANY HOTEL
Edinburgh

A very discreet brass plate on the front of the building identifies the Albany Hotel, which is actually a series of three 1812 Georgian townhouses. Albany Street is typical of Edinburgh's business and financial district, with the imposing facades of 19th-century townhouses lining both sides of the very wide New Town boulevards.

Pauline Maridor took over the hotel in 1982, and she is almost always there to welcome her guests. This is a modest, unassuming small hotel, just around the corner from the shopping district. With BBC-TV, Scottish-TV, and the Playhouse Theatre close by, Pauline often has guests from the media and entertainment fields. In fact, she told me that members of the Black Ballet Jazz Company and the French Ballet of Nancy had just been there for the Edinburgh Festival.

Since the hotel is a listed historic building, there are limitations on the amount of renovation that can be done. For instance, Pauline is not allowed to put in a lift (elevator), which means that you can get your exercise going up and down the beautiful Adams spiral staircases. There are three of them with lovely Adams cupolas over the third floor.

The guest rooms are simply furnished in a contemporary style, with those on the back looking out over a very pretty little walled hillside garden with green lawns, flowers, a rowan tree, and ivy and various plantings. This little garden area is also used for outside dining when weather permits.

The guest rooms are equipped with color TV, radio, telephone, and makings for coffee or tea, and they all have private bathrooms. If you like, a continental breakfast can be served in your room.

P.M.'s Restaurant in the basement is open for breakfast, lunch, and dinner, and offers an extensive menu, featuring traditional Scottish dishes.

This is an informal and quiet little hotel, and if you're planning to attend the Edinburgh Festival in late August be sure to make your reservations months in advance.

THE ALBANY HOTEL, 39 Albany St., Edinburgh EHI 3QY. Tel.: 031-556 0397 or 0398. Telex: 727079. A 21-guestroom small in-town hotel, a few minutes' walk from the center of town. Restaurant is open for breakfast, lunch, and dinner; reservations necessary. Closed Christmas and New Year's. Convenient to buses and the downtown shopping district. Pauline Maridor, Proprietor. (See Index for rates.)

Directions: From Princes St., enter St. Andrews Sq. and turn right onto Queen St., then left on Dublin St. Take first right on Albany St. There is parking on the street or in a nearby car park.

THE OPEN ARMS HOTEL
Dirleton, East Lothian

"Our guests find that the Open Arms is perfectly suited to the visitor who wants to be near Edinburgh, but prefers to stay in the country."

Arthur Neil, the managing director of this village hotel, was explaining some of the interesting sights and activities of this corner of Scotland, which borders on both the North Sea and the Firth of Forth.

"We have eight golf courses within easy driving distance," he commented. "The sandy local soil enables the golfer to play in almost any weather, summer and winter. There are also many beaches and numerous beauty spots nearby."

We were enjoying a chat in the drawing room and he noticed that my attention was drawn to the ruins of the famous Dirleton Castle, just across the quiet village street.

"Our guests love to roam inside of those walls," he said. "It's one of the most famous ancient monuments in the British Isles. Time has dealt most graciously with the old 11th-century castle—it has taken on a great mellowness of age."

I had seen quite a few of the carefully kept guest rooms, each with its own private bath. Mr. Neil made a point of mentioning that service is available in the rooms at no extra cost.

We did have a moment or two to talk about some of the items on the menu, including a mussel and onion stew, something which I must confess I had never heard of until visiting the Open Arms.

Mr. Neil spoke at some length of his interest in encouraging the young people of Scotland to become involved in the hotel business; he has set up some standards for industry practice and training programs that I found most admirable.

Arthur Neil is also the proprietor of the Howard Hotel, located in a very pleasant residential area of Edinburgh. When telephoning either one or the other hotel, arrangements can be made for either place.

Incidentally, the symbol on the stationery and brochures for the Open Arms is a stylized version of a young lady in a colorful costume with long hair curling over her shoulders holding her arms out with such bountiful offerings as oranges, apples, pears, grapes, and other fruits and vegetables. The motto of the house is, "Where welcome ever smiles and farewell goes out sighing."

THE OPEN ARMS HOTEL, Dirleton, East Lothian. Tel.: (0620 85) Dirleton 241. U.S. reservations: 800-243-1806. A 7-guestroom village hotel, 20 mi. east of Edinburgh. Open every day in the year for breakfast, lunch, tea, and dinner. Within a short drive of many historic and scenic attractions and adjacent to active sports such as tennis, golf, fishing, walking, and riding. Arthur Neil, Managing Director. (See Index for rates.)

Directions: From Edinburgh: follow A1 to Berwick, using Musselburgh Bypass and watch for roundabout indicating A198 to No. Berwick on the left. The road passes through Gullane to Dirleton.

GREYWALLS
Gullane, East Lothian

Greywalls is the Americans' "golf club away from home." It's a mashie-niblick shot from the fairways and greens of the world-famous Muirfield golf links. The great and near-great of golfdom have played Muirfield, and the hotel guestbook includes such names as Palmer and Nicklaus.

To avoid any misunderstanding, the proprietor of Greywalls, Giles Weaver, points out that being in residence at the hotel does not automatically provide an introduction to Muirfield. "To play, one has to make one's own arrangements with the Secretary." So come prepared with letters from your home club and other documents—they take such things seriously at Muirfield. Not everyone can be accommodated.

So much for golf. I can assure any golfers that even if they cannot play Muirfield, the ten other courses in East Lothian contain some surprises and challenges.

As suggested earlier, Greywalls has a definite clublike atmosphere. Several of the drawing rooms are lined from floor to ceiling with books and have cheery fireplaces. The furniture is deep and comfortable, inviting conversation with new acquaintances.

The rather opulent guest rooms overlook the fairways and greens of Muirfield and the Firth of Forth beyond. On the opposite side of the hotel

there are some gorgeous gardens with many roses and beautiful delicate purple irises, which were in bloom during my visit.

Greywalls is a luxurious, highly reputable country house hotel. Guests are made to feel as if they are in a private home, and there is a casual and natural atmosphere.

The amenities are numerous, including fresh fruit and good books in the rooms, as well as telephones and TV's. There is a call button in both bedrooms and bathrooms to summon the bellman, if needed. Everything has been done, as the saying goes, "to the nines."

GREYWALLS (Pride of Britain), Duncur Rd., Gullane, East Lothian EH31 2EG. Tel.: (0620) 842 144. U.S. reservations: 800-323-7308. A 23-guestroom elegant country house hotel, immediately adjacent to the famous Muirfield golf links on the Firth of Forth and 19 mi. from Edinburgh. Breakfast, lunch, dinner served to non-residents. Open every day in the week. Closed during the winter. It is wise to check in advance for accommodations at any time. In the historically rich and beautiful natural area of scenic beauty in East Lothian. Golf and many other sports available nearby. Giles Weaver, Proprietor. (See Index for rates.)

Directions: From Edinburgh take the A1 through Musselburgh and then watch carefully on the left for A198, which leads eastward to Gullane. Turn left at the end of Gullane Village at the signpost; Greywalls is 300 yds. further on.

THE PHILIPBURN HOUSE HOTEL
Selkirk

It is possible to drive from London to Edinburgh in one day, but please don't do it. A much more enjoyable, maybe even a more *civilized,* way is to take it in easy stages and spend two nights at each stop along the way. This book is based on that premise.

After an enjoyable trip through the lovely Scottish Lowlands (I'm sure you will agree they have been misnamed), one of the stops might well be the Philipburn House in Selkirk, south of Edinburgh in the Borders.

This country house hotel is set in the heart of Sir Walter Scott country in the Dale of Ettrick and Yarrow. The original house was built in 1751 and the exterior has that wonderful feeling of Scottish austerity that at times can be most attractive.

The interior has obviously been well designed and coordinated, and the lounges, poolside restaurant (oh yes! I said poolside), and public rooms all have a wonderful glow about them, partially provided by some extremely attractive pine woodwork.

I was seated at one of the tables in the poolside restaurant, talking with Anne Hill, who with her husband, Jim, is the owner of Philipburn House, about what Americans would find entertaining and diverting while on a holiday in Scotland.

"Just imagine that it's morning now," Anne began, "and the sun is already warm—slanting over the nearby Border hills, and the scents of pine, heather, and peat are in the air. Your American friends can spend a day in the hills with Davy Fordyce, our resident guide, who is a sort of craggy person with a warm and friendly personality and a grand sense of humor. A walk with Davy provides a rich insight into the history and romance of the Borderland, the hills, the forests, the rivers, the lochs, the ancient towers, the poetry, the legends, the songs, and the rich wildlife that abounds in our territory. How's that for starters?"

I had to admit that I was already convinced. Other activities that provide a holiday atmosphere include horseback riding in all seasons (because there is an indoor riding school nearby), 200 miles of trout and salmon fishing, which can be arranged, garden and woodland walks, golf, swimming in the pool, quite a rarity for Scotland.

Each accommodation is different, including spacious country house bedrooms, family suites, poolside suites, and cottages. All of these look over the lawns and woodlands to the hills beyond. All have private' bathrooms and color television.

Anne continued, "We believe that dinner here is the highlight of the day and, perhaps after a last dip in the pool, I meet all the guests and help them with the difficult task of trying to choose from the menu items. We have such traditional dishes as freshly caught fish, as well as pheasant stuffed with raspberries and wrapped in bacon, roast pork stuffed with apple, fillet of sole, mallard duck, and venison served with poached pears, cherry port, and cranberry sauce."

During my stay I saw no other Americans, but lots of British families with children, and since my idea of travel is not only to look at the scenery but to meet the people, here's a wonderful opportunity to meet our British cousins as they enjoy a good holiday. By the way, there is much entertainment and diversion for children with provisions for serving them at teatime, giving their parents an opportunity to relax for a few moments. The Hills have three children of their own and believe that people need a holiday as much as, if not more than, the children, so they provide as many things as possible to entertain the younger generation.

THE PHILIPBURN HOUSE HOTEL, Selkirk TD7 5LS. Tel.: 0750 20747/21690. A 16-guestroom (private baths) country house hotel about an hour from Edinburgh. Breakfast, lunch, tea, and dinner served daily. Open year-round. Swimming pool on grounds. Ample facilities to amuse young people. Golf, fishing, shooting, and hill walking. Jim and Anne Hill, Proprietors. (See Index for rates.)

Directions: Locate Selkirk, south of Edinburgh. Coming from the south on A7, ignore the right turn in the middle of Selkirk and continue on over the river towards A708. A sign for Philipburn House is at a T-junction.

SHIELDHILL COUNTRY HOUSE HOTEL
Quothquan, Bigger, Lanarkshire

I was quite excited to begin my stay at Shieldhill Country House because it is one of the oldest, most historic structures I have had the opportunity to visit. The small Norman castle was built in 1199 and sits surrounded by the rich farmlands of the Clyde valley. Pathways wind through manicured grounds inviting guests to explore the woodlands and gardens.

Partners Christine Dunstan and Jack Greenwald still can't believe the hotel they first purchased in 1987 has gone through such a successful transformation. Christine says that when they first saw the house, "It was ghastly, quite ghastly!" Run as a hotel since 1959, Shieldhill had been operated by a variety of owners and had become rundown and rather seedy.

Christine is a Scotswoman who, with her scientist husband, moved to California in the 1960s and set up her own travel business after her three children were grown. She then took on another challenge: opening a successful bed and breakfast in Santa Barbara. This success motivated her to try her luck back in her native Scotland, and with her fellow travel colleague, Jack, she purchased Shieldhill.

Restoration began in earnest, and by the time decorating was completed to Christine's standards, they had spent a good deal of money. ". . . I wanted the hotel to have a really nice atmosphere," she said emphatically.

And the atmosphere is lovely, yet warm and relaxed. The eleven spacious guest rooms, all named after Scottish battles, are decorated with Laura Ashley wallpapers and fabrics. Four-poster beds, cozy chairs in sitting areas, and wonderful views of the countryside make the rooms inviting. All have private baths, some with Jacuzzis.

The four common rooms are also very comfortable. A cheerful fireplace warms the Oak Lounge and, named in honor of Christine's American home, the California Room has plants, easy chairs, and a great view over Clyde. The first-floor library is well stocked with books, and is a non-smoking room.

Chef Brian Graham is a master in the kitchen and offers guests elegant dinners emphasizing unusual flavor combinations. Supreme of guinea fowl, stuffed with fresh herbs from the hotel's garden, in a grapefruit and honey sauce is just one example. "I mainly use Scottish produce— salmon, venison, scallops, oysters, Oban mussels, and smoked trout," Brian explained. He is also familiar with the American palate and serves wonderful salads.

Shieldhill is close to golf courses, only an hour's drive to Edinburgh or Glasgow, and an easy drive to the enchanting Lake District, home of Beatrix Potter.

By the way, be sure to watch for Shieldhill's resident castle ghost, "The Grey Lady." Some say she still walks the halls.

SHIELDHILL COUNTRY HOUSE HOTEL, Quothquan, Biggar, Lanarkshire ML 12 6NA. Tel.: (U.S.) 011 44 899 20035; (Southern CA) 818-345-7704, Andrea; (Scotland) 0899 20035. An 11-guestroom (private baths) elegant, restored Norman castle in the Clyde Valley. Open Mar. thru Dec. 24. King and queen beds. Full breakfast included; lunch and dinner available. Centrally located for sightseeing. No pets. Christine Dunstan and Jack Greenwald, Proprietors; E. Jane Shillan, Manager. (See Index for rates.)

Directions: From Biggar, take B 7016 (Carnwath) 4 mi. Turn left onto Shieldhill Rd. Go 1½ mi. to hotel.

KIRROUGHTREE HOTEL
Newton Stewart, Wigtownshire

Patrick Heron, an industrial architect, built Kirroughtree House in 1719, and the hotel has developed quite a historic story since then. The name Kirroughtree is of Gaelic extraction. Originally, the estate consisted of 6,000 acres and stretched as far east as Palnure. In 1792, two extensions were made to Kirroughtree when a turret was added above the red dining room, and in 1890 the Regal suite was built as a library. And a bit of intrigue: in the 1890s three tunnels were discovered running from the hotel to Wigtown Bay, apparently used to smuggle goods from the coast over to Ireland.

The 18th-century mansion is furnished in the Rococo style. French doors that lead to the croquet lawn and terrace were originally the main entrance to the house when the lawn was used as a parking place for carriages. The oak-panelled lounge emphasizes comfort and relaxation. Famed poet Robert Burns used to recite poetry to the Heron family members and their guests from the staircase that rises from the lounge.

All twenty-two guest rooms have private baths and are individually decorated. Central heating, color television, and direct dial telephones assure comfort.

A full English breakfast and a four-course dinner, highlighting French cuisine, show the chefs at their best. Local produce and high quality poultry, seafood, and meats are a matter of course. I particularly appreciated the two separate dining rooms—one for smokers, and one for non-smokers. The wine list is varied, and the cocktail bar is a charming place to enjoy an aperitif.

Lawn tennis, pitch and putt, croquet or bowls may occupy your time, or play a round of free golf at two local courses. Fishing for salmon and trout is available on nearby lochs, and clay pigeon shooting can be arranged. Kirroughtree Hotel has something for everyone.

KIRROUGHTREE HOTEL, Newton Stewart, Wigtownshire DG8 6AN. Tel.: 0671-2141. A 22-guestroom (private baths) 18th-century mansion in beautiful Galloway. Open Feb. 4 to Jan. 4. All sized beds. Four-course dinner and breakfast included; lunch available. Free golf, fishing, clay pigeon shooting nearby. Children over 10 welcome. Pets by arrangement. Raymond Dilks, Proprietor; Andrew Donohoe, Manager. (See Index for rates.)

Directions: From Preswick to Ayr, then to Girvan and onto Newton Stewart, follow signs for Dumfries. The hotel signpost is on the main road.

KNOCKINAAM LODGE HOTEL
Portpatrick, Wigtownshire

Even now I can close my eyes and experience once again the sunset at Knockinaam. The setting is breathtaking, for the lodge sits in its own little naturally created row of rugged cliffs, and the broad expanse of lawns invites a walk toward the sea among the box hedges and the wild flowers and roses.

I was reminded of the coast of northern California—Carmel, Monterey, and even farther north. The entire experience of the sea, sky, and the rugged cliffs impressed itself upon me forever.

The owners of Knockinaam are two very attractive people, Connie and Marcel Frichot. They've done a perfectly splendid job of infusing the entire hotel and the staff with their enthusiasm.

Marcel puts it this way: "Most people come to Knockinaam for the peace and relaxation, but the guests who feel so inclined can walk, fish, play golf, visit the gardens at Logan and Castle Kennedy, or simply explore one of the few areas of Scotland as yet largely undiscovered."

Connie joins in, "Yes, I should say quite undiscovered, particularly by

North Americans. There are many larger, smarter hotels offering more facilities, but what we have is unique and we think that our guests enjoy the homey feeling, as well as the really serious attention given to our food. Furthermore, in these difficult times when everything is very expensive, you can still rely on a friendly smile and a good word. When guests arrive, we do our best to make them feel welcome. Their spirits are lifted when they catch the first glimpse of Knockinaam and its beautiful setting. Once inside, they need to relax, so we offer them something refreshing, explain to them how the telephone works, and carry their luggage upstairs."

I would hope that many of the readers of this book will break away from the standard practice of many first-time visitors to Scotland and make a real effort to visit this southwest corner. It is actually less than two hours' drive from Prestwick, and passengers on the night flight from North America can be here at Knockinaam between 10 and 11 a.m., allowing them an almost two-day stay, even though they may remain for only one night. The car ferry to Ireland is just a few moments away and not likely to be as crowded as some of the better-known terminals.

Knockinaam Lodge is a little out of the way, but it is a rewarding, relaxing experience and travelers should plan to spend a minimum of two nights.

KNOCKINAAM LODGE HOTEL (Pride of Britain), Portpatrick, Wigtownshire DG9 9AD. Tel.: 077-681-471. USA: 800-323-3602. A 10-guestroom (private baths) seaside country house hotel on the extreme western end of the Scottish Lowlands. Breakfast, lunch, and dinner served. Open Easter to Jan. Excellent walking, fishing, golfing, swimming, and driving nearby. Convenient for a first overnight stop after landing at Prestwick. Connie and Marcel Frichot, Proprietors. (See Index for rates.)

Directions: Portpatrick is 119 mi. from Carlisle (A75) and 101 mi. from Glasgow (A77). From Stranraer, travel south on the A77 toward Port-

patrick and 3 mi. after the village of Lochans, turn left at the main hotel sign.

MARINE HOTEL
Troon, Ayrshire

If you are flying in or out of Prestwick Airport, the Marine Hotel can provide sensible accommodations either the night before your departure or the day of your arrival.

Actually, the building is rather impressive for its size alone. It's a big, multistoried, red sandstone building that provides holiday accommodations for Britons and their Continental neighbors who enjoy the game of golf. It stands between the Royal Troon and the Portland golf courses and I saw many golfing holiday-makers arriving and departing, complete with their golf bags.

There are two restaurants—the Fairways Restaurant, overlooking the bay and golf courses, and Crosbie's Brasserie, a lively restaurant/bar offering imaginative and inexpensive meals from morning until the "wee small hours." There is also an impressive sports and leisure club, available free of charge to guests staying in the hotel.

Bedrooms are comfortable and all have private bathrooms and the other British hotel amenities.

MARINE HOTEL, Troon, Ayrshire KA10 6HE. Tel.: (0292) 31-4444. A large, conventional hotel (private baths) a few minutes from Prestwick Airport. Open year-round. Breakfast, lunch, and dinner served daily. Quite convenient to many nearby golf courses. Located in Robert Burns country; his cottage at Alloway and other Burns memorabilia nearby. (See Index for rates.)

Directions: Troon is to the west of M6. Follow any of the roads to the middle of town and make inquiries.

DRIVING IN THE SCOTTISH HIGHLANDS

Motoring in the Highlands is marvelous. It is also very different. Fortunately, by the time I had reached this incredibly beautiful country I had quite a few days of driving on the left side of the road so that my reactions were good.

The entire experience from the broad expanse of the extraordinary scenery to the minutiae of the individual plants, flowers, trees, houses, rocks, animals, and clouds make it sensational backroading.

Like the fjord country of Norway, the White Mountains of New Hamp-

shire, the Grand Canyon of Arizona, and the Himalayas of Tibet, the Scottish Highlands have a wildness completely their own. One of the qualities I like is that, with all of the ruggedness, there is a certain gentleness, because almost everything is covered with green grass and heather. It is only the mountain crags that are without vegetation.

Sheep and cattle in the road are a way of life. The roads in the Highlands are so curvy and twisty that when I took a moment to look at a loch or a glen I frequently found myself confronted by a cow in the road.

Much of the time I was traveling on roads only wide enough to accommodate one car. However, they were all paved and in good shape. There are turnouts every 50 or 100 yards, and the courtesy of the road determines which car going in the opposite direction should pull over and wait for the other car. The question naturally comes as to what happens when two cars meet in the middle between two turn-off places? My experience was that everyone was quite considerate and very frequently there would be two cars backing up, each expecting to allow the other car to continue. Cars traveling at a leisurely pace also pull over to the side, allowing those who are traveling faster to pass. Ninety per cent of the time great courtesy is shown by all concerned and everyone acknowledges with a friendly wave of the hand.

Quite a few Scottish innkeepers will hold a telephone reservation only until five o'clock in the afternoon. Some of the popular American credit cards are only good in the more luxurious hotels, although traveler's checks are accepted. I carried British traveler's checks and had no problems. I was never able to buy gasoline (petrol) with anything except cash.

Watch out for bank holidays; change money or traveler's checks the Friday before; I got caught on a few Mondays with no pounds sterling.

There is a lot of sunshine and also a lot of "Scottish mist." I was glad to have a lightweight nylon jacket with a hood.

GLEDDOCH HOUSE
Langbank, Renfrenshire

Gleddoch House is a charming Scottish country house with wonderful guest rooms named after fabulous Scottish birds and is located only twenty minutes from the city of Glasgow. Yet it seems worlds away. The original house was built in 1927 for ship builder Sir James Lithgow. The building is similar to a French chateau, painted white, with exposed stone framing around the windows and doors.

Many of the magnificent pictures and furnishings originally belonged to the Lithgows. Combined with contemporary pieces, old and new blend together to create a homey atmosphere. The light and spacious common rooms display wonderful carved oak panelling, astragalled windows, working fireplaces, and molded plasterwork. Fresh flowers enhance the rooms during the summer, and doors open onto the terrace or garden during warm weather.

The thirty-three guest rooms are equipped with television, radio, tea and coffee facilities, trouser presses, and leather-topped desks. The Ptarmigan Room has a great, high-powered telescope and a four-poster bed. All rooms have private baths.

The hotel bar offers a wide selection of whiskies, including a blend created for the hotel. Formerly the billiards room, the bar is lined with green baize and sports branch water pumped up from Gleddoch's own spring.

Head chef Charles Price uses local fresh fish, game, meats, and vegetables from the hotel's garden to create superb meals. Rattan-backed carvers, floor to ceiling windows, and linen-draped tables make the dining room relaxed and comfortable. I enjoyed a wonderful dinner of breast of duck, cooked pink and served in a sherry and tomato essence. The wine list is extensive and includes a fine selection of clarets and ports.

Guests at the hotel have access to the Gleddoch Club where they can enjoy an eighteen-hole golf course, sauna, pool, billiards table, and squash court, all only a two-minute walk from the hotel. Pony trekking is also available.

GLEDDOCH HOUSE, Langbank, Renfrenshire PA14 6YE. Tel.: 047-54-711. A 33-guestroom (private baths) traditional Scottish country house 15 minutes from Glasgow, and 1 hour from the Preswick airport. Open all year, except a few days at Christmas and New Year. King, double, and twin beds. Full breakfast included in tariff; lunch and gourmet dinner available. Situated on 250 acres overlooking the River Clyde and Loch Lomond Hills. Squash, billiards, sauna, and lounge bar available on grounds. Pets by arrangement. Smoking in public rooms only. Gleddoch Hotels, Proprietors; C. J. Longden, Manager. (See Index for rates.)

Directions: Take M8 motorway toward Glasgow. Take the B789 Langbank/Houston exit. Follow signs to the left and then right after ½ mi., the hotel driveway is signed on the left.

THE ISLE OF COLONSAY

Anyone looking for a truly "different" travel experience, where there is practically no commercial intrusion and where it's possible to feel the thrill of being alone and secluded, will enjoy the Isle of Colonsay.

Although visitors are very much encouraged to come to Colonsay and to enjoy its special attractions, it does not offer any synthetic entertainments. There are no tourist traps, no amusement arcades, or fun fairs. Nor are there day-trippers, because the ferry only runs twice a week. Caravans (camping vehicles) are not allowed, and only educational and scientific organizations are given permission to camp in tents.

There is one general store, used by all of the islanders. The arrival of the ferry is an Event, and guests of the Isle of Colonsay Hotel invariably hurry down to the dock to watch the unloading.

However, for anyone who is content with a holiday built around the natural amenities and social life of a small Scottish island, Colonsay has plenty to offer. In the summer, there are several beaches for bathing and picnicking. The walking is superlative along the beaches, roads, and paths, and among the rocks and cliffs and several caves, which were probably inhabited as long as six thousand years ago. There is much of interest to the archeologist and antiquarian, including various standing stones and ancient ruins.

Colonsay is the larger of two islands in the Outer Hebrides, joined at low tide by a narrow sandy beach called the Strand. The second is Oronsay Island, which lays claim to a most important event in history—it is said to have been where St. Columba landed on his way to Iona from Ireland in the middle of the 6th century.

ISLE OF COLONSAY HOTEL
Isle of Colonsay, Argyll

This story began in Ireland a few years ago when I first met Kevin and Christa Byrne, who are now the hoteliers at the Isle of Colonsay Hotel. At that time, these two attractive young people, graduates of Trinity College in Dublin, had enthusiastically embarked on a career of hotelkeeping.

A short time later I received a letter from Kevin, who is a tall red-bearded man with a fascinating gift of conversation, to the effect that they were moving to the Isle of Colonsay to take over the hotel.

So I found myself on the ferry from Oban, arriving at the wharf, where the selfsame Kevin was waiting in a former London taxicab to drive me to his small hotel, in sight of the ferry dock.

Kevin immediately enveloped me with his enthusiasm. "I'm glad you're coming here now," he said. "We've put things in beautiful shipshape order, but it's been a lot of work. Christa has really been magnificent, being both mother and hotelier. Ah, here we are." He pulled into the small parking lot, scattering some of the ubiquitous sheep.

Kevin was right, the additions were shipshape and the accommodations were clean, comfortable, and, without a doubt, cordial. Furthermore, he

had a very good chef, and the menu included Colonsay oysters and other local seafood, as well as hearty and tasty native lamb.

Guests become involved with each other almost immediately, exchanging experiences at the end of the first day and joining forces on subsequent days. There's ample opportunity to meet the islanders, because the hotel has the only pub on the island.

I spent almost a whole day on a walking excursion of one portion of the island with two American women. We climbed over fences (legally) and followed rocky roads over cliffs and moorland, sandy beaches, and lily-filled lochs, rhododendron woods, cultivated lands, farms, and hills. It was a day to be remembered.

During one of my long conversations with Kevin, I remarked that someone ought to write a book about Colonsay.

"Somebody already has," he replied with great glee, whereupon he presented me with a copy of a book entitled *The Crofter and the Laird,* by John McPhee (Farrar, Straus and Giroux, New York). Author McPhee visited the island in the late 1960s because he, like so many other McPhees, McAfees, and other permutations of the name, have ever been drawn back to the land of their ancestors. The people he wrote about still live on the island, including the schoolmistress with whom I visited on the very last day of school.

A recent letter from Kevin told a tale of the extensive improvements he and Christa have accomplished since my last visit. All the double guest rooms now have private bath/showers, and there are three new self-catering chalets that will be suitable for families. Along with a number of other amenities they have added to make their guests more comfortable, they have also developed some services and facilities for visiting yachtsmen.

Because the railroad station in Oban is right next to the ferry dock, it's possible to reach Colonsay using public transportation from any point in England and Scotland. A chartered boat ride around the islands is also a singular experience. Automobiles are not necessary, and the hotel has bicycles.

Please check all sailing schedules and other important details with Kevin Byrne when making bookings.

I believe I've presented Colonsay as it really is. Incidentally, the hotel is the only such accommodation on the island. If it's "your kind of place," you'll love it.

ISLE OF COLONSAY HOTEL, Colonsay Island, Argyll PA61 7YP. Tel.: (095 12) 316. An 11-guestroom (mostly private bath/showers) village inn located on an island 37 mi. from Oban. Full central heating. Open every day in the year. Breakfast, lunch, tea, and dinner served. Exceptional hill and muir walks. Bicycles and boats available. Primitive and challenging golf course; fishing. Kevin and Christa Byrne, Resident Proprietors. (See Index for rates.)

Directions: Colonsay is, with the aid of the railroad and the ferry, available to all parts of Britain. The train station is a few steps from the ferry dock. All sailings are from Oban (Railway Pier). Check with hotel for days and hours of sailing (2½ hrs.); meal service provided on board. Cars may be left on mainland; really not needed on island.

ARDANAISEIG
Kilchrenan, Argyll

Ardanaiseig is in Argyll, in the heart of the mountainous region, over which the Clan Campbell held undisputed sway for centuries. This gracious mansion, built in 1834, was until recently a family home.

The first owner was so inspired by the setting of his new house on the shore of Loch Awe that he began planting a great garden. A number of conifers and other rare trees still stand. The grounds are replete with rhododendrons and azaleas.

The guest rooms have big, chintzy chairs, polished tables, and fresh flowers, and the entire atmosphere is warm and relaxed. Each bedroom has its own bathroom.

The hotel has its own private pier on the loch and boats from which to fish or explore and picnic on the many islands not too far away. There is a fishing beat on the River Awe and various hill lochs for the serious fisherman.

Ardanaiseig is a most pleasurable experience.

ARDANAISEIG (Pride of Britain), Kilchrenan, by Taynuilt, Argyll. Tel.: (08663) 333. U.S. reservations: 800-323-3602. An impressive Scottish country house hotel, just a short distance from Oban. Breakfast, lunch, and dinner served daily. Two-night minimum stay. Closed mid-Oct. to Easter. Woodland trails, croquet, tennis court, and clay pigeon trap. Michael and Frieda Yeo, Resident Directors. (See Index for rates.)

Directions: Take A85 east from Oban and watch for hotel sign.

TAYCHREGGAN HOTEL
Kilchrenan, by Taynuilt, Argyll

Even if you will never visit Taychreggan Hotel, please write the proprietors, John and Tove Taylor, and tell them I suggested you ask for the brochure of the hotel. With many excellent full-color photographs and an engaging personal description, it is one of the best I've seen anywhere. As I was on my way from Connel across A85 toward a luncheon at Creggans Inn, I saw a sign for Taychreggan Hotel leading down a country road. It was just on a whim that I decided to see what was at the end of the road.

What I found was the little village of Kilchrenan, a cluster of houses and a post office, and a little farther on, the Taychreggan Hotel.

It is situated on the shore of Loch Awe, which, at twenty-four miles, is the longest fresh-water loch in Scotland.

The older part of the building was originally a drovers' inn. In subsequent years, substantial additions were made to the old stone house and further imaginative construction has created a three-sided cobbled courtyard. The fourth side of this very sunny environment is a glassed-in passageway connecting the old house with the new.

I was quite disappointed that Mr. and Mrs. Taylor were not in residence during my brief visit, but I was much impressed with the cordiality of the staff.

There are traditional bedrooms, as well as some that have been more recently created. The decor is plain and simple; good straight colors and pine. The overall effect is one of light and warmth.

One of the great advantages of staying at the Taychreggan is the opportunity to meet and perhaps engage the services of the local ghillie for a fishing guide. Of course he knows all of the waters and islands of

Loch Awe and is ready for serious fishing with a generous dollop of humorous anecdotes.

I was not there for dinner, but the menu included Scottish as well as Continental main courses. My whim to visit Taychreggan turned out to be a good one and I would recommend that travelers plan on spending two nights, not only to enjoy the hotel, but also the many outdoor diversions within a few miles, at most, of the hotel.

A departing young American couple were enraptured with Taychreggan and full of regret that they had engaged a room for only one night.

Reader Comment: "Thank you so much for leading us to this delightful spot. Our room was charming, with matching wallpaper and curtains— there were even matching padded coat hangers. Plants and flowers were everywhere."

TAYCHREGGAN HOTEL, Kilchrenan, by Taynuilt, Argyll PA35 1HQ. Tel.: (08663) Kilchrenan 211. U.S. reservations: 800-243-1806. A 17-guestroom (14 with private bathrooms) lochside hotel in the western Highlands. Open from Easter to mid-Oct. Rates include dinner. Breakfast, lunch, tea, and dinner served. Riding, sailing, fishing, shooting, walking, gardens, and historic places, as well as many day trips. John and Tove Taylor, Proprietors. (See Index for rates.)

Directions: From A85 turn off at Taynuilt onto B845 for Kilchrenan. Follow B845 to the village; the hotel is just beyond.

ISLE OF ERISKA HOTEL
Ledaig, Connel, Argyll

Robin Buchanan-Smith leaned back in his chair and raised his eyes to heaven. Because he is the Reverend Buchanan-Smith, it occurred to me that this particular attitude was not unusual for him at all. However, this time he was pondering a question I had put to him about his innkeeping philosophy.

He returned for the moment to more terrestrial environments. "I believe that it's 'taking care of people.' Looking after people means personal attention, and I drill this into our small, youngish staff at every opportunity.

"My wife, Sheena, and I keep an eye on everything, and fortunately, the staff is quite dedicated. It's really like a house party. Eriska combines the two oft-forgotten ideals of the modern world—Romanticism and Realism."

He paused for a moment to add a dollop of cream to my cup of tea and continued, "One of our guests stayed here and then went back to California, saying that he had seen everything. He was referring to the fact that there was a British prime minister seated in our parlor, smoking a nine-inch cigar and reading Jane Austen. The prime minister was Harold Macmillan."

Eriska's setting on the shores of the Firth of Lorne is superb. It is on a small island one mile by half a mile, and is reached by a private bridge — this little bridge is important, because it does create a marvelous feeling of being set apart.

On this sylvan island, the hotel stands in the middle of a lovely green lawn dotted with maple and copper beech trees, and accented with rhododendron, wild orchids, sea pinks, and irises.

The building is Scottish Victorian baronial, and true to its tradition, has turrets and battlements from which there are additional and revealing views of the mountains and firths. I was intrigued to learn that there were trekking ponies available from stables right on the hotel grounds, as well as tennis and fishing. There is also water skiing and wind surfing on the firth. The English-style croquet, played with great politeness, was for blood. The feeling of being on a Highland estate is heightened by the presence of roe deer, badgers, heron, and even, on occasion, golden eagles. The milk and cream are from a herd of Jersey cows and there are well-tended vegetable gardens.

The interior is characterized by log fires, wood-paneled walls, and elegantly decorated plaster ceilings. The drawing room where the P.M. smoked his cigar, enjoys a view of the lawn and firth. The guest rooms all have their own private bathrooms.

At tea that afternoon, I joined four other Americans who had just returned from an excursion to the islands of Mull and Iona.

Oddly enough, it was Jim Mellow from St. Louis who first recommended that I visit the Isle of Eriska. He particularly made note of the roast pheasant and the breakfasts that would have pleased Pangloss.

Later, as I was walking on the shore of the firth, I caught a snatch of conversation from a young hand-holding couple . . . "This is the most romantic place I could ever imagine. It far exceeds my greatest expectations."

Reader Comment: "When we first arrived it was a rainy, damp day, and we had tea and scones by the fire. It was delightful."

ISLE OF ERISKA HOTEL, Ledaig, Connel, Argyll PA37 1SD. Tel.: (063 172) Ledaig 205. A 16-guestroom elegant country house hotel on an island in Scotland's western Highlands, 100 mi. from Glasgow. Open early April to end of Nov. Lunch, dinner served to non-residents. Fishing, riding, croquet, tennis, water-skiing, wind-surfing, beach walking on grounds. Speed boat excursions around the island. Sailing, golf nearby.

Stunning views of Loch Linnhe and the Atlantic Ocean. Many castles and places of historic and natural interest nearby. Robin and Sheena Buchanan-Smith, Resident Owners. (See Index for rates.)

Directions: From Glasgow, take A82 past Loch Lomond to Tyndrum, then A85 to Oban, turning left onto Fort William Rd. at Connel on A828. Cross Connel Bridge, proceed 3 mi. to Benderloch and look for hotel signs.

ARDSHEAL HOUSE
Kentallen of Appin, Argyll

"That is Loch Linnhe, and beyond are the hills of Morvern. Strontian Pass leads out to a point that is about as far west as you can get on the British mainland."

Bob Taylor, resplendent in kilts, and I were standing in the window of the billiard room of Ardsheal House looking down across the broad meadow to the loch and the mountains beyond. We were enjoying the absolutely magnificent show being put on by nature, presumably for our special benefit. Overhead, the deeply stratified clouds were parting and closing, allowing unexpected bars of brilliant sunshine to spotlight the hills and the loch, a sight truly beyond words.

He continued my geography and history lesson: "This is an area known for bloody battles and feuds among the Highland clans," he said. "There

are many tales of Bonnie Prince Charlie. In fact, this house, built in 1545 by the Stewarts of Appin, was totally sacked by the Duke of Cumberland during the uprisings of 1745. What is here was rebuilt on the old foundations in 1760. Later sections were built in 1814, and this wing with the billiard room, in 1850.

"Ardsheal plays an important part in Robert Louis Stevenson's *Kidnapped*. It was only a mile or so from here where the infamous murder of Appin took place, providing Stevenson with a great deal of material for his book."

It comes as a surprise to many of the guests at Ardsheal House that Bob, a Princeton graduate, and his wife, Jane, and their sons, Brigham and Jason, are from the United States. Previously they had been pursuing successful careers in banking and advertising, but decided that they wanted to try something as a family that provided them with a greater opportunity for expression—a broader challenge.

To make a long story short, on a trip to Scotland they discovered this historic house, and the family decision was made to convert it to a country house hotel. They are at Ardsheal from April to November. In the winter, they return to their home in New Paltz, New York.

The reception hall is paneled in oak and there's usually a cheery fire blazing on the old stone hearth. A glassed-in porch on the lochside is made for watching sunsets and seals (or monsters) or for enjoying the peace and beauty of the Scottish Highlands. The dining room faces the garden and another glassed-in extension brings the flowers and sky even closer.

All of the spacious guest rooms have private baths, and all the beds are provided with electric blankets.

"Because we are Americans, we can appreciate the fact that our overseas guests frequently enjoy lots of activity. We have our own tennis court, and there's fishing, sailing, and boating, as well as horseback riding nearby. We try to persuade Americans to enjoy the British sport of hill walking and I think we've got some of the best starting right at our doorstep."

At dinner that evening, which included Loch Linnhe salmon, I made the acquaintance of Ray and Mary Rendall from Northumberland, and we discovered that Ray and I had both been in India at the same time and had a few "old soldier" stories to exchange. They had been there for a three- or four-day holiday, and Mary was particularly complimentary about the menu, which has received a glowing review by Craig Claiborne in the *New York Times*.

Ardsheal House is just off A82, the principal road from Oban to Inverness, a few miles south of Fort William. Due west is Mallaig and the Isle of Skye.

There's a postscript to my pleasant stay at Ardsheal House, which took place the following winter, when Bob and Jane drove from New Paltz and I drove from the Berkshires, all meeting at the Redcoat's Return Inn in Tannersville, New York. It was a most enjoyable reunion and another chance to talk about Ardsheal House. It would be just another month when the Taylors would be heading back to their beloved Kentallen of Appin, enthusiastically looking forward to another season. The Scottish adventure would continue.

ARDSHEAL HOUSE, Kentallen of Appin, Argyll PA38 4BX. Tel.: 063-174-227. A 13-guestroom country house lochside hotel overlooking the spectacular view of the western Scottish Highlands. Approx. 17 mi. south of Fort William. Breakfast, lunch, tea, and dinner served every day in the year from Easter through Oct. Minimum stay of 2 nights with advance booking. Tennis on the grounds. Hill walking, beach walking, sailing, riding, pony trekking, fishing, and golf nearby. No credit cards. Jane and Bob Taylor, Proprietors. (See Index for rates.)

Directions: From Glasgow take the A82 to Crianlarich. Continue on A82 to roundabout at Ballachulish Bridge; then follow A828 toward Connel and Oban. Ardsheal is about 4 mi. on the right. Well signposted.

INVERLOCHY CASTLE
Fort William, Inverness-shire

In Scotland, the word "castle" means a great many different things. Sometimes it means a fortress that may have withstood many attacks. However, Inverlochy Castle is a totally benign place, built by the first Lord Abinger in 1863 near the site of a 13th-century fortress. Turrets and battlements aside, it resembles a sumptuous Italian villa or an elegant French chateau.

The two-story-high great hall has lavishly frescoed ceilings, large oil paintings, and opulent furnishings; all dominated by a crystal chandelier that seems suspended in space. Inverlochy played host to Queen Victoria in 1873, and in her diary she wrote, "I never saw a lovelier or more romantic spot."

The dining room and other drawing rooms, as well as the unusually large guest rooms, are all beautifully decorated and fitted with fine, elaborately fashioned furniture.

Such a castle should have a princess to preside over it, and indeed there is one: Mrs. Grete Hobbs. This attractive, sophisticated woman is the owner, and is originally from Copenhagen. We talked about what is involved in providing hotel accommodations in a castle.

"I've been fortunate enough to travel to a great many different countries in the world. And this house has many things I found most attractive while traveling."

The house and grounds of Inverlochy Castle are entirely private, and are not open to non-residents for viewing.

INVERLOCHY CASTLE (Relais et Chateaux de Campagne), Fort William, Inverness-shire PH33 6SN. Tel.: (0397) 2177. Telex: 776229. A luxurious 13-guestroom private castle hotel, about 3 mi. north of Fort William. Dinner provisions for non-residents are limited. The western Highlands scenery and other impressive centers of natural beauty are within a pleasant drive. Tennis and fishing are available at the castle; golf, riding, and walking are available nearby. Open from March to Nov. Mrs. Grete Hobbs, Proprietor. (See Index for rates.)

Directions: Inverlochy Castle is 3 mi. from the center of Fort William on the A82, and approx. 6 mi. from Spean Bridge. The entrance is set back from the road, but is well signposted.

KNOCKIE LODGE
Whitebridge, Inverness-Shire

Built as a hunting lodge in 1789, Knockie Lodge is located in a beautiful, secluded area 800 feet above Loch Ness. Birch, pine, and larch trees guard this bit of heaven, an oasis hidden from civilization. Sheep bleat in nearby pastures, and you just might awaken to the crow of an early-rising rooster. Ian and Brenda Milward opened Knockie Lodge in 1983 because, according to Ian, "It felt like a private house and we wanted guests to feel they were staying in our private house, not a hotel."

Ian is quite friendly and welcomes guests in the proper attire of the area, a kilt. The lodge is attractively furnished in comfortable antiques highlighted by the Milwards's personal collectibles. Logs and peat burn in the drawing room fireplace, and guests are welcome to a "help yourself" bar that harbors a fine selection of malts and an extensive wine list.

Dinner is a wonderful five-course affair, served by candlelight, featuring a special menu every evening. I particularly enjoyed my dinner of roast guinea fowl with bacon rolls and bread sauce, which was accompanied by red cabbage, roast potatoes, and a mixed green salad. Dessert included blackcurrant and mint parfait, or a luscious plum and sour cream tart with brown sugar and cinnamon.

The ten guest rooms are all centrally heated and have private baths. While furnished with antiques, the rooms are modern and very comfortable. Each room has a direct dial telephone.

The area around the lodge offers a wide choice of outdoor activities. The abundance of lochs give even the most choosy fisherman a challenge, or you can stay put and fish in the lodge's private lochs. Deer hunting is available by arrangement, or for the nonsportsman, wildlife abounds for photographic studies, sailing excursions can be arranged, and even pony trekking is possible. An eighteen-hole golf course is within an hour's drive, or chalk up a cue in the lodge's new billiards room.

Knockie Lodge is a relaxing, charming place to stay while in the Highlands. A number of historic spots are within an easy drive, and the Milwards are happy to help you plan your day.

KNOCKIE LODGE, Whitebridge, Inverness-Shire, IVI 2UP. Tel.: 045-63-276. A 10-guestroom (private baths) comfortable lodge located high above Loch Nan Lann, close to Loch Ness. Open April thru Oct. King, double, and twin beds. Full Scottish breakfast and dinner included; bar lunch available. Close to historic points of interest. Fishing, golf, hiking, sailing, pony trekking. Pets by arrangement. Ian and Brenda Milward, Proprietors. (See Index for rates.)

Directions: Take A82 Glasgow/Inverness Rd. as far as Fort Augustus. Then B862 for 8 mi. until Knockie Lodge sign directs you to the left.

DUNAIN PARK HOTEL
Inverness

The Scottish Highlands have always had a particularly romantic pull for me. With heather-clad, windswept stretches of headlands, lovely lochs surrounded by forests, and the many historic points of interest, the Highlands offer exceptional opportunities for the traveler.

Ideally situated for touring the Highlands, Dunain Park Hotel sits on six secluded acres of garden and woodland just two and one-half miles from the capital of the Highlands, Inverness. The Georgian country house was originally built as a shooting lodge in the 1700s. Since then an extension has been added in the Victorian style.

I was pleasantly surprised to be welcomed by the owners of the hotel, Ann and Edward Nicoll, rather than a management team. Ann and Edward consider the Dunain Park their home. "Ann left dairy farming and I gave up teaching so we could live in this country setting and work where we live," Edward commented as the three of us had tea and homemade shortbread in the luxurious lounge. A log fire spit and crackled, warming the leather settees and brocaded chaise lounges.

The lounge shares a spectacular view with the dining room of the Caledonian Canal. Each evening drinks are served in the lounge while guests are given a choice of the evening's menu. As the chef, Ann laughingly told me, "I cook almost twenty-four hours a day!" Breads are baked daily, and Ann prides herself on her dessert buffet. Along with local venison, grouse, pheasant, seafood, and Scottish beef and lamb, seasonal vegetables are picked fresh from the hotel's walled garden. A good selection of wines, liqueurs, brandy, vintage ports, and malt whiskies is available.

After dinner I returned to my room to read up on "Nessie," the famous monster of Loch Ness. The hotel has six guest rooms in the main house and two additional suites in the converted coach house. All have private baths, telephone, color television, and radio. My room had an impressive four-poster bed, and was decorated with traditional antiques and oil paintings. For guests' relaxation, an indoor swimming pool, complete with wave machine and sauna, is offered.

Over a full Scottish breakfast in the morning, I made my plans for sightseeing and questioned Edward on the *real* truth about "Nessie." He just smiled, and with a wink suggested that I might be one of the lucky ones to see her. Did I? I'll never tell.

DUNAIN PARK HOTEL, Inverness IV3 6JN. Tel.: 0463-230512. An 8-guestroom (private baths) secluded country house in the Highlands, only 2½ mi. from Inverness. Open all year. All sized beds. Breakfast included; lunch and dinner available. Loch Ness, Culloden Battlefield, Cawdor Castle, Fort George nearby. Salmon and trout fishing, hiking, golf, indoor swimming pool. Ann and Edward Nicoll, Proprietors. (See Index for rates.)

Directions: Located on the left hand side of A82 Rd. from Inverness to Loch Ness and Fort William. 1 mi. from town boundary.

INVERNESS AND LOCH NESS

When I asked Alistair MacPherson of the Loch Ness House Hotel about the famous Loch Ness monster, a beatific smile crossed his handsome Scottish face.

"Most people know two things about Inverness. It's where the best English is spoken and where the Loch Ness monster is a neighbor. I've never seen the monster myself, but it's often been described as the world's greatest mystery. It was first recorded by the 7th-century monk Adamnan. He related how it attacked one of Saint Columba's party, only to be deterred by an invocation from Columba himself. From that day the monster has never harmed another human being. Of course, it's the subject of serious scientific study by expeditions all over the world. Everything from space-age technology to yellow submarines have been used to track down this creature. Much of the equipment and many of the results can be seen at the Loch Ness Centre in nearby Drumnadrochit."

For centuries Inverness has stood at the crossroads of the Highlands, the historical starting point and goal of travelers in the North. Now improved roads and new bridges bring much of the Highlands within a few hours' drive.

Inverness is a good center for traveling in all four directions and visiting the many castles and historic spots. For example, a monument at nearby Culloden marks the site of the last pitched battle on British soil. It was fought in 1746 between the Duke of Cumberland's forces and the Jacobites, marking the end of Bonnie Prince Charlie's struggle for the throne. There's also Cawdor Castle, which has strong associations with Macbeth *and Shakespeare.*

The wild Highlands to the north and west have always held a strong attraction for visitors to Scotland.

THE CLIFTON HOTEL
Nairn, Nairnshire

J. Gordon Macintyre, the hotelier at the Clifton Hotel in Nairn, is a man of many gifts. Among them is the mastery of the simple declarative sentence. With this in mind I'm going to use his prose to describe this hotel. Let me say that Mr. Macintyre himself is a very elegant gentleman, and on the occasion of my meeting him he was wearing an absolutely smashing beige suit with champagne-colored shoes. As we toured all of the guest rooms and public rooms I realized that the decorations, furnishings, and ambience were really an expression of his individuality. But enough of that. Let's hear what he has to say.

"The Clifton Hotel, with only grass and trees between it and the sea, overlooks the whole stretch of the Moray Firth and commands an unrivalled view of the Ross-shire and Sutherland hills. The beach, tennis courts, and swimming baths are only two minutes' walk away, and the hotel is equidistant to both golf courses. We can obtain fishing, shooting, and riding by arrangement, given advance notice.

"Many things go towards the unique atmosphere of this small, charming, and very personal hotel—a Victorian house, most decoratively revived and carefully restored, abounding with flowers, paintings, colour, and an interesting collection of objets d'art. A sense of the theatrical, backed up by cleanliness, really good food, and masses of hot water, make this an ideal establishment in which to relax and unwind from the stresses of modern living.

"The hotel has only sixteen guest rooms on two floors. Each room is individually designed and decorated and all have private baths. We have several rooms with really *enormous* beds. The public rooms include a writing room, a television room, a bar, and the drawing room, where a log fire is always burning, except in the very warmest weather. The restaurant is the cornerstone of our cardinal reputation. Also, for the last three years we have served lunch in the small but exquisite Green Room, with a menu that features fish and seafood along with other dishes.

"During the winter months, from October to May, a number of plays, concerts, and recitals are staged in the hotel.

"The evening meal includes six to eight main courses. The dining room also serves as a theatre and recital hall during the winter months."

Believe me, the Clifton Hotel in Nairn is one of the most singular experiences in the British Isles.

THE CLIFTON HOTEL, Viewfield Street, Nairn. Tel.: (0667) Nairn 53119. A 16-guestroom (mostly private baths) elegant hotel in a resort town on the shores of the Moray Firth. Lunch and dinner served daily. Open from late Feb. to early Nov. Conveniently located to enjoy day trips to the northern and western Highlands, as well as golf and recreation nearby. J. Gordon Macintyre, Proprietor. (See Index for rates.)

Directions: Nairn is on the A93, which runs east and west between Inverness and Banff. The best procedure is to make inquiries in the center of town for the Clifton Hotel.

THE NORTHEAST CORNER OF SCOTLAND

Scotland isn't really very large, but there is so much to see! For instance, the entire Grampian region and in particular the northeast corner is tucked away from the busy through routes. Looking toward the sea, it's virtually undiscovered by visitors. It's a land of fishermen and farmers, with fishing villages nestling under the cliffs along the coast and small farm villages and market towns dotting its rolling interior. There are miles of peaceful main roads and quiet little side roads for excursions and picnics.

Robert Bruce was here and it was the home of many a character in fact and fiction. There are many castles, great and small houses, gardens, and countryside areas, many maintained by the National Trust for Scotland.

I visited this area in late June, which is supposed to be the threshold of the "high season." I found it uncrowded, very comfortable, and largely undiscovered by the overseas visitor to Britain.

For room rates and last time for dinner orders, see Index.

PITTODRIE HOUSE HOTEL
Pitcaple, Grampian, Aberdeenshire

I hope that everybody who visits Scotland will take a few extra days to spend in Aberdeenshire. This area to the north of Aberdeen and south of the Firth of Moray has the largest group of ancient castles and historic houses in Scotland, and the rolling countryside with its busy farms, sweeping horizons, vast meadows and woodlands is a joyful experience. Along the coastline are old fishing villages where hearty Scotsmen still ply their ancient endeavors.

The Pittodrie House Hotel is wonderfully located to visit all of Aberdeenshire. It sits in an estate of 3,000 acres of mixed arable, forest, and hill land, with the peak of Bennachie providing a dramatic backdrop.

In June, the private road leading through the parkland to the hotel was lined with Queen Anne's lace and the rhododendrons were in glorious profusion. I emerged from the forest, following the sweeping curve to the left, and there sat Pittodrie House, dominated by a three-and-a-half-story, vine-covered tower with additions on both sides.

The entrance is through a massive door and into a reception area that features an almost overpowering staircase. "Perfect," I thought, "for a descending bride or a nude."

My host, owner Theo Smith, told me that his grandfather had purchased the property in 1900, and he had opened it in 1977 for the first time as a hotel. "The family paintings and antique furniture have remained in the reception rooms and guest rooms, and I hope we have kept the atmosphere of a family home rather than a hotel."

As one might expect of a castle in Scotland dating to 1480, Pittodrie House has some interesting history. The original building was burned down by the Marquis of Montrose; he was eventually executed in 1650. The main building was a Z-plan castle and this was rebuilt in 1675; the traces of this early history lend an air of antiquity to the place.

The lounges have very high ceilings and many oil paintings that date back two or three hundred years—there is even one of His Royal Majesty, George III. There are gorgeous tapestries, many sporting prints, highly decorated mirrors, rugs that seem almost priceless, and furniture I would expect to find in either a castle or a museum.

Many of the guest rooms have four-poster beds, and enjoy views of the meadows, forests, and parkland. It is really quite romantic. All guest rooms have color TV, radios, and private baths.

Pittodrie House seems to run off in all directions because there have been many new sections added over the years. Theo grew up in this house and he said it was a great place to play "hide and seek."

One of the bathrooms contains a Victorian shower that I'm certain must have been a marvelous feat of engineering in its time, and is still in use today. The water spray comes not only from overhead, but from three sides as well.

Theo excused himself to attend to a wedding party and suggested that I might be interested in seeing the walled garden. In typically British fashion, he said, "It's really quite nice, actually." This was the understatement of the day.

The walled garden is one of the most extraordinary I've ever seen. It covers three acres divided into a series of small gardens, each about the size of two tennis courts. There were gardeners wearing rubber boots working among garden pools, rose gardens, and a lavish display of flowers of every type and description. Part of the garden was devoted to vegetables served at the hotel.

At Pittodrie House, in addition to the incredible setting, the extensive acres, the Billiard Room, the fantastic gardens, and that incredible bathtub . . . they also make their own ice cream!

PITTODRIE HOUSE HOTEL, Pitcaple (by Inverurie), Grampian, Aberdeenshire AB5 9HS. Tel.: (046 76) Pitcaple 202. U.S. reservations: 800-243-1806. A 12-guestroom (private baths) country house hotel in a restored 15th-century castle, 20 mi. from Aberdeen. Open every day of the year except Christmas Day and Boxing Day. Lunch and dinner served to non-residents. Tennis, squash, snooker, and croquet available on grounds. Fishing and hill walking nearby. Pittodrie House is convenient to all of the National Trust properties and other great houses and castles in Aberdeenshire. Theo Smith, Owner. (See Index for rates.)

Directions: From Aberdeen take the A96 toward Inverness to Inverurie. Continue on, taking the first turning to the left (1½ mi.) signposted to

Chapel of Garioch. At the village take the first right fork at the shop and follow signs for hotel.

TULLICH LODGE
By Ballater, Aberdeenshire

Tullich Lodge is a most spectacular country house hotel in the Scottish Baronial style. Built of pink granite and located on five acres of woodlands and gardens, the hotel has been operated for the past twenty-two years by Neil Bannister and Hector MacDonald. If longevity breeds quality, then Tullich Lodge's owners certainly have garnered well-deserved gold stars.

It isn't often that I encounter a hotel of this high-class standard that welcomes children and pets. In fact, I can't remember when I had the pleasure of staying in a hotel that serves children's high tea in the kitchen so parents may dine on their scones and clotted cream in peace.

While the lodge is furnished with elegant antiques, the atmosphere is anything but presumptuous. The common rooms invite relaxation. Furnished in the late Victorian style, the drawing room has open views across Strathdee and Lochnagar. Neil told me that during a storm, the effect is quite memorable. A bit of historic trivia: Menuhin has tickled the keys of the room's old Broadwood grand piano which, incidentally, only responds to early 19th-century works. Across the hall, the sitting room is decorated in chintz and offers a variety of books.

While the bedrooms are small, beds are large and comfortable. Antiques again add the perfect touch to the decor, and all but two rooms have private baths.

A full Scottish breakfast and fabulous five-course dinner are included in the room tariff. Guests gather in the informal bar before dinner for a selection of madeiras, sherries, or malt whiskies while the dinner menu is reviewed. A well-researched wine list is also available. Adjoining the mahogany-panelled dining room, guests are served a fixed menu that has received enthusiastic comments. The chef uses fresh vegetables from the lodge's garden, fish from Aberdeen, and local meats. Other specialties follow the seasons. Breakfast is just as wonderful, featuring porridge, meat, fruit, cheeses, coffee, and teas.

The area surrounding the hotel has good hiking trails and a golf course. Historic points of interest include stone circles and ruined medieval castles. But guests' real enjoyment will come from the tranquil surroundings, the intimate atmosphere, and the wonderful, somewhat eccentric hoteliers.

TULLICH LODGE, by Ballater, Aberdeenshire AB35SB. Tel.: 03397-55406. A 10-guestroom (9 private baths) Victorian country gentle-

man's house. Open Apr. to Nov.; 2 night minimum. Queen, double, and twin beds. Full Scottish breakfast and dinner included; bar lunch available. Hiking, golf, and medieval castle ruins nearby. Children and pets welcome. Neil Bannister and Hector MacDonald, Proprietors. (See Index for rates.)

Directions: ½ mi. east of Ballater on the A93 Aberdeen Braehar Rd.

PORT-AN-EILEAN HOTEL
Strathtummel, Tayside, Perthshire

The leading sailboat had reached the buoy marking the far end of the course and was now coming about, ready to sail a broad reach on the final leg of the course. "Sometimes," said Gordon Hallewell, "they set their spinnakers."

Gordon and I were seated in the lounge of the Port-an-Eilean country house hotel, the bow window providing us with an excellent view of Loch Tummel and the almost daily sailboat race. The hotel, standing in twenty acres of natural woodland and formal gardens with magnificent views of lochs and mountains, was once the Duke of Athol's shooting lodge. It is at the start of the legendary "Road to the Isles" and at the geographic center of scenic Scotland.

"We are open from mid-April to mid-October," he said. "Many of our guests find that a holiday in early spring or autumn finds the countryside most beautiful. The roads are less crowded and log fires are most welcome in the evening after a good dinner."

From the very moment I had stepped through the front door I was impressed with the unusual number of contemporary oil paintings. Gordon explained that he and his wife, Evelyn, are collectors; I believe they have successfully blended some landscapes by modern painters among the more traditional works of earlier periods.

The general architecture and design of the building can be characterized as Scottish Victorian baronial, and the high-ceilinged drawing rooms and dining rooms are very elegant, with handsome wallpapers and many framed prints and originals providing a rich complement to the rugs and furniture.

"We're quite well situated for the guests who would enjoy a few days of rest and relaxation," he remarked. "It's possible to tour both the west and east coasts within a day or to take a short drive to Edinburgh, Inverness, or Aberdeen. We have facilities available for shooting and fishing. There are several beautiful walks that start right here at the hotel."

Gordon then suggested that we take a tour of the guest rooms and perhaps even look at the kitchen. As we wound our way up the handsomely paneled open staircase, Gordon told me that there are ten guest rooms, all with their own private baths. Many of them have a magnificent view of the loch. "The Duke wanted to provide his sporting guests with the best of accommodations," he said. The Hallewells have taken great pains to furnish the rooms in an appropriately Victorian style.

Returning to the first floor, Gordon handed me the menu for the evening, saying, "We always have trout and salmon from the loch, and venison and Scottish lamb in many different variations. Our approach to cuisine concentrates on the good cooking of a limited menu. Besides offering breakfast, tea, and dinner to non-residents, we can also supply hearty packed lunches for our houseguests who want to spend a day out-of-doors."

As we strolled on the lawn next to the loch, Gordon noted that the sailing dinghies were all at the far end of the loch and told me the view was so admired by Queen Victoria that it has since been called "The Queen's View."

PORT-AN-EILEAN HOTEL, Strathtummel (near Pitlochry), Perthshire. Tel.: (088 24) Tummel Bridge 233. A 10-guestroom (private baths) lochside country house hotel, almost in the geographical center of the Scottish Highlands, 10 mi. from Pitlochry. Open from mid-April to mid-Oct. Breakfast, tea, and dinner served daily to non-residents. Fishing and boating available at the hotel; 5 golf courses and hill walking nearby. All of the delights of Scottish Highlands are within an easy driving distance. No credit cards. Mr. and Mrs. Gordon Hallewell, Resident Proprietors. (See Index for rates.)

Directions: Follow A9 north of Pitlochry, then turn west from bypass on B8019 to Kinloch Rannoch. Hotel is 9 mi. along this road on left.

THE CAIRN LODGE
Auchterarder, Tayside

"Well, Bruce," said one gentleman to the other, "have you got your golf clubs in the boot?" The two of them were looking out the bay window of the drawing room at the velvety putting green. (It's impossible to reproduce the Scottish burr on the printed page.) The atmosphere was informal and the conversation lively in this very pleasant room, with its tall windows framed by draperies in shades of apricot and avocado. There were two or three groups of guests enjoying light lunches, with their chairs drawn up to coffee tables. I had stopped in for a spot of lunch, on the recommendation of Jess Miller at Hillhead of Dunkeld, and was relishing my smoked salmon sandwich.

The lady sitting nearest to me, who was originally from Brazil, had just told me that Scottish rolls were called "babs," and that her mushroom soup was wonderful and the babs were lovely, light, and soft.

On my arrival, lunch was going full tilt, with guests being shown to their tables in the lovely, very gracious dining room, where a more formal and extensive lunch was being served.

I would have to call Cairn Lodge a real "find." It has a warm, informal quality that made me feel immediately at home. The rooms are light and airy, and the furnishings and decorations are both comfortable and rather elegant, with many fresh flowers and plantings. There are lots of books, magazines, and newspapers in evidence. In addition to the pleasant drawing room, where light lunches and afternoon refreshments may be enjoyed, there is a most attractive little lounge, which looks out on a pretty garden. Just off this room is an enclosed sun room with easy chairs, also looking out on the garden, where there are masses of roses, along with lots of other flowers and an expanse of green lawn. A little outside patio with white garden furniture is another area where refreshments are served.

The five guest rooms (plans are afoot for an additional five or ten rooms) are all beautifully and individually furnished and immaculately kept. They all have color TV, the makings for tea and coffee, and plates of fresh fruit.

The menus look enticing, with such dishes as langoustine tails with orange cream sauce, veal cutlets with raspberry vinegar, and venison with wild mushrooms. The main course is served with fresh vegetables and there is a nice selection of interesting appetizers. I saw the sweets trolley and everything looked absolutely scrumptious.

Golfers come to this area for the great courses—the famous Gleneagles is a mile away. The Auchterarder course is across the street, and there are several other well-known courses nearby.

The Cairn Lodge is in a residential neighborhood, and is named for the tall mound of stones, called a cairn, at its side entrance, which was constructed by a local man, John Campbell, in commemoration of Queen Victoria's Diamond Jubilee in 1897. It provides a convenient landmark for guiding you to a most pleasant sojourn at an extremely friendly and delightful place.

THE CAIRN LODGE, Orchil Rd., Auchterarder, Tayside PH3 1LX. Tel.: (07646) 2634. A 5-guestroom (private baths) attractive country house hotel in a residential section of Auchterarder, in the Strathearn Valley between Stirling and Perth. Breakfast included in tariff. Breakfast, lunch, and dinner served to the public by reservation. Closed Christmas and New Year's week. Putting green on grounds. Gleneagles, St. Andrews, Muirfield golf courses nearby. Fishing on the Earn and Tay rivers, shooting, hill walking, pony trekking, swimming, wool shops, antiques, and

Auchterarder Heritage Center with displays and exhibitions of Scotland's last working textile steam engine. No pets. Gilberto Chiodetto, Managing Director. (See Index for rates.)

Directions: Coming north on the A9, Auchterarder is well signposted. In Auchterarder take the first left onto Orchil Rd., continue 200 yds. to the lodge on the right.

AUCHTERARDER HOUSE
Auchterarder, Perthshire

Stepping into the magnificent marble entrance of the Auchterarder House, I could see why the present owners, Ian and Audrey Brown, and their three sons had been captivated. Once the country home of famous Scottish industrialist and art patron James Reid, the imposing Scottish baronial has turreted Victorian architecture. The Reid family spared no expense when they enlarged and improved the house, and their interest in art and the highest quality of craftsmanship is apparent throughout the splendid mansion.

The Browns purchased Auchterarder House in 1984 and proceeded, through dedicated hard work, to develop a most exclusive and beautiful hotel. In keeping with the tradition of the country house, the Browns have created a gracious atmosphere. Ian told me, "We want guests to feel like they are in a house rather than a hotel."

One certainly does feel at ease, whether in the richly panelled, book-lined library where guests can relax and meet fellow travelers, or the billiards room with its vaulted ceiling and fine woodwork. On sunny days, doors are thrown open to the adjacent croquet lawn. The airy conservatory is a room I will long remember. A traditional "wintergarden" provides a colorful array of blooms, even when snow surrounds the house. Deep window boxes and graceful hanging planters overflow with pink and red flowers. In fact, sprays of fresh flowers are placed throughout the house.

The ten guest rooms are furnished in period pieces and named after Scottish clans. The rooms are large and airy and all have private baths. The Stuart Room still has its unique, original Victorian bath. Besides the usual amenities such as telephone, radio, and color television, trouser presses and hair dryers are also supplied.

All meals are available at Auchterarder. Dinner is a flavorful adventure, cooked to order. I had a wonderful steamed loin of lamb, succulently wrapped in leeks. Other unusual choices included fillet of turbot and scallops on a spaghetti of cucumber and a mersualt wine sauce, and breast of duck in pastry lattice. All dinners are served with seasonal vegetables, and followed by the traditional cheese tray and elegant desserts.

Because of Auchterarder's central location, only a one-hour drive from either Edinburgh or Glasgow, and a few miles from historic Perth, all types of sightseeing trips are possible. The house's seventeen acres of gardens provide a lovely morning's outing, and private shooting and fishing can be arranged.

The Browns are most kind and pleased to help you in any way to make your stay at Auchterarder House memorable.

AUCHTERARDER HOUSE, Auchterarder, Perthshire PH3-1DZ. Tel.: 0764-63646/7. A 10-guestroom (private baths) gracious Scottish baronial country house only 1 hour from Edinburgh and Glasgow. Open all year. Double and twin beds. Breakfast included with tariff; lunch and four-course dinner available. Hiking, shooting, fishing; close to points of historic interest. Pets by arrangement. Smoking permitted. Audrey, Ian and Paul Brown, Proprietors. (See Index for rates.)

Directions: Follow main routes to Auchterarder. On entering the town, turn onto B8062—signposted Grieff.

NIVINGSTON HOUSE HOTEL
Cleish, Kinross-Shire

I came to Nivingston House Hotel on the recommendation of a friend who raved about the dinner he had enjoyed there. What I found was not only fabulous food but a charming Scottish country hotel run by a couple who make warmth and hospitality what it should be.

Allan and Pat Deeson have been operating the hotel since 1983 and have created a stylishly comfortable environment. The converted Victorian farmhouse, parts of which date back to 1725, nestles at the foot of the Cleish Hills on fourteen acres of landscaped grounds. Two croquet lawns, a practice golf net, and a putting green offer guests outdoor entertainment.

Laura Ashley color-coordinated linens and wallpapers add to the country feeling of the seventeen guest rooms. The ambiance is restful and inviting. The rooms are outfitted with hair dryers, radios, televisions, tea making facilities, and direct dial telephones, and all have private baths.

A full Scottish breakfast is available in the morning, but it was dinner I worked up my appetite for during an afternoon of golf at the famous St. Andrews course just outside nearby Edinburgh. (By the way, I didn't do too badly; I broke 100! But I think my seasoned caddie had a bit to do with my success.)

"A Taste of Scotland" was emphasized on the dinner menu as I glanced over the evening's options. I settled on cream of Orkney oatmeal vegetable soup to start, then had a wonderful loin of pork, pan fried with a creamy Stilton, celery, and walnut sauce. The Stilton cheese in Scotland is exceptional and really put the crowning touch on the tender pork loin. Fresh local vegetables are served alongside, and dinner is complete with sweets, cheese, and hot coffee.

The hotel has full liquor service, so after such a satisfying meal, guests can retire to one of the lounges or the library for a liqueur or after-dinner drink and possibly a bit of bragging with other golfers.

Nivingston House is halfway between Edinburgh and Perth and is ideally located for visits to surrounding points of interest, such as Vane Farm Bird Sanctuary, a boat trip to Loch Leven Castle where Mary Queen of Scots was imprisoned, or a jaunt to the trout farm at Crook of Devon.

NIVINGSTON HOUSE, Cleish, Kinross-Shire KY137LS. Tel.: 05775-216. A 17-guestroom (private baths) converted Victorian farmhouse/country hotel at the foot of the Cleish Hills. Open all year. Various sized beds. Breakfast included; lunch and dinner available. Close to golf, fishing, and points of historic interest. Children welcome; pets by arrangement. Pat and Allan Deeson, Proprietors. (See Index for rates.)

Directions: Take Exit 5 from M90 then B9097 towards Cleish.

Rates for a room for two people for one night with breakfast, except where noted, are included in the Index of this book. They are not to be considered firm quotations, but should be used as guidelines only.

Ireland

Ireland is a land of old stone walls that are grown over with honeysuckle and roses, a land of fields, farmhouses, and small villages. In Ireland it is possible to find an old gate standing abandoned because the great house that it once served no longer exists.

It is a conservative land, bordering on the austere. The houses are very much alike and individuality is expressed by different-colored trims.

Essentially, the countryside charm lies in the fact that Ireland is still an agricultural country, and everywhere I traveled there were fields with either crops or cattle. The villages on the back roads have very few restaurants, although there are restaurants located on main highways.

There aren't many of the intrusions of modern life in Ireland. Television and radio are found everywhere, but only in a few of the accommodations that I visited did I find them in the guest rooms.

Public telephones can usually be found, one to a village, near the post office.

Frequently, the road passes by some of Ireland's stately homes with their decorated ceilings, tapestries, picture galleries, fine fireplaces, and furniture. These are found in all of the counties of Ireland. There are also many gardens that are open to the public.

There are over one hundred 18-hole golf courses in Ireland, including Portnarnock, near Dublin, described by Arnold Palmer as "the finest in the world."

There are very many interesting connections between Ireland and America. For example, there were several Irish-born signatories to the Declaration of Independence. During the American Civil War nearly 150,000 natives of Ireland served in the Union forces. The first recorded celebration of St. Patrick's Day was in 1762 in New York City. In 1779, the first St. Patrick's Day Parade was held in New York City. Apparently, the Irish have always been fond of coming to America; one legend says that the first Celtic arrival in North America was St. Brendan, the Navigator, around A.D. 550.

Irish-Americans have also had significant influence on literature and drama in the United States. The Nobel Prize went to playwright Eugene O'Neill in 1936, and novelists with an Irish heritage include F. Scott Fitzgerald, James T. Farrell, and John O'Hara.

GETTING TO IRELAND FROM BRITAIN

You can fly from London, Manchester, or other points, landing at Dublin or Shannon airports. You can take the train or drive on the A40 to Fishguard, boarding the car ferry for Rosslare or Cork. I would recommend driving, since cleanliness and convenience aboard the ferry are not the best. Also, there is no help with the luggage.

ACCOMMODATIONS AND FOOD IN IRELAND

Basically, I visited two kinds of accommodations in Ireland. The first type is converted country houses, mansions and castles similar to those I saw in England and Scotland. The menus are frequently both English- and French-oriented.

These somewhat luxurious country mansions and castles are really resort-inns. Most of them have rooms with private baths and serve an elaborate meal. In most cases, I found them owner-operated and comfortably informal. There are usually quite a number of recreational facilities on the grounds, and since they are located in resort areas, there are plenty of additional sports and recreational activities nearby.

The second type of accommodation that I have listed is the farmhouse. Those that I saw had five or six bedrooms and resembled the American farmhouse with the individuality and creativeness of the owners expressed in terms of bright curtains, multicolored sheets, flowered wallpaper, and very comfortable living rooms where the guests and family gather to watch TV or talk. In all cases cleanliness is very important. I understand that the Irish Tourist Board checks the farmhouses to make certain that high standards are being maintained.

The food was generally right off the farm at all farm accommodations that I visited, and this is one of the main points of pride. Meals are very informal, and all the guests sit around a big table, very often with the family.

Incidentally, all of these offer bed and breakfast. Partial or full board is also obtainable for a longer period of time.

TRAVELING IN IRELAND

Sooner or later anyone traveling in the Irish countryside has to get directions from one village to another. Irish signposts are in two languages. Most of the time one of them is English. The main problem is that the signs only direct the traveler from one village to the next and very seldom to villages beyond. I found that when the village I was looking for was not on my map I had to stop and ask directions. These directions were given in a wonderfully charming, polite, melodious manner and always ended up with the assurance that "you can't miss it." Well, "miss it" I did—quite a few times, in spite of some of the most intricate detail that accompanied each direction.

The most frequent direction was "straight on." One of the problems was that "straight on" usually led to another four-way crossroads and it was necessary to go through the whole process again.

As in Scotland and England, driving is on the left side of the road. I found very few traffic tie-ups even in the larger cities.

RESERVATION SERVICES

For bookings in hotels, guesthouses, farmhouses, and cottages, contact your nearest travel agent or contact the Central Reservation Service, Bord Fáilte, 14 Upper O'Connell St., Dublin 1, Ireland. Tel.: (01) 735209. Telex: 32462. Here you can book all types of accommodations, including cabin cruisers and horse-drawn caravans.

Throughout Ireland you will see a sign displayed by farmhouses and houses in town and country offering accommodations that have been inspected and approved by the Irish Tourist Board.

Rock of Cashel

IRELAND

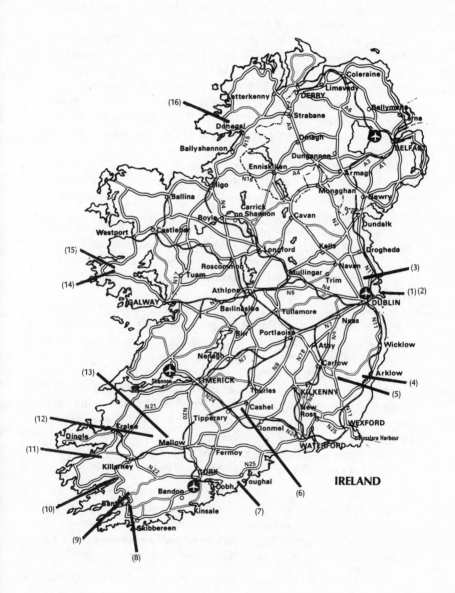

(16)

Coleraine
etterkenny
DERRY
Limavady
Strabane
Ballymena
Larne
Donegal
Omagh
BELFAST
Ballyshannon
Dungannon
Sligo
Enniskillen
Armagh
Newry
Ballina
Carrick
on Shannon
Cavan
Dundalk
Boyle
Monaghan
Westport
Castlebar
Longford
Kells
Drogheda
(15)
Roscommon
Mullingar
Navan
(3)
Tuam
Trim
(14)
Athlone
(1) (2)
GALWAY
Ballinasloe
Tullamore
DUBLIN
Birr
Portlaoise
Naas
Nenagh
Athy
Wicklow
(13)
Shannon
Carlow
Arklow
LIMERICK
Kilkenny
(4)
Thurles
(5)
(12)
Cashel
New
Ross
Tralee
Tipperary
WEXFORD
Dingle
Mallow
Clonmel
(11)
Fermoy
WATERFORD
Rosslare Harbour
Killarney
(10)
Bandon
Youghal
(6)
Cobh
(9)
Kinsale
(7)
Bantry
(8)
Skibbereen

IRELAND

EGAN'S HOUSE
Glasnevin, Dublin

Johnny Egan was fullback captain of the Irish Gaelic football team that played in New York, Boston, and Philadelphia in 1970. In fact, he made three trips to America as a footballer.

This is one of the interesting bits of information I learned during a pleasant evening at Egan's House, a guest house in a very quiet section of downtown Dublin called Iona Park. In a city that has many impressive hotels, Egan's is modest in demeanor, but big on friendliness and service. There are twenty-six rooms in all and each room has its own private bath—quite unusual for a small hotel. The hotel consists of two Dublin townhouses that have been connected, and so there are several different stairways to the second floor.

Dinner is available with a variety of selections, and as Betty Egan explained, "We only serve fresh vegetables and fresh meats. We also offer continental breakfasts or the American-type breakfast with things like scrambled eggs and bacon."

Betty mentioned another service for their guests that I think is quite thoughtful: it's possible to use Egan's as a forwarding address to hold mail.

The whole atmosphere is very informal and homey, and I noticed that there were many experienced travelers who found the place much to their liking.

Overseas guests arriving at Shannon Airport can phone Egan's when they get to the outskirts of Dublin and good directions will be provided. Guests arriving at the Dublin Airport can take either a cab or bus—those directions will also be provided by telephone.

Betty Egan, knowing that I was leaving very early in the morning, gave me a tray with a big bowl of cornflakes and some milk and a flask of coffee to sustain me for the long flight back to New York. She has a little store with all kinds of small items people might have lost or run out of, such as shaving cream, toothpaste, shampoo, and a few souvenirs of Ireland.

Egan's Hotel is small and unassuming, and a great way to get acquainted with the informal friendliness of Ireland.

Note: Not everyone agreed with my enthusiastic observations about how homey and friendly Egan's is. One gentleman named Sullivan felt that it was "too casual with not enough attention paid to important details." I will, with your permission, fall back on an old English saying which I think describes Egan's at this time: "Good value for the money."

EGAN'S HOUSE, 7 Iona Park, Glasnevin, Dublin 9. Tel.: (01) Dublin 303611 or 305283. A 26-guestroom in-town guest house in the middle of Dublin, 15 mi. from the airport. Breakfast and dinner served daily. Convenient to all of the Dublin shops, museums, and other attractions. Mr. and Mrs. John Egan, Proprietors. (See Index for rates.)

Directions: If you are arriving at Dublin Airport, I'd suggest a taxi to Egan's Hotel. From there, arrangements can be made to pick up a rental car in Dublin city. If arriving by car, have a Dublin city center map available to note directions, and telephone the hotel for specific directions from outside of Dublin.

KILRONAN HOUSE
Dublin, Ireland

Josephine Murray, the owner of Kilronan House, is a friendly, energetic, and warm hostess. She has owned the black and white Victorian bed and breakfast inn for the past twenty-five years and spares no effort to make guests feel welcome. She and her friendly golden labrador, Oscar, met me as I checked in. I liked Josephine immediately. As she showed me to my room, she proudly pointed out that the inn's breakfast menu had recently won an award as Dublin's best.

Kilronan House is located in the heart of Dublin and is ideally situated within walking distance of the city's most famous landmarks: Trinity College; Mansion House; Leinster House, the seat of parliament; the National Museum; the National Gallery and more. St. Stephen's Green offers a delightful park, and nearby Grafton Street is lined with exclusive shops.

The atmosphere of Kilronan House is restful in contrast to the surrounding city. A cozy drawing room/lounge is furnished in antiques, including display cabinets that house Waterford crystal. Wines and sherry are available and can be enjoyed in this spacious room.

Guest rooms are intimate, with thick curtains that adequately block the light. Each room is equipped with a tea/coffee maker, direct dial telephone, color television, hair dryer, robes, and shower. All rooms have chairs, and some have reading lamps, while pastel colors and modern teak furnishings make the rooms warm and inviting.

When I went down to breakfast in the morning, I looked forward to the award-winning meal Josephine had mentioned the evening before. I wasn't disappointed. Beginning with fresh fruit and juices, I was served prunes, a fruit salad, porridge, muesli, bacon and eggs, pudding, fresh tomatoes, homemade scones with honey and jam, and fresh coffee. I could see why the judges had been impressed.

After such a hearty feast, I needed some exercise, so I strolled off to visit St. Patrick's Cathedral where celebrated Irish writer Jonathan Swift had been Dean in the 1700s. Dublin is a wonderful city to visit, and Kilronan House offers a balm to travelers: seclusion, ideal central location, comfort, and reasonable rates.

KILRONAN HOUSE, 70 Adelaide Rd., Dublin. Tel.: 01, 755266. Fax: 782841. An 11-guestroom (10 with private showers, 1 with bath/shower) Victorian guest house within walking distance of most landmarks and tourist sights. Open Jan. to Dec. 23. Full breakfast included. Central heating. Double and twin beds. No pets. Smoking permitted. Josephine Murray, Proprietor. (See Index for rates.)

Directions: Go straight on O'Connell St. past Trinity College, up Kildare St. to St. Stephens Green. Go right at Shelbourne Hotel to T-junction on Adelaide Rd. Kilronan House is on right.

MOYGLARE MANOR HOTEL
Moyglare, Maynooth, County Kildare

Located only fifteen miles from the center of Dublin, the Moyglare Manor Hotel offers warm hospitality in a luxurious atmosphere highlighted by antique furnishings and magnificent decor. The 18th-century Georgian country house is located on a great limestone plain that is surrounded by hundreds of acres of parkland and mountains. The area has been home to some of the world's most outstanding horses and still has many breeding farms and race tracks.

Owner Nora Devlin has been a hotelier for some time. Along with her daughter and son-in-law, Nora came to Moyglare Manor Hotel in 1983 and brought with her an impeccable sense of style. Vases of fresh flowers are scattered everywhere, highlighting beautiful antiques from the extensive family collection.

While antiques appear in all the rooms, don't let the luxury fool you; the emphasis at Moyglare Manor is on personal service and relaxation. The seventeen guest rooms are welcoming. Dramatic accents, like canopied four-poster beds, add charm to the comfortable rooms. All rooms have private baths, telephones, and televisions on request. Most rooms have spectacular views of the surrounding countryside.

The lounge offers a relaxing spot to unwind after a day of golf or horseback riding. A log fire beckons guests to enjoy a restful hour with a drink from the bar before dinner. Both dinner and breakfast are served in the elegant dining room. The cuisine is excellent and varied, and the chef makes use of fresh fruits and vegetables from the hotel's gardens. Breakfast is included in the room tariff and is wonderful. I began with fresh orange juice, then had stewed prunes, a tender scramble of eggs and smoked salmon, and finished with rich, hot coffee.

While Dublin is only a half-hour drive away, you may decide to stay near home and visit one of the four golf courses that are within ten miles of the hotel, play tennis, or enjoy a real treat—an early morning fox hunt.

Whatever your preference, the Moyglare Manor family will make your stay memorable and pleasant.

MOYGLARE MANOR HOTEL, Moyglare, Maynooth, Co. Kildare. Tel.: 01-286351. A 17-guestroom (private baths) luxurious Georgian country house, 18 mi. from Dublin. Open all year round except 3 days at Christmas. King, queen, and double beds. Full breakfast included; lunch and dinner available. Close to horseback riding, golf, and tennis. No pets; smoking restricted. Nora Devlin, Proprietor; Shay Curran, Manager. (See Index for rates.)

Directions: From Dublin, take Galway Rd. Turn right at Maynooth, approx. 1½ mi.

MARLFIELD HOUSE HOTEL
Gorey, County Wexford

Mrs. Mary Bowe and I were in the sumptuous, but comfortable, drawing room of the Marlfield House, discussing the problems of keeping a country house hotel in Ireland in general, and the dinner menu for the previous evening, Friday, the 12th of October, in particular.

"I usually have twelve or fourteen starters and nine or ten main courses," she said. "It's a bit limited tonight."

I glanced down the list of offerings and it seemed more than sufficient to me. The starters included Kilmore crab salad, butter-fried sea trout, and soused herring. There was a choice of three soups, and among the main dishes were roast ribs of beef in a Béarnaise sauce, grilled turbot, seafood pancakes, scallops in cream, and pork chops Normandy. The vegetables were from the garden. Mrs. Bowe told me that they make their own ice cream and butterscotch sauce.

While we were discussing the dinner menu, houseguests and other people from the nearby area had begun dropping in for the Saturday bar lunch. Mrs. Bowe excused herself several times to greet her guests, and this gave me an opportunity to observe the scene.

The drawing room takes up one end of this beautiful old country house, set on thirty-five acres of woodland about one mile from the town of Gorey on the Courtown Road. Marlfield House was the former residence of the Earls of Courtown. My attention was caught by the beautiful flower arrangements on the tables and on the baby grand piano in one corner, and also by the several tastefully chosen country prints. The room had very high ceilings with decorated moldings and there was a handsome marble fireplace.

Mary Bowe rejoined me and suggested that we had better take a tour of the bedrooms before guests began to check in. I followed her up the very impressive winding staircase that curves around a sparkling crystal chandelier hanging from the two-and-a-half-story ceiling. There were fourteen double guest rooms, all with baths, and all furnished most appropriately. Those on the top floor have a panoramic view of the fields and the low hills of county Wexford.

We took just a moment or two to look at some of the beautiful and frequently rare trees on the grounds, including a flowering ash tree, many oaks and evergreens, beeches, and pink and white flowering chestnut trees. She called my attention to a very sturdy California redwood. "We have quite a lot of birds here and about thirty wild ducks. Our two peacocks always amuse our guests."

Marlfield House, situated midway between Dublin and Wexford, is within a short drive of beaches, rugged mountains, and richly timbered valleys, and is in what is known as the "Garden of Ireland."

Reader Comment: "This is a delightful place," writes Marilyn Schubert. "We think that it is one of the best decorated and furnished country houses in Ireland. The Conservatory is most unusual, and Charlie and I both thought that Mary Bowe is a lady of considerable grace, style, and talent."

MARLFIELD HOUSE, Gorey, Co. Wexford. Tel.: (055) 21124. A 14-guestroom country house hotel on Ireland's southeast coast, 57 mi. from Dublin. Closed Dec. 10 to Feb. 14. Lunch, tea, dinner served to non-residents. County Wicklow with beautiful beaches and mountains is nearby; Mount Usher Gardens, Russborough House, and other celebrated beauty spots within easy driving distance. Grass tennis court, croquet on grounds. Golfing, sea bathing, hunting, and fishing nearby. Children over 6 allowed under strict supervision. Mrs. Mary Bowe, Proprietress. (See Index for rates.)

Directions: Gorey is on the Dublin-Wexford Rd.; just before Gorey, turn left before the road goes under the railroad bridge and proceed on the Courtown Rd. Hotel entrance is on right.

LORUM OLD RECTORY
Bagenalstown, County Carlow

I liked Lorum Old Rectory and Betty Young immediately. She was a most accommodating and entertaining person and, like many of my Irish friends, a great conversationalist. She explained that she and her daughter run this 130-year-old, cut-stone farmhouse, while her son-in-law runs the farm.

All of the rooms in the Old Rectory are pleasant and homey—they are not luxurious, but clean and comfortable. One of the first things that attracted me was all of the books that are to be found on shelves throughout the house.

Guests all gather around the table in the evening and enjoy a real Irish farm meal that includes many homemade preserves, breads, pâtés, and the like. Salmon and trout have been freshly caught from nearby streams.

"We've had quite a few visitors from your book," she wrote in one of her recent letters. "Americans who are looking for the 'real Ireland' come for a night and decide to spend two or three, because we are located quite conveniently for many of the attractions of the south of Ireland. In the evening after dinner we spend a lot of time sitting and visiting. That's one of the nicest things about keeping a guest house, sooner or later all of the world comes to us.

"I am only here for six months of the year now, but my daughter, Bobbie, is running things beautifully. I do hope you will stop on your next visit to Ireland."

LORUM OLD RECTORY, Bagenalstown, Co. Carlow. Tel.: (0503) 75282. A 5-guestroom rural guest house in the southeast of Ireland, 64 mi. from Dublin. Breakfast and dinner served to houseguests only. Open year-round except Christmas. Tennis, golf, river fishing, riding nearby. Within convenient distance of the sea. Beautiful mountain scenery nearby. Betty Young and Bobbie Smith, Proprietors. (See Index for rates.)

Directions: Bagenalstown is south of Carlow, just off the road to Kilkenny. From Carlow, go to Leighlinbridge and then turn sharp left for Muine Bheag. At Muine Bheag take the Borris Rd. Lorum Old Rectory is 4 mi. out on the left side. (All of these are on map.)

KNOCK-SAINT-LOUR HOUSE
Cashel, County Tipperary

I was sitting in Mrs. O'Brien's kitchen enjoying a cup of tea and watching her prepare the evening meal. "Tonight it is ham and chicken," she said, "and we'll have roast pork tomorrow night."

Mrs. O'Brien loves flowers. The house is surrounded on three sides by a truly intricate rock garden of myriad colors. "My mother tends the flowers outside," she said, "and I do the arranging on the inside. It keeps both of us very busy, but we love it."

Color is found throughout the house. Each bedroom is pastel-hued with harmonizing sheets and pillowcases and curtains.

Knock-Saint-Lour House is a farmhouse and almost everything served is homegrown. "I do a lot of freezing in the summer and early fall," she explained, "so that we have our own produce through most of the year."

I noticed a donkey grazing in a nearby field. "Oh, that's for the children. They love it."

She pointed out that there was a good view of the famous Rock of Cashel through one of the kitchen windows. "Everyone wants to visit there."

KNOCK-SAINT-LOUR HOUSE, Cashel, Co. Tipperary. Tel.: (062) 61172. An 8-guestroom (private and shared baths) farmhouse serving dinner and breakfast. Just 1½ mi. from the town of Cashel, where the famous Rock of Cashel is located. Open all year except Christmas. Golfing, tennis, horse riding and pony trekking available nearby. Mrs. Eileen O'Brien, Proprietress. (See Index for rates.)

Directions: Knock-Saint-Lour is on the Dublin-Cork Rd. (N8), just south of Cashel.

BALLYMALOE HOUSE
Shanagarry, County Cork

The Ballymaloe House is one of Ireland's manor house accommodations. The house is part of an old Geraldine Castle, rebuilt and modernized through the centuries, one portion dating back to the 14th century. It is in the middle of a 400-acre farm on the Cork–Ballycotton road about two miles from the coast of southern Ireland.

Fifteen of the thirty guest rooms are in the main house and there are other lodging facilities in a 16th-century gatehouse and other farm outbuildings.

My room was located on the front, overlooking a very pleasant terrace and some beautiful fields and meadows that stretched out to some low hills a few miles away. I understand that this particular part of Ireland is not developed as a tourist area as yet. The coastal area is just a few minutes away.

After leaving Mrs. Young's in Bagenalstown, I followed the main road south through Thomastown and into Waterford, which is the home of the famous Irish Waterford crystal. From there, the main road heads southwestward with frequent glimpses of the Irish coast, passing through Dungarvan and Youghal. At Ladysbridge, I began another "cat and mouse" game of directions to try to find Shanagarry, the town closest to Ballymaloe. It is quite beyond my limited description to explain how I arrived, but it took at least four stops.

I arrived in the late afternoon and had time enough for a good long soak in the tub and few moments' rest before coming down for dinner.

Shortly before dinner I met some other houseguests in one of the living rooms who were on holiday from Dublin. I realized then that there were a great many children in residence and discovered that it was a long weekend. My new acquaintances had two children and explained that they had been in Ballymaloe several times because the golf, tennis, and swimming is free during July and August.

Dinner was very informal, served by waitresses in attractive costumes who were efficient and answered questions in a very pleasant manner. The menu offerings were basically English and Irish, rather than Continental.

After dinner I took a short walk in the gathering darkness, strolling on the country lanes between the fields of ripening wheat. The lights of Ballymaloe gleamed softly and occasionally I could hear the delighted cries of some young people who were being allowed to stay up a little longer because it was a special occasion.

After many centuries of existence, I felt that Ballymaloe had really come into its own.

Reader Comment: Marilyn said that this was the place where Charlie was proud he was an Irishman. "Norman, we had a wonderful time here and I was amazed to find out how much of the family is involved. We met another couple at dinner from Belfast and then went on to visit a monastery with them. It was very special." (Ballymaloe apparently made a big hit with both Charlie and Marilyn.)

BALLYMALOE HOUSE, Shanagarry, Co. Cork. Tel.: (021) 652531. A 25-guestroom country house hotel, 3 mi. from the sea on Ireland's southern coast. Lunch and dinner served to non-residents. Closed Dec. 23 to 27. Tennis, golf, swimming pool, fishing, in July and Aug. on grounds. Allen Family, Proprietors. (See Index for rates.)

Directions: From Cork Road: On Midleton Bypass, take Cloyne-Ballycotton Rd. toward Shanagarry. Ballymaloe House is on L-35, 2 mi. beyond Cloyne.

BANTRY HOUSE
Bantry, County Cork

As I drove through the filigreed black iron gates and up the graveled drive, I felt as if I had been dropped into a set from the film *Wuthering Heights*. Before me a fabulous Irish country house awaited—classical lines drawn out in colonnades, arches, and pavilions of improbable lengths, Gothic towers and battlements trailing off to courts and stable yards.

My reverie was suddenly broken by the honk of a trombone. As I entered the Bantry House reception area, the mysterious trombone player appeared in the person of Mr. Egerton Shelswell-White, a descendant of the White family who purchased the mansion in 1739, and the present owner. "Hello! You caught me practicing," he laughed. "Welcome to Bantry House."

Egerton is a trombonist with the Cork School of Music Symphony Orchestra and a relative of the infamous second Earl of Bantry. The Earl had a great vision when he began modification and redecoration of this Queen Anne house during the second quarter of the 19th century. During his continental travels he amassed a wonderful collection of furniture, tapestries, and works of art that now make up the spectacular museum area of the mansion. He also designed the grounds, which are laid out as a formal Italian garden, and a "staircase to the sky," rising to steep terraces overlooking Bantry Bay.

The wing, which houses the refurbished guest rooms, is actually on the side of the house that overlooks the formal gardens. Guests share common areas that include a sitting room, billiards room, television room, and dining room. Bedrooms are comfortable, with modern private bathrooms and telephones. Of course, the decor is museum quality and adds to the wonderful manor house atmosphere.

Egerton and his wife live on the premises and give tours of the museum wings. They joined me for a breakfast and, over coffee, told me a bit of the family history. "I could have been an earl; but somewhere along the line there was no male heir to carry on the name, so we lost the title," he explained. They have certainly made the best of the situation and live with their dog Pip, enthusiastically sharing the treasures their ancestor so fervently collected.

Bantry House is one-half mile from the town of Bantry and offers an excellent base for touring the area. The scenery is spectacular, and the West Cork and Kerry artists' studios are quite interesting.

As I left the magical spell of Bantry House, I took one look back and momentarily felt like the Lord of the Manor.

BANTRY HOUSE (not the Bantry Hotel), Bantry, Co. Cork. Tel.: (027) 50047. A 10-guestroom (private baths) spectacular Irish country house on acres of formal gardens with museum quality decor. Open all year. King and twin beds. Full breakfast included; dinners to be offered soon. Overlooks Bantry Bay. Near town, artists' studios, sporting activities. No pets. Smoking permitted. Mr. and Mrs. Egerton Shelswell-White, Proprietors. (See Index for rates.)

Directions: From the city of Cork, go 60 mi. on N71. Entrance on right on outskirts of town.

SEAVIEW HOUSE HOTEL
Ballylickey, Near Bantry, County Cork

Ideally situated to tour west Cork and the Kerry regions, the Seaview House Hotel sits on five acres of manicured grounds in the tradition of the country house that it is. Owner Kathleen Sullivan greeted me as I checked in and gave me a personal tour of the 100-year-old Victorian. "I take real pride in this place," she told me. "It's my family home."

Her sense of pride is obvious in the pleasant atmosphere she has created at Seaview House. The main lounge, reading room, television room, and cocktail bar are all quite comfortable and provide ample opportunity to mingle and get to know other guests.

The eighteen guest rooms are all decorated in bright colors, with antiques and lovely fabrics. Chairs and reading lamps are provided, and all rooms have private baths. While I found the decor a bit unexciting, all the rooms were warm and cozy and very clean.

A traditional Irish breakfast is included with the room tariff, and lunch and dinner are both available. One evening I enjoyed hors d'oeuvres, drinks, and conversation with other guests as we sat in front of a blazing fire in the main lounge prior to dinner. We continued our discussion of Bantry Bay over a wonderful five-course meal featuring seafood dishes. The meal included a selection of appetizers, soup, five main-course choices, and luscious homemade desserts. A well-stocked wine cellar complements the meal.

Seaview House is located near two golf courses. Fishing, shooting, and pony trekking can be arranged. Or you may just want to sit at the umbrella-topped table on the lawn and ponder the views to Bantry Bay and the mountains beyond. Whatever you choose, Kathleen and her staff are very friendly and hospitable and will try to make your stay most relaxing.

SEAVIEW HOUSE HOTEL, Balleylickey, Near Bantry, Co. Cork. Tel.: (027) 50462. An 18-guestroom (private baths) Victorian country house on 5 acres. Open Apr. 1 to Oct. 31. Queen, double, and twin beds. Traditional Irish breakfast included; lunch and dinner available. Dinners approximately $20/person. Golf, fishing, hunting, and pony trekking nearby. Ideally located for touring west Cork and Kerry. Pets accepted. Kathleen Sullivan, Proprietor. (See Index for rates.)

Directions: On Rte. 71, 3 mi. from Bantry on the main Bantry/Glengarriff Rd.

PARK HOTEL KENMARE
Kenmare, County Kerry

When I think of Ireland, I think of a climate that is a bit crisp, cool, and often blustery. But I was surprised to find areas that are really quite mild. The Park Hotel Kenmare is situated in such a mild climatic area. This small, but luxurious hotel is on the lovely Ring of Kerry, a spectacular round-tour of the west coast region with its lakes, mist-shrouded rocky hills, and gorgeous views. I was amazed to see subtropical vegetation peeping out here and there around the ten acres of parkland on which the almost 100-year-old Victorian hotel is located.

Originally a railway hotel, the present Park Hotel Kenmare was opened at Easter in 1897 as the "Great Southern Hotel Kenmare." The wonderful stone exterior still blends harmoniously with the surrounding landscape. While the hotel has maintained its old-world charm, modern amenities have been successfully blended to provide comfort. The immaculate interior is offset by beautiful antique furnishings, Flemish tapestries, and unique art treasures.

As I had a glass of wine in the drawing room before dinner, I enjoyed the restful view out its large windows overlooking the lake garden. An inveterate eavesdropper, I couldn't help but overhear one of the other guests regale his friends with the tale of his exceptional day on the nearby links—one of the "Big Six" golf courses of Ireland.

The hotel offers a classic Irish bar and memorable gourmet dining. Dinner is served in the formal dining room where wall scones and magnificent fluted glass chandeliers add to the ambiance. Tables are set with heavy Irish linen tablecloths and Rosenthal china. Ireland has a reputation for fine seafood, and I couldn't pass up the Irish salmon with wild-mint sauce. Unusual additions to the meal were nettle soup and a chilled almond soufflé for dessert.

Breakfast is more traditional. Fruit, juice, and cereal are served with a variety of egg dishes, meats, puddings, scones, and tea or coffee. Both meals are included with your room fee.

The guest rooms are furnished with antiques, some with gorgeous four-poster beds. Most rooms have baths and all have direct dial telephones. The rooms are intimate and spacious and exude an air of ease and contentment.

The hotel is only a short walk from the picturesque little Irish country town of Kenmare, where horse-drawn carriages still travel up and down the streets and shopping is available. The hotel's staff are most willing to recommend all sorts of additional outings, which might include fishing and horseback riding.

The Park Hotel Kenmare should not be missed.

PARK HOTEL KENMARE, Kenmare, Co. Kerry. Tel.: (064) 41200. Telex: 73905. Fax: (064)41402. A 49-guestroom (40 private baths) luxurious grand hotel overlooking Kenmare Bay. Outstanding service. Open Easter to Jan. Double and twin beds. Wheelchair access, TV, tennis, croquet on grounds. Golf, swimming, fishing, horseback riding, historical sites nearby. No pets. Francis Brennan, Proprietor. (See Index for rates.)

Directions: Kenmare is 60 mi. southwest of Cork on the N22.

CARAGH LODGE
Caragh Lake, County Kerry

"The Ring of Kerry"—doesn't that have the most wonderful, melodious sound? Among the beautiful nature spots that are either on or near the Ring of Kerry, which is really an automobile road for our purposes, are Tralee Bay, Dingle Bay, Bantry Bay, and Healy Pass. In southwest Ireland within a few hours' drive of Dublin and an even shorter distance from Shannon Airport, the Ring has a great appeal for many people.

Charlie and Marilyn Schubert, former owners of the Barrows House in Dorset, Vermont, stopped at nearby Caragh Lodge on their trip to Ireland, and they were telling me about it.

"Marilyn and I have always wanted to see the Ring of Kerry and this was one of the stops that we had planned for many months ahead. It exceeded all of our expectations.

"Now here's the funny part. We found Caragh Lodge, although not without some most amusing roadside conversation and instruction from a young man with a donkey cart. It is on a small rise overlooking Caragh Lake and is back from the road so that the atmosphere is quiet. As we pulled into the courtyard, the innkeepers came to the door to greet us, and Marilyn grabbed my arm and said, 'We know these people; I'm sure they have been to the Barrows House.' They had indeed been our guests, and now we were theirs. We were all surprised and delighted at this happy coincidence."

Surrounded by nine acres of parkland, with lovely gardens and spectacular scenery, the lodge has a really magic setting, with the greenness of the countryside, the blue skies, and the lake combining to lift one into another world. It's particularly attractive when the gorse is in bloom.

With all of the possibilities for recreation, one could spend several days there. There's swimming, fishing, and boating on the lake and horse riding nearby, along with all of the interesting auto touring. The lodge has an all-weather tennis court, bicycles for hire, and a sauna chalet.

Charlie was particularly interested in the fact that there were seven 18-hole golf courses all within a reasonable driving distance.

There are three extra-sized rooms in the main building that have been furnished in excellent taste with private baths. There are additional rooms in other buildings also.

The à la carte menu features sirloin steak, lamb chops, and chicken Cordon Bleu, and some of the house specialties include fresh warm smoked salmon and poached trout with butter sauce. Of course, everything is as local as possible. Dinner reservations are necessary.

Marilyn summed things up for me. "You know, I'm an early riser so I was up while the dew was still on the grass, and there was a wonderful thin cloud over the lake. I walked into the woods and could almost see the 'little people' scampering out of the way. I'd say that Caragh Lodge, with its lovely warm innkeepers, spectacular scenery, and magic setting, is really a jewel."

And I would agree as well.

CARAGH LODGE, Caragh Lake, Co. Kerry. Tel. 066-69115. A 10-guestroom secluded lodge in the Ring of Kerry holiday area. Breakfast is included in the room rate and dinner is served every night, reservations necessary. Open from spring to October. Lake swimming, all-weather tennis court, table tennis, sauna, boating, bicycling, and fishing on grounds. Many golf courses and riding stables nearby. No pets. Michael and Ines Braasch, Proprietors. (See Index for rates.)

Directions: Caragh Lake is 1 mi. off N70 between Killorglin and Glenbeigh.

ASSOLAS COUNTRY HOUSE
Kanturk, County Cork

As I approached Assolas Country House I had a faint will-o'-the-wisp feeling that I had been there before. Like the proprietors of many other country houses in Britain and Ireland, the Bourkes had permitted the vines to find their way up the rough stone walls, and the contrast of the green leaves against the gray stone created a most fetching effect.

I crossed the stone bridge, pausing for a moment to watch the swans on the water and admire what I am sure are some of the finest gardens in all of Ireland. Plantings of tulips around the trees were a lovely touch. The size and beauty of the trees were quite overwhelming.

Assolas is a 17th-century manor house with low, round turrets on either end. It has been the home of the Bourke family for over seventy years. The setting is nothing if not sylvan, with a delightful river coursing through the grounds.

I stepped inside the house and, typical of me, I had entered the wrong door at the back, walking into an immaculate country kitchen. I was greeted by Hugh Bourke and his son, Joe, who was already at work doing the early preparation for the evening meal. I learned subsequently that he does all the cooking. He clattered about the place with his pots and pans while his father and I chatted a bit. Then Hugh led me into the drawing room, where there was a jolly fire in the fireplace, comfortable sofas and chairs, a huge mirror, and many paintings. We were joined by his wife, Eleanor, who has a very pleasant, natural quality, and we sat and talked about Americans in Ireland, inns in North America, and the joys and problems of being the owner of a 300-year-old country house.

"We had a gentleman who left unexpectedly this morning, rather

unhappy," Eleanor said. "He was terribly upset when he discovered that there was no telephone or TV in his room. We bade him farewell and good luck with his accommodations in the future."

Hugh showed me to my unusually large guest room. I admired the lovely view of the gentle Irish landscape and he assured me that all of the views are almost equally enticing. He also mentioned that a few of the rooms boast whirlpool baths.

We started talking about the menu at Assolas and he explained that "we have what we call progressive Irish cooking, and whenever possible we use fresh local produce and home-grown fruit and vegetables. Joe has proved to be a magician in our kitchen. He's got a bit of a reputation for both leg of lamb and leg of pork."

Hugh and I sauntered down to the drawing room and out into the sunny Irish countryside. In answer to my inquiry about guest activities, he said, "Our guests can enjoy lawn tennis and boating. Salmon fishing is available on the Black Water River.

"If you are into golf," he remarked, "we have several golf links, including some international championship courses within easy reach."

Later that evening, Hugh pulled me aside and said, "I've been thinking about your feeling that you've been here before, and I believe this is the answer." He handed me a large, handsome fashion catalog of Etienne Aigner clothing that had been photographed at Assolas. The models, two young women and a young man, were posed in various settings around the estate—against wonderful old stone walls, on a bundle of hay in the barn, in front of beautiful old trees, beside the river. Assolas provided a wonderful setting.

Of course, this was where I'd seen Assolas before. Hugh remarked that often their guests have that same feeling of déjà vu.

ASSOLAS COUNTRY HOUSE, Kanturk, Co. Cork. Tel.: (029) 50015. A 10-guestroom (private baths) comfortable country house in the southwest touring region of Cork and Kerry. Breakfast and dinner served to residents and travelers. Reservations necessary. Light lunch available. Open most of the year. Tennis, croquet, boating, trout and coarse fishing as well as salmon fishing. Challenging golf courses within a short distance. Convenient to Killarney, the Ring of Kerry, the Dingle Peninsula, Bantry Bay, Blarney Castle, and historic Limerick. Children under 12. No pets. The Bourke Family, Proprietors. (See Index for rates.)

Directions: From Cork, take N20 north to Mallow, then take N72 west to R576. Look for signs to hotel.

LONGUEVILLE HOUSE
Mallow, County Cork

It was at Longueville House that I had my most intriguing contact with Irish history. Michael O'Callaghan, the resident owner of this handsome Georgian manor house, and his wife, Jane, entertained me royally with a high tea that included some simply fabulous homemade ginger cookies. (I unashamedly pocketed two of them as I was leaving.) Jane, as a Cordon Bleu–trained chef, has won several awards for her cuisine and supervises all the cooking.

The house overlooks one of the most beautiful river valleys in Ireland, the Blackwater Valley. The central portion was built about 1720 on a 500-acre wooded estate, then the property of an ancestor of Michael O'Callaghan. As Michael said, "Since then, Longueville has had a checkered history." Now, it has been considerably enlarged and is an excellent country house hotel surrounded by an area particularly rich in scenery.

The size of the building took my breath away. The entrance is through a stately arch, and the first thing I noticed approaching the front entrance was a tremendous brass lock on the door. The center hallway and reception area are most elegant, as are the library, living room, smaller parlors, and dining rooms. The impressive main staircase rises to the full height of the house on both sides and repeats from the second to the third floor. One of the most unusual areas is a glass conservatory, left over from Victorian days, that contains many tropical plants, tree, and flowers. All the guest rooms that I saw were comfortable, large, and very tastefully furnished.

Over tea I asked Michael about the outdoor sports and recreation in the area. He replied, "Well, athletic salmon abound, as do trout, in the river that runs across the southern boundary of our estate. We are just a few miles from the south coast where there is good sea fishing and shore angling. There are eighteen golf courses in the county, including one at

Mallow, which is free to our guests. We have horses and ponies available for trekking nearby.

"Many of our guests spend a great deal of time on the back roads here in County Cork, and driving out to the coast to some of the places of great natural beauty such as Glengarriff, Blarney, and Limerick. Killarney is one hour away.

"There are many castles in this section of Ireland that are open to the public, and quite a lot of history was made in this vicinity. For example, the oak trees that you see out the window were planted in the formation of the English and the French battle lines at Waterloo," he said.

"What about the history that took place nearby?" I asked.

"Well, this part of Ireland was known as Rebel Country," Michael said. "The O'Callaghans had owned this land for 100 years, including the remains of a castle which you can see from our front windows. It is one of my fondest wishes to completely restore this monument and make it available once again. When Cromwell's army invaded Ireland this was one of the few places that was not burned. Cromwell's son-in-law, who was in charge of the army, stayed nearby."

I could see that Michael was beginning to warm to his subject, and I settled back comfortably in the luxurious chair to get a good lesson in Irish history.

LONGUEVILLE HOUSE, Mallow, Co. Cork. Tel.: (022) 27156 or 27176. A 20-guestroom country house hotel situated west of Mallow on the Killarney Rd., 54 mi. from Shannon Airport. Open from Easter to Oct. 20. Dinner served to non-residents by telephone booking. Fishing on grounds;

horse riding, complimentary golf nearby. Michael and Jane O'Callaghan, Resident Owners. (See Index for rates.)

Directions: From Shannon: take the road to Limerick, then the Cork Rd. into Mallow. Take the Killarney Rd. for 2 mi. west. From Dublin; take the Cork Rd. to Mitchell's Town and then on to Mallow. Continue on, following above directions on the Killarney Rd.

THE BURREN

Ireland is certainly a land of surprises, and one of the most paradoxical and contradictory surprises is the Burren, a 100-square-mile region in county Clare that provides endless browsing and opportunities for discovery.

Eerie and yet fascinating, the landscape of the Burren appears bleak, yet is far from barren. There are very few trees or shrubs and apart from one small stream there is no trace of a river. Yet the Burren supports a selection of flowers and plants that are found elsewhere as far north as the Arctic regions and in climes far south of Ireland.

Rock and stone predominate, and in their own way support the luxurious growth of rare flowers. Because the area has been inhabited for 4,000 years, the region is dotted with monuments representing almost every century of man's habitation.

There are forts, ruined castles, caves, tombs, limestone pavements, cairns, abandoned churches, turloughs (dry lakes), and most of all, rare Burren plants that are a delight to the botanist.

Just outside the Burren at the village of Kilfenora there is an interpretive center that gives visual and sound explanations of the geology, botany, and history of the area.

Be prepared to be amazed by the Burren. Information is available on the area at Gregans Castle Hotel.

CASHEL HOUSE HOTEL
Cashel, Connemara, County Galway

Here's a bit of Relais et Chateaux de Campagne luxury in one of Ireland's beauty spots.

The setting is typical of Connemara. Surrounded on three sides by rugged mountains, Cashel House Hotel stands at the head of Cashel Bay in a fifty-acre award-winning garden of flowering shrubs and woodland walks. During my late October visit, there were literally thousands of yellow flowers in bloom, whose gay colors were shown to great advantage against the rather austere white lines of a Georgian-style house. I could hear songbirds who evidently found the exotic flowering shrubs, including rhododendrons, azaleas, camellias, and magnolias, much to their liking.

In contrast to the exterior, the interior furnishings with antiques and 19th-century paintings have many bright colors interspersed with gentle pastels. There were a number of paintings throughout all of the public rooms and dining rooms.

I arrived during the Sunday lunch, and among the local well-dressed Galway patrons was a table of beaming clergymen, who were also enjoying the noontide comestibles.

The resident owners are Dermot and Kay McEvilly. They passed me back and forth between the two of them because Sunday lunchtime is one of the busiest of the week.

From Kay I learned that Dermot is in charge of the kitchen and the menus. "He places a great deal of emphasis on seafood because we're so close to the water," she said. "We have fresh turbot, sea trout, and salmon, as well as scallops from Cashel Bay. Lamb and beef are plentiful. We serve them in many varieties of sauces. The vegetables come from our own garden whenever possible.

"I think the main emphasis here is on a restful holiday," she said. "Our guests can use our hard tennis court or swim from our little private beach, golf at Ballyconneely, or fish in any of the lakes and rivers. A lot of them go in for mountain climbing, bird watching, horse riding, or just driving around on a picnic. We have two good day trips from Cashel House, which are shaped like a figure 8. I believe that guests using these excursions can see most of Connemara."

This was another place that Marilyn and Charlie Schubert liked very much. They spoke of its "wonderful, warm feeling" and of the numerous small cozy sitting rooms with fireplaces and beautiful gardens.

"Kay McEvilly gave us a delightful table by the window overlooking the gardens. We had a wonderful dinner that night of Irish salmon and lobster Newburg. We talked with Dermot and Kay, and as one-time fellow-innkeepers we had much to talk of."

The beauties of Connemara provide a splendid backdrop for the understated elegance of the Cashel House Hotel.

CASHEL HOUSE HOTEL (Relais et Chateaux), Cashel, Connemara, Co. Galway. Tel.: (095) 31001. U.S. reservations: 800-223-6764. Telex: 50812. A 32-guestroom country house hotel located in the Connemara area of county Galway, 174 mi. from Dublin. Open from March to Nov. 1. Golf, fishing, boating nearby. McEvilly Family, Proprietors. (See Index for rates.)

Directions: From Galway, Cashel can be reached via the N59 Oughterard–Clifden Rd. Plainly marked on the map. (Note: There is another Cashel in county Tipperary.)

ROSLEAGUE MANOR HOTEL
Letterfrack, Connemara, County Galway

The visit to this country house hotel began with a sinking sensation. It all happened this way:

Driving on the Connemara coastal road between Clifden and Leenane, I saw the sign for the Rosleague Manor Hotel, remembered Peter and Moira Haden's recommendation, and turned into a pleasant, woodland road that afforded many glimpses of a splendid bay. Just as I pulled into the car park of a Georgian house, I felt the left front corner of my automobile descending and experienced the said sinking sensation. I had a flat tire.

From that point on, it was all uphill. Anne Foyle, one of the resident owners of the hotel, was good enough to ask a young man to help me change the "tyre," and also conducted me on a tour of the house, which wound up with tea in the library.

"We are essentially a friendly, family-run hotel with much emphasis on what I think is superb home cooking," she said. "My brother, Patrick, is the principal chef."

Her eyes sparkled when I remarked on the unusual number of oil paintings. "Yes, Patrick and I, as well as our mother, are art lovers and we've had a great deal of enjoyment in supplementing the period furniture with bright spots of color."

Characteristic of Georgian houses, the public rooms in the main part of the house have high ceilings and very comfortable, conversation-inviting furniture. A pleasing collection of English bone china was displayed on one wall of the dining room; I believe Anne said it was English Derby, which is basically white with a wide blue border.

The guest rooms in the older portion of the house are large and decorated with harmonious draperies, bedspreads, and wallpaper, as are the bedrooms in the newer part of the house. All have private bathrooms. All of them have a view of Ballinakill Bay.

Back in the main sitting room, Patrick, resplendent in his chef's whites, joined us for just a few moments. He was making his preparations for the evening's repast.

"The one thing that we insist on is fresh food," said Patrick. "Everything comes locally—the vegetables are either from our own garden or are grown nearby, the meat all comes from Galway, and the fish comes from the bay out there. At the beginning of the season we have salmon—that's the main attraction, especially for the tourists. We also serve lamb, veal, and beef. Most of our dishes are served with sauces that give some of them a very nice French touch."

Anne was able to fill me in a little bit more on this beautiful section of Ireland. "Mountains dominate the Connemara landscape," she said. "There are many picturesque, hidden villages, and the coastline, as you've already seen, has dozens of little bays interspersed with very wide beaches. Ireland's language, customs, and crafts are kept alive in Connemara.

"Our guests can fish for salmon or sea trout, enjoy pony trekking, golf, or hill climbing. I think one of our principal virtues is the traffic-free roads."

And so my visit at Rosleague Manor, which began with a sinking sensation, ended with a real lift as I drove out of the driveway, taking one last look at Ballinakill Bay, encircled by the Twelve Bens Mountains. The water looked warm and there were lazy ripples tempting me to stay even longer.

Reader Comment: "This place put us in mind of an American inn—we loved it. Anne Foyle was not there but we had a lovely visit with Patrick, her brother, who was kind enough to show us all around the inn. He well remembered changing your 'tyre.' We were very impressed, as you were, with the beautiful paintings. You didn't mention the very high quality shops that are located in Letterfrack. Charlie had to drag me away by the heels."

ROSLEAGUE MANOR HOTEL, Letterfrack, Connemara, Co. Galway. Tel.: 095-41101. A 16-guestroom country house hotel in the west of

Ireland, 100 mi. from Shannon Airport. Open from Easter to the end of Oct. Lunch, tea, and dinner served to non-residents. Salmon and sea trout fishing, pony trekking, golf, and hill climbing nearby. Anne and Patrick Foyle, Resident Proprietors. (See Index for rates.)

Directions: Letterfrack is located on the coastal road in the Connemara section of Co. Galway between Clifden and Leenane.

GLENCOLMCILLE

Since I've returned from Glencolmcille I have been amazed at how many people also have either been there or have heard about it. It is located in the southwest corner of county Donegal on a peninsula of land thrust out into the Atlantic about 170 miles northwest of Dublin.

Glencolmcille comprises five parallel glens, each opening out to beautiful expansive beaches and the sea. Within a radius of five miles there are twenty-three lakes, three rivers, and countless streams. The mountains end in precipitous cliffs that hurl defiance at the changing moods of an unpolluted ocean. One of these cliffs is reputed to be the highest in Europe at 1,972 feet.

The lore, legends, antiquities, scenic views, tranquility and peace of Glencolmcille are such that the area is extremely popular among the Irish themselves. I caution against arriving in high season without advance reservations.

Besides all these things I have enumerated, Glencolmcille is very well *known in Ireland because of the efforts of Father McDyer, who has become the guiding spirit of a cooperative known as the Glencolmcille Association.*

Briefly, and with apologies to Father McDyer, whose small booklet I am paraphrasing, the isolation, poor land resources, and the tyranny of landlordism all conspired in their own way to subject Glencolmcille to massive emigration over the past 150 years.

Father McDyer saw the need for providing a way for the people of the area to help themselves and, among other things, a Holiday Village was built and new industries were fostered. There is an excellent folk museum and a crafts shop.

I have a suggestion: whether you're going to Glencolmcille or not, send $2 in American currency to the manager of the Glenbay Hotel, request an inn brochure and a copy of The Riches of Glencolmcille *by J. McDyer. The booklet contains not only the history of the area, but also several walks in the countryside and some excellent four-color photographs. I promise the reader an unusual literary journey.*

I shall quote briefly from this booklet: "I hope you are not a careless driver, for, although the road to the car park overlooking the cliff (2,000 feet) is quite safe, the driver must proceed very slowly and keep his eye riveted on the road until he parks his car. On the right side of the road driving upwards there can be seen many outcrops of large flagstones, from which the mountain Sliabh a Liag takes its name. I hope, too, that the day is fine and that you brought your luncheon basket and your camera for here you can remain for a long time, absorbed by the riot of colours, the majesty and the peace, and entranced by the distant prospect of the mountains of Connaught far across the bay. It is also an engaging thought as you look westwards that there is no land between you and the American continent. Looking downwards you will see the seagulls gliding lazily on the air currents or occasionally plummeting toward the fish beneath."

The booklet is the next best thing to being there, and being there is to catch a brief glimpse of the magic of Ireland.

GLENCOLMCILLE HOTEL
Malinmore, Glencolmcille, County Donegal

This is the only hotel in the Glencolmcille area. The accommodations are warm and comfortable and the menu is adequate. The hotel also has frequent Irish gatherings and songfests.

Oddly enough, for an accommodation that seems rather remote, there is also a telex service available and arrangements can probably be made by a North American travel agent.

GLENCOLMCILLE HOTEL, Malinmore, Glencolmcille, Co. Donegal.
Tel.: 073-30003 Telex: 33517 DWPEI. A 20-guestroom (private baths)
conventional hotel on Ireland's west coast, 142 mi. from Dublin. Open all
year. Breakfast, lunch, dinner served to non-residents. (This particular
section of Donegal is extremely popular and reservations must be made
considerably in advance in the high season.) Bicycles, deep-sea fishing,
boat trips, archeology, folk museum, evenings of Irish music and dancing,
tennis, and sandy beaches all available. (See Index for rates.)

Directions: There are several different choices of roads from Dublin or
Shannon to Donegal town. From there follow the road west through
Killybegs to the farthest end of the peninsual.

FROM DONEGAL TO DUBLIN VIA NORTHERN IRELAND

The shortest distance between Donegal town and Dublin is to travel
across the Black Gap, following the signs to Pettigo, Kesh, Irvinestown,
and Enniskillen. This road leads through two border-crossing points
which, I must confess, I was through before I had even realized it. It
introduced me to the Erne Lakes that afford some of the most beautiful
scenes in Ireland.

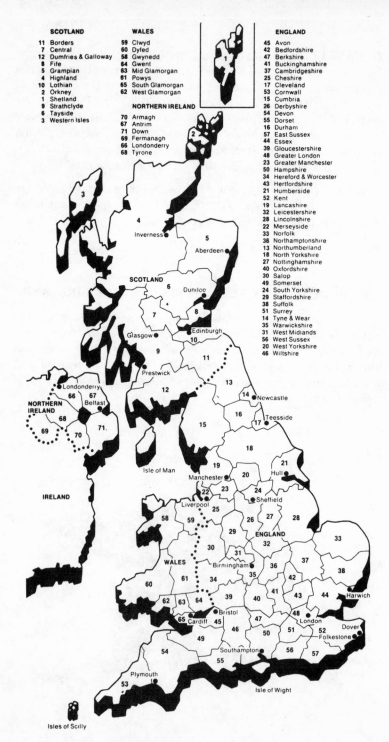

INDEX

The following alphabetical listings under each country provide approximate rates in British pounds sterling (£) for two people for one night, including breakfast. In most cases, these rates include the Value Added Tax (VAT) of 15%. However, it is always wise to check the rates and what they cover when you make the reservation. There are a few places where breakfast is not offered with the room tariff, as well as others where *both breakfast and dinner* ARE included in the room rate. This latter situation is identified in the listing as "MAP" (Modified American Plan). (American Plan includes 3 meals.) These rates are estimated through 1990.

ENGLAND

Rates shown are for lodgings and breakfast for two people for one night; in most cases, inclusive of VAT (Value Added Tax, 15%). Prices are in British money; pounds sterling (£). Check exchange rate. Rates are estimated through 1990.

	RATES	PAGE
Abbey Court, The 20 Pembridge Gardens, London	£95	26
Abbey Hotel Abbey Street, Penzance, Cornwall	£55–70	105
Alverton Manor Tregolls Road, Truro, Cornwall	£85	103
Angel Hotel, The Bury St. Edmunds, Suffolk	£80–100*	56
Beaufort, The Beaufort Gardens, London	£140-195	29
Buckland-Tout-Saints Groveton, Devon	£85–115	99
Calcot Manor (near Tetbury) Tetburh, Gloucestershire	£85–120	130
Castle Hotel, The Taunton, Sumerset	£95–135	114
Cavendish Hotel Baslow, Derbyshire	£65–75	147
Chewton Glen Hotel New Milton, Hampshire	£138–165	79
Collin House Hotel Broadway, Worcestershire	£61–69	138
Combe House Hotel Gittisham, Devon	£80–103	96
Congham Hall King's Lynn, Norfolk	£77–90	54
Crosby Lodge Crosby-on-Eden, Cumbria	£75	181
Crudwell Court Crudwell, Wiltshire	£70–85	124
Dedham Hall Dedham, Essex	£31–48	52
Dukes Hotel St. James's Place, London	£180*	32
Durrants Hotel George St., London	£72–95*	33
Eagle House Church Street, Bathford, Avon	£34–44	123
Eastnor House Hotel Stratford-upon-Avon, Warwickshire	£40–46	139
Ebury Court Hotel Edbury St., London	£75–90	30
Esseborne Manor Hurstbourne Tarrant, Andor, Hampshire	£78–100	87
Farlam Hall Hotel Brampton, Cumbria	£120–160**	182
Feathers Hotel, The Woodstock, Oxfordshire	£60–105	38

*Breakfast additional   **MAP

*Breakfast additional   **MAP

LONDON

Rates shown are for lodgings and breakfast for two people for one night; in most cases, inclusive of VAT (Value Added Tax, 15%). Prices are in British money: pounds sterling (£). Check exchange rate. Rates estimated through 1990.

*Breakfast additional   **MAP

WALES

Rates shown are for lodgings and breakfast for two people for one night; in most cases, inclusive of VAT (Value Added Tax, 15%). Prices are in British money: pounds sterling (£). Check exchange rate. Rates estimated through 1990.

	RATES	PAGE
Bontddu Hall Hotel Bontddu, Gwynedd	£64	196
Bwlch-Y-Fedwen Country House Hotel Penmorfa, Gwynedd	£54–60**	197
Crown at Whitebrook, The Whitebrook, Gwent	£46–56	191
Egerton Grey Porthkerry, South Glamorgan	£65–75	190
Llwyn Onn Hall Wrexham, Clwyd	£52–63*	201
Llwynderw Hotel Abergwesyn, Powys	£100–160*	195
Plas Bodegroes Pwlheli, Gwynedd	£50–60	198
Sygun Fawr Country House Hotel Beddgelert, Gwynedd	£32	199
Ty Mawr Country House Hotel Brechfa, Dyfed	£42	192

SCOTLAND

Rates shown are for lodgings and breakfast for two people for one night; in most cases, inclusive of VAT (Value Added Tax, 15%). Prices are in British money: pounds sterling (£). Check exchange rate. Rates estimated through 1990.

Albany Hotel, The Edinburgh	£50	206
Ardanaiseig Kilchrenan, Argyll	£124–168**	220
Ardsheal House Kentallen of Appin, Argyll	£100–136**	224
Auchterarder House Auchterarder, Perthshire	£100–140	238
Cairn Lodge, The Auchterarder, Tayside	£65	236
Clifton Hotel, The Nairn, Nairnshire	£68–76	230
Dunain Park Hotel Inverness	£45–78	228
Gleddoch House Langbank, Renfrenshire	£97–125	216
Greywalls Gullane, East Lothian	£100–115	208
Inverlochy Castle Fort William, Inverness-shire	£160	226
Isle of Colonsay Hotel Isle of Colonsay, Argyll	£80–100**	218
Isle of Eriska Hotel Connel, Argyll	£103–120	222
Kirroughtree Hotel Newton Stewart, Wigtownshire	£116–124**	212
Knockie Lodge Whitebridge, Inverness-shire	£100–144**	227
Marine Hotel Troon, Ayrshire	£92	215
Nivingston House Hotel Cleish, Kinross-Shire	£70–100	239
Open Arms Hotel, The Dirleton, East Lothian	£55–88	207
Philipburn House Hotel, The Selkirk	£70–90**	209
Pittodrie House Hotel Pitcaple, Aberdeenshire	£66–80	232
Port-an-Eilean Hotel Strathtummel, Perthshire	£44	235
Shieldhill Country House Hotel Begger, Lanarkshire	£88–119	211
Taychreggan Hotel Kilchrenan, Argyll	£100**	221
Tullich Lodge By Ballater, Aberdeenshire	£148**	234

*Breakfast additional   **MAP

IRELAND

Rates shown are for lodgings and breakfast for two people for one night; in most cases, inclusive of VAT (Value Added Tax, 15%). Prices are in British money: pounds sterling (£). Check exchange rate. Rates estimated through 1990.

**MAP

About the Author

In addition to his successful career as a travel writer, Jerry Levitin is an inn and bed and breakfast consultant who works from experience—he owned and operated an urban inn in San Francisco for five years. Previously, he had been a Court Commissioner for the city and had practiced law for 21 years.

He and his family live in Napa Valley, California.